Table of contents

Course Handbook………………………..1

Instruction of a Student……………....47

The Book of Knowledge………………129

Advice from Tayba Students………….149

Study Guide……………………….....185

Study Tips for Distance Learners..…...190

TAYBA FOUNDATION

STUDENT HANDBOOK

TAYBA FOUNDATION

ADAB 100 How to Study Islam
Fall 2016

August 15- December 15th, 2016
Instructors: Tayba Faculty

This handbook is designed to provide the information you need to help you complete the course. It is split into four sections, please read them all carefully:

1. Course information
2. Advice on studying for this course
3. Assignments and grades
4. Information on Tayba Foundation

At Tayba, we realize the unique and difficult situation our students are in (such as lack of money, high security, changing of locations without notice, solitary confinement, etc) and we will accommodate any reasonable situation for a student who sends us a written explanation. If you feel unable to complete the course for any reason, contact us to see if we can help.

ADAB 100 is a correspondence course. We will not meet in a classroom at any time. We will not have any phone tutoring sessions scheduled.

To succeed in this class, you must be proficient in managing your time well and being self-motivated to go through the material and ask questions when you need to.

Section 1: Course Information

Course Description

This course welcomes you as a student. You have set your foot on the path of learning the religion and striving to perfect your faith and practice. Staying on this path requires commitment, consistency, and an understanding of the etiquette of seeking religious knowledge. This course provides a valuable introduction on how to study Islam, one of the most important factors in success being the etiquette of learning. This course also provides a number of learning strategies to aid you in mastering the material you are learning. Our tradition is deeply rooted in proper manners; or the right way of doing things. For this reason, the scholars have always stressed its importance in training new students in order that they may be fit to benefit from their studies.

This course includes two major works on this subject, the first being "Instruction of the Student and the Method of Learning" by Imam Zarnuji, it is of the utmost importance that one has deep respect for the knowledge one is studying and its people. Imam Ghazali (Allah be pleased with him) mentioned that, "We didn't attain unto this knowledge except by way of humility".

Course Objectives

The student will meet the following learning objectives:

*Know the concept of adab as it relates to studying Islam
*Strategies on practical implementation of those lessons
*To be very familiar with two traditional texts on the subject

Course Instructors

There are a number of instructors who contributed to developing this course, as well as being available to answer questions and grade your assignments at the end of the semester.

Please see Section 4, "Information on Tayba Foundation" to read their biographies.

Disability Support Services

Students who believe that they may need accommodations in this class are encouraged to contact TAYBA.

Inclusivity Statement

Tayba Foundation supports an inclusive learning environment where diversity and individual differences are understood, respected, appreciated, and recognized as a source of strength. We expect that students, faculty, administrators, and staff within Tayba Foundation will respect differences and demonstrate diligence in understanding how other people's' perspectives, behaviors, and worldviews may be different from their own.

Academic Dishonesty

The Tayba Foundation's Student Code of Conduct and Honor Code strictly prohibits any form of academic misconduct. Academic misconduct includes, but is not limited to, plagiarism, cheating, fabrication, and knowingly or recklessly encouraging or making possible any act of plagiarism. Academic misconduct is an unacceptable activity in scholarship and is in conflict with academic and professional ethics and morals. All incidents of alleged plagiarism or other forms of academic dishonesty will be investigated and violations of academic integrity will result in a consequence that may result in a failing grade and/ or expulsion from the program.

Communication between Students and Instructor

Students are encouraged to stay in contact with the instructor(s) to ensure that all questions are answered and all assignments are clearly understood. We encourage you to use the written mail correspondence to communicate with your instructor, or email for those who have access. Feel free to ask questions, enquire about courses or class assignments, ask about grades or to report technical problems with quizzes or course materials.

Please note that <u>questions about the course should ***not*** be submitted with your course assignments</u>, all questions should be submitted separately.

By e-mail: When sending e-mail, always include "ADAB 100 How to Study Islam" in the subject line of the message.

By letter: Please briefly include the subject of your letter on the envelope, for example "ADAB 100 question about assignment". This will help us to respond to your letters more quickly.

Please be sure to write your Name and ID number on all communication with Tayba Foundation, particularly on all of your assignments.

By phone: We welcome pre-paid phone calls from students (*unfortunately we do not currently have the budget to accept collect phone calls*). Please note that the hours our office manager will make sure to be available to take calls are <u>11:00 am - 2:00 pm PST (California time zone) Tuesdays, Wednesdays and Thursdays</u>. We will try to take calls at other times but unfortunately we cannot guarantee somebody will be available outside of the set hours. If your call goes straight to voicemail we are taking another call so please try again.

You may also consider giving the message to a family member or friend with whom you are in contact with. That person could then email us or phone us and we can answer an inquiry if you give them permission to receive information on your behalf about your studies.

Textbook and study materials

The main text used for this course is the book "Instruction of the Student" written by a classical scholar in Islam, al-Zarnuji. You will be provided with a copy of the original Arabic text, and the English translation. We have also included a translation of "the Book of Knowledge" written by Imam al-Ghazzali.

Lesson Overview

Lesson 1: The definition of knowledge and fiqh (understanding) and their virtue.
Lesson 2: Intentions while learning.
Lesson 3: Choosing a subject, teacher, study partner and Steadfastness.
Lesson 4: Honoring knowledge and those who carry it.
Lesson 5: Seriousness, perseverance and aspiration.
Lesson 6: Prioritization and the amount to study.
Lesson 7: Depending on Allāh.
Lesson 8: The time of acquirement.
Lesson 9: Compassion and advice.
Lesson 10: Benefit and Procuring Etiquette
Lesson 11: Waraʾ (scrupulousness) while studying
Lesson 12: That which Increases memory and what causes forgetfulness.
Lesson 13: That which increases sustenance and that which decreases it. That which increases and decreases lifespan.
Lesson 14: Book of Knowledge of Imam Al-Ghazali

Detailed Schedule, Fall 2016

A key to success in a correspondence class is to keep up and not get behind. The deadlines listed below are designed to help you succeed in this class by encouraging you to keep up with your work throughout the semester. You are free to submit your work before the final deadline, however please note that tests and papers will **NOT** start to be graded until January 2017. You will receive a postcard confirmation in the mail once we have received your work. Submit all tests and the term paper together.

Suggested timeline to keep up with the coursework:

August/ September: Lessons 1-4
September/ October: Lessons 5-8
October/ November: Lessons 9-14
December: Submit all assignments together (**DO NOT SUBMIT TESTS SEPARATELY. INCLUDE YOUR NAME AND ID NUMBER ON ALL ASSIGNMENTS**)

(**DO NOT SUBMIT INCOMPLETE WORK. THIS TAKES A LOT OF OUR OFFICE TIME TO NOTIFY YOU OF WHAT IS MISSING. PLEASE SUBMIT A COMPLETE PACKET AND IF YOU CANNOT, THEN WAIT UNTIL YOU CAN**)

__Final Deadline to submit exam and the essay is December 15th, 2016.__
__If, for any reason, you are unable to submit the coursework on time, please provide a brief note explaining the reason for late submission.__

Section 2: Advice on studying for this course

This text has been studied by both young and old alike. It is of the utmost importance that all Muslims dedicate a portion of their precious lives to gaining sacred knowledge, and this text is one of the best ways to begin. As for motivation to study, it should suffice us that Allah has honored knowledge and its people in His Book. Allah has said:

- Are those who know equal to those who do not? Nay they are not equal (Quran 39:9)
- Ask the people of knowledge if you do not know (Quran 16:43)
- Only the scholars have deep fear of Allah (Quran 35:28)

Also, the many sayings of the Messenger of Allah ﷺ should be enough to motivate us to desire to seek knowledge such as, "Seeking knowledge is incumbent on every Muslim."

When we look to the scholars of all generations, we find much praise about the stations of knowledge, such as the answer of Imam Malik when he was asked, "When does studying become blameworthy?" He answered, "When does ignorance become praiseworthy?"

Despite all this praise of knowledge by Allah in His Book, the sayings of His Messenger ﷺ and the many sayings of the righteous people, we still find that many people have little, if any, desire to gain knowledge. We also know that this is a sign of the end of time because our Noble Prophet ﷺ said:

> Allah will not take away knowledge all at once. Rather, He will take it away by taking away the scholars. Then, the people will make the ignorant ones their leaders and they will give answers without knowledge so they will be misguided and they will misguide.

So, if we do not want to make ourselves another sign of the end of time, we must be a part of reviving the sciences of this *deen*.

To do that, we have to go back to the texts that have been passed down to us by our pious predecessors and wholeheartedly begin to study and implement them. One of the poets has said, "Those who have come before us have left for us nothing other than to follow their footsteps." The *ummah* is in desperate need of people who have a deep understanding of this *deen*, those who can aid in alleviating the suffering caused by ignorance. Just as the sacred texts have been preserved, so too has the method to study them.

Traditionally, the Islamic method of learning began at age seven lunar years, with memorization of the Qur'an. During that time students would also acquire the necessary tool of the Arabic language. Then they would go on to study Islamic Creed (*aqīdah*), Islamic Jurisprudence (*fiqh*), Arabic grammar (*nahw*), Foundational Methodology (*usul*) and many other sciences. All the texts that were studied were committed to memory, as this was one of the main ways of preserving the knowledge. Even if a person did not have access to his books for whatever reason, whether they were stolen or destroyed, the river of knowledge continued to flow.

Imam Shafiʿī said, "My knowledge is with me when I walk in the streets, and not in a trunk at my home." Imam Ghazzali once spent a great amount of time copying various manuscripts by hand. Once, when he was on a journey, they were stolen. Imam Ghazzali told the thief, "Do not take my knowledge." The thief responded by saying, "What kind of knowledge is it if a person like me can take it?" From that time on, Imam Ghazzali resolved to never study anything except that he would memorize it.

When the Mongols invaded Iraq, the river ran red and black. Red from the blood of those killed and dumped in the river and black from the books that were thrown in. here were many great works that were lost and never recovered but thanks to the many *huffadh*, or "those who preserve" (i.e. memorize), the most important of those books were saved. One scholar, Ibn Al Qassar, told the people in Iraq to bring scribes to write what he says as he could recite from memory the contents of the books that were destroyed. This station, however, was not something gained overnight; rather it took years of strenuous study. We too hope that we can produce people of knowledge that can relieve some of the pain that humanity is experiencing.

One of the most beautiful examples of where our *huffadh* (those who have memorized the Qur'an) have done this is during the transatlantic slave trade. In those horrible conditions, in the depths of those ships, one of the only things that gave the stolen people comfort, whether they were Muslim, Christian or pagan, was the Qur'an reciters. The Noble Carriers of the Book of Allah who were ripped from all they had, including their clothes, could not have the Qu'ran ripped from their hearts. In their pure hearts, they also carried some of the sacred texts of Islam, such as the *Risala of Ibn Abi Zayd*.

Some of them put what they carried in their hearts on paper when they got a chance, and now those manuscripts are being preserved in museums throughout America. We too want huffadh whose recitation of the Qur'an and the sacred texts can echo throughout the wilderness of North America and once again bring comfort to the suffering souls of the children of our father Adam, upon him be peace. This dream can become a reality through texts like these.

Although traditionally these texts were studied one on one with a teacher who would give the commentary orally and guide the student during the course of his studies, we realize that many people do not have access to a teacher who can do this. We decided to try a new method, in the same way that when water is not available for ablution (*wudu*), one does dry ablution (*tayammum*). , along with a translation of the text.

The hope is not that one will study and memorize in the English medium, but rather the student will use it as a means to increase his or her understanding of the Arabic language. Without the Arabic language, one will never gain a deep understanding of the way of Islam. One of the scholars, Al Hilali, said, "The most important aspect of knowledge is aqeedah, then fiqh, then purification of the heart and then Arabic which is a tool that is needed to begin." So, even though Arabic is ranked fourth in importance, it is needed to access the rest. Nabigha said, commentating on this opinion, "It seems from his statement that Arabic is studied even before aqeedah." We find people will learn a language for the love of a woman or to get a job, so where are those that will learn Arabic for the love of Allah Almighty and His Messenger ﷺ.

This method gets one's eyes used to reading the Arabic, the tongue used to reciting it, the ears used to hearing it and the hands used to writing it. This has been the traditional way of studies throughout the Muslim lands and is a way that is in tune with the *fiṭra* (natural disposition). One man who was guided to this method of learning and greatly benefited from it was the *shaheed*, El Hajj Malik El Shabazz, or Malcolm X. He says in his biography in chapter 9, "Saved";

> I spent two days just riffling uncertainly through the dictionary's pages. I'd never realized so many words existed! I didn't know which words I needed to learn. Finally, just to start some kind of action, I began copying.
>
> In my slow, painstaking, ragged handwriting, I copied into my tablet everything printed on that first page, down to the punctuation marks. I believe it took me a day. Then aloud, I read back, to myself, everything I'd written on the tablet. Over and over, aloud, to myself, I read my own handwriting.
>
> I woke up the next morning, thinking about those words- immensely proud to realize that not only had I written so much at one time, but I'd written words that I never knew were in the world. Moreover, with little effort, I could also remember what many of those words meant.

Malcolm, may Allah have mercy on him, began this process after being frustrated over not being able to express himself in the English language, as his mother tongue was the slang of the streets. For those that are frustrated over not being able to access the Arabic language, this process we have at Tayba will benefit them as well.

It will take time and effort but if you persevere, you will be victorious, *in sha Allah*. Knowledge is a precious thing and Allah will only let you have it if you struggle. Even for the Messenger of Allah ﷺ, revelation was received only after experiencing great pain. At the first revelation, the Angel Gabriel , squeezed him three times and then our Messenger r began reciting. Each squeeze was unbearable but he was being shown that knowledge can only be received by those who endure hardship. In the story of our Masters Moses alayhis salam and Khadr alayhis salam, when the former was going to seek knowledge from the latter, Moses alayhis salam said, "We have become tired because of our journey" (Quran 18:62).

One must also struggle to gain knowledge by staying up late into the night or getting up before dawn. Imam Shafi'i said, "Whoever seeks lofty things will stay up late at night. Whoever seeks lofty things without struggle will have wasted his life seeking the impossible. The one who seeks pearls dives into the ocean." El Hajj Malik El Shabazz said when recounting the long hours he spent reading every night, "That went on until three or four every morning. Three or four hours of sleep a night was enough for me. Often in the years in the streets, I had slept less than that."

With this in mind, one must also realized that his body has a right over him, so give it rest from time to time. Traditionally, schools set aside two days a week for rest. A student should pursue personal interests, spend time with friends or do other light study.

We hope that for those that receive this book it will be the beginning of a lifelong journey of seeking knowledge. This process will include moving from this text to other texts moving through the beginning texts, to the intermediate and then on to the advanced texts. The same will be for the other subjects of *'aqīdah, usul, seerah*, and the many other sciences of Islam. You can correspond with Tayba to clarify anything that is obscure.

With this as a beginning, we hope to increase the number of Muslims who have deep understanding of the deen who can then move to spreading the correct message of Islam. If we want the best for ourselves and our families, we must strive to get this understanding, or *fiqh*. Our Master Muhammad ﷺ said, "Whoever Allah wants good for him, He will give him deep understanding (*fiqh*) of the *deen*."

We ask that Allah accept all of our actions and gives us success in following the way of our Master Muhammad ﷺ. We ask all those that receive this book to pray for those who aided in putting the study package together and for their families and teachers.

Advice on How to Study this Course Material

1. Work your way through the texts provided in this course. Take a short section at a time.
2. Write your own notes.
3. Keep track of any questions that you have and send those to Tayba in writing being sure to mention the course name in your letter.
4. Use any methods of study that you have found beneficial to master material. Every student will have different methods that work for them.

Section 3: Course assignments and grades

Assignments that you must complete

There are **three** separate assignments that you must complete:

1. One multiple choice exam. It is provided along with this packet. There are 100 multiple choice questions, worth 100 points.

2. An essay worth 50 points.

3. A second essay, also worth 50 points.

The exams are "open book" and so you may use your book and notes during exams. Before starting an exam, you should study the material as thoroughly as you would for a closed-book test in a classroom.

Grades

Your grade will be based on the number of points you earn on the multiple-choice exam and the essay, and one term paper. There are 200 points available. Submit the multiple-choice exam and both essays together (**DO NOT SUBMIT ESSAYS or TESTS SEPARATELY**)

The 200 available points will be distributed as follows:
- 1 exam worth 100 points total
- 2 essays worth 50 points each (100 points total)

Essay Directions

Each essay should be between 4-6 pages typed or handwritten. Make sure to **double space** between lines. If you will be writing the paper by hand, you should make sure to write as clearly as you can. Cursive or print are both acceptable for handwritten papers. Make sure to write in blue or black pen, not pencil, unless you do not have access to a pen. If your handwriting is small, please write a little larger for this paper.

If you have trouble writing a paper of this length, try speaking from your heart and have someone take notes. Take those notes and write out a paper based on them. Do not be intimidated

by this paper. We are not trying to assess your essay skills, grammar, punctuation, spelling, etc. Those are important and you should work on them. But you will be graded on this essay on content. The content will be based on whether you answered the topics.
Be creative.

Essay #1 Topic: "How can you implement the lessons of this course in your personal, family, and communtiy life?"

This essay assignment is designed to promote active learning and critical thinking about the application of this knowledge you gained in your personal, familial, and community environments. It gives students an opportunity to show the knowledge that they gained from the course as well as from any supplemental or prior knowledge

The purpose of this paper is to show that not only have you learned the actual technical aspects of the book, but that you can relate them to your personal, familial, and community life. You want to show how the study of this text has changed you. You can focus on all three aspects equally (personal, family, community), or you can focus on one area more than the others (or even just one area). The goal of this paper is to show us how you, as an individual, will work to implement the knowledge that you learned.

Essay #2 Topic: Strategies and Methods of Learning: Past and Present

For this essay, you will discuss two topics; strategies or methods of learning that you had previously and then strategies of learning that you gained through this text. We would like to see what tools of learning you have come to this course with. Here are some questions to get you thinking about the topic (you don't have to answer them one by one:

What things have you developed on your own for learning over the years? What tools of learning have been taught to you? How did they impact your learning? What tools of learning did you gain from this course? What are some things that you found very profound? What things have you already tried from this course and found benefit from? What were things that motivated you to learn in the past? What things from this course sparked motivation to learn?

Essay Writing Made Easy

All essays should have an *introduction*, a *body,* and a *conclusion.* A balance of these 3 sections is important. A good rule of thumb is:

Introduction: 10 %   **Body:** 80 %   **Conclusion:** 10 %

Helpful Tip: Before you dive into your essay, create an outline to help organize your thoughts.

Step1:

The first thing you need to do is answer your topic or research question.

For example: **How has the knowledge you have learned from "The Abridgement of Al-Akhdari," affected your personal, family, and community life?**

- Ask yourself what topics, from the text, will you reflect on? Wudu, Tawba, Ghusl, Prayer etc.
- Think about how the knowledge you have learned has affected your personal, family, and community life.
- Ask yourself some specific questions: (for example)
  - How has the act of tawba changed my life with my parents?
  - After learning the importance of ghusl, how has it changed my understanding of cleanliness?
  - How has the act of promoting good and forbidding evil affected my relationship with the brothers in my community?

Step 2:

In this step you want to narrow your ideas further. An average essay will make a general statement of what was learned and briefly mention what affect it had on your life. A <u>*strong*</u> reflective essay will:

- ✓ State what was learned
- ✓ State how it has affected an area of your life
- ✓ Provide personal examples
- ✓ Give an insight to the outcome

(Example)

1. Promoting Good and Forbidding Evil
   - Give a brief statement on what this means
   - Discuss how you tried to implement what you learned
   - Give examples of the success or obstacles you encountered
   - Provide an insight as to why you encountered problems
   - Talk about how it made you feel

Step 3:

Create a thesis

This is probably the most important part of the essay. Every essay must have a thesis statement. The thesis statement is one or two sentences, in your **introduction**, that contains the focus of your essay and tells the reader what the essay is going to be about. You want to make sure your thesis piques the interest of the reader.

(Example of Average thesis)

1. *"For the purpose of this essay I will talk about wudu, tawbah, and ghusul and how they have affected me in my personal, family, and community life."*

This thesis is correct. But it is also unimaginative.

(Example of an interesting thesis)

2. *"Knowledge is the key to freedom," is a statement I have heard throughout my life. I have never truly understood its meaning until I began studying sacred knowledge. What I have learned has had a profound effect on all areas of my life.* **(Then you can list the topics you will discuss)**

This thesis pulls the reader into wanting to read further to find out what the author has to say. Don't worry if a thesis extends a little beyond the two sentence norm. Sometimes you need to build up to what you want to talk about.

Important Note: Now that you've organized what your thoughts and ideas are you can start your essay.

Introduction

The introduction is the first paragraph and the point of entry for your essay. It is where you will introduce your thesis.

Body of the essay

The body of the essay is where you will discuss your three points. Each paragraph will focus on one topic. To make your paragraphs effective follow these guidelines:

Paragraph 1, 2, & 3

- Topic sentence
- Supporting sentence
- Concluding sentence

1. The **topic sentence** introduces the point you will talk about.
2. The **supporting sentences** provide details to support the topic. Use examples, your opinion or personal accounts to give more value to your topic.
3. The **concluding sentences** sum up what you've said in the paragraph and pave the way for your next topic sentence.

Conclusion

Your conclusion is your last chance to highlight your point of view to your readers. The impression you create in your conclusion will leave a long lasting effect with your reader long after they've finished the essay. The end of an essay should bring a sense of completeness and closure to your discussion.

Final Note

A strong essay is not just well organized thoughts and ideas. It is also important to pay attention to spelling, grammar, punctuation, and vocabulary.

Basic Grammar Rules

- For every sentence, your subject and your verb need to be in agreement. The most common mistakes are with the verb "to be."

subject	present	past
I	am	was
He	is	was
She	is	was
It	is	was
You	are	were
They	are	were
We	are	were

- Only use capital letters for proper nouns and at the beginning of a sentence. Proper nouns are specific names of people, places or things.

Common Noun	Proper Noun
teacher	Murabit al Hajj
city	Los Angeles
document	Declaration of Independence

- When a sentence is complete use appropriate punctuation.
- Sentences should be complete thoughts and not fragments. For example: *(fragment)* **went to the ballpark.** *(complete)* **He went to the ballpark.**
- Do not use double negatives. Double negatives are two negative words used in the same sentence. For example,
    - That won't do you no good.
    - I ain't got no time for supper.
    - Nobody with any sense isn't going.
    - I can't find my keys nowhere.

Vocabulary

A rich vocabulary is important for effective writing. Refrain from using slang words.

diss	disrespect
bling	jewelry
ain't	is not
bogus	fake

Final Thought

Writing takes practice. The more you write the better you get. Don't be disappointed if you do not get a masterful grade the first time around. This is a learning process aimed at improving your skills.

If you have any questions or concerns, the Tayba staff is here to help.

Letter from Tayba team member

As salamu alaikum,

My name is Khadija and I work with Tayba Foundation helping to develop the courses. I became Muslim in 2004, following almost ten years of searching for the truth. I would like to personally congratulate you on becoming a student, and on taking this course "How to Study Islam".

Please consider this a significant step on your path to perfecting your faith and practice. As you begin on your path, you may be experiencing some strong emotions, including a very strong desire to learn and act. Your job now is to harness that positive energy, and use it in a way that ensures you can maintain and grow in this religion.

A point on maintaining and finding balance

Maintaining is an important point, and I remember being advised early on, not to take too much on and not to try to implement everything I read or hear. At the time I could not understand where this advice was coming from, but several years on it is now clear. It's about finding balance in our devotional acts, including our studies. Know that it takes time to master a new concept or subject, and it takes time to truly establish an act in our lives, and we cannot do it all at once. So we need self-discipline to make sure we are prioritizing that which is most important.

Distance learning - why being "disconnected" isn't necessarily bad

While the social aspects of a usual college environment can bring advantages, remember that it can also bring numerous distractions. Rather than seeing that disconnection as a negative thing, we can see it as being a positive aid in our studies. Through distance learning, we're protecting ourselves from all kinds of things that can potentially get in the way of our goal.

Islam can be described as a social religion, though "time out" is also encouraged in order to reflect and focus entirely on Allah. My belief is that while environmental factors may have some effect on our success and growth, what's most important is our own desire to learn and improve ourselves and our relationship with Allah.

There's only ME to motivate myself

If it helps, keep in mind that at least one Tayba team member (and likely more than that) will be reading the work you return to us at the end of each semester. The whole office looks forward to receiving your work and letters, we even publish some of them online and print large copies to show the public at conferences. We recently made a calendar from our students' artwork which has been widely distributed in the community.

Second, find practical ways to keep yourself motivated. I know, easier said than done. But maybe there's something somebody said to you that had an effect, or maybe a particular image you can bring to mind that reminds you why you are on this path. If you have a notebook, consider writing a message to yourself when you are feeling particularly motivated, to read at times when you need a boost.

Lack of resources, or opportunity to focus?

Don't feel down about your "lack" of learning resources. Remember the goal; it isn't to read or watch as much as you possibly can, it's to truly benefit from what the Prophet (God bless him and grant him peace) has given to us. Resources such as the Internet can be very useful to a student, though in the early stages of learning, it can sometimes be more of a hindrance than a help.

When I first started learning about Islam, I used the Internet a lot and searched for just about anything and everything. In my experience, the Internet can be a dangerous place particularly at this time as it's difficult for the beginner to distinguish between truth and falsehood. Often we don't know what we're looking for, and we may not really understand what we're reading. We may not know how all the things we read fit together, and how to handle differences when we come across them.

You are blessed to have one clear path of studies, along with guidance through the courses in the correct order. You also have protection from incorrect and potentially harmful material. It's really no different from what people on the outside or those attending an institution in-person need. In fact all of our courses are based on texts that students all over study and benefit from.

One thing I would like to mention in closing is please do your best to stick with this program. Consistency is a sign of sincerity, and God willing, this will pay off much more greatly than taking bits and pieces of knowledge here and there. Do not be tempted to go only with self-directed study, rather benefit from the tried and tested path which Tayba is offering. I wish you all the best in your studies and in your growth as a Muslim, and I ask that you remember all of us at Tayba in your prayers,

Wa salam
Khadija

Section 4: Information on Tayba Foundation

Tayba's Mission

Our mission is to provide Islamic correspondence courses at the post-secondary level to the incarcerated and formerly incarcerated through our Distance Learning Program. We've seen the transformative value of higher education and are wholeheartedly committed to establishing the processes that enable our students to inherit a contributory role that will facilitate their self-improvement and allow them to reclaim a future, even beyond the walls of the prison.

Tayba's History

The Tayba Foundation was established in 2008 to provide current and formerly incarcerated men and women with quality Islamic education geared towards the refinement of their thinking and behavior, positioning them to transition to society more productively. Although founded in 2008, Tayba's roots began in 2002 when Shaykh Rami Nsour began teaching prisoners via phone, guiding them through classical Islamic texts and answering questions related to their newfound faith. Over the next few years, under the umbrella of the Zaytuna Prison Outreach Program, these students engaged in serious distance learning with Shaykh Rami, learning Theology (Aqida), Islamic Jurisprudence (Fiqh), Spirituality (Tazkiya), Character Development (Akhlaq) and other associated disciplines. Those students went through enough learning to be able to teach other inmates.

It was through this effort that both the need for Islamic Education and its positive transformative effect became apparent. Consequently, in 2008, Tayba Foundation was formally established as an independent organization to impart and educational curriculum to inmates, with the underlying goal of spiritual nourishment and character rectification. Tayba Foundation is a registered non-profit 501(c)3 educational and charitable organization located in the S.F. Bay Area, but serving all states.

Between 2008 and 2015, Tayba Foundation has:

- Developed an educational curriculum incorporating traditional Islamic knowledge and accounting for special inmate needs

- Developed an administrative infrastructure to assess, enroll, grade and manage student participation

- Developed processes to comply with rules and requirements of the prison system

- Facilitated integration into society of released inmate students

- Grown to a student body of over 600 students, with hundreds more currently on the waiting list to enroll.

The Tayba Team

Shaykh Rami Nsour, Founding Director & Teacher

Rami Nsour was born in Amman, Jordan and moved to the United States at the age of 9. During his college years, he attended Zaytuna classes taught by teachers in the San Francisco Bay Area, notably, Shaykh Khatri bin Bayba, Shaykh Abdullah bin Ahmedna and Shaykh Hamza Yusuf. With their encouragement, Rami embarked on a journey to study at the well acclaimed mahdara (college) of Shaykh Murabit al Hajj bin Fahfu in Mauritania in 1998. There, he was blessed with deep studies with beloved and respected teachers such as Murabit Muhammad al-Amin bin al-Shaykh, Murabit Ahmed Fal bin Ahmedna, Shaykh Abdullah bin Ahmedna, Shaykh Tahir ibn Murabit al Hajj and Shaykh Sa'd Bu among others. Rami completed studies in the various subjects of Qu'ran, 'Aqeedah (Belief), Fiqh (Law), Nahu (grammar), Ihsan (spiritual purification), and adab (manners) and received traditional teaching license (ijaza) to transmit what he learned. Within the area of Fiqh, he also completed the final text of Maliki fiqh, Mukhtasar Khalil, with memorization and has been granted permission by his shuyukh to teach.

In addition to his extensive study of fiqh, he was afforded the unique opportunity to attend one-on-one sessions with his teachers where he would engage them in countless hours of discussion on the application of fiqh in general and specifically for those living in the West. He was also afforded the opportunity to learn practical applications of Islamic law (fiqh) during an extraordinary 'in-residence' experience.

Rami has translated traditional Islamic texts from Arabic to English, including various works on Maliki fiqh and several works of the great Mauritanian scholar, Shaykh Muhammad Mawlud. Rami has dedicated much of his time in teaching, conducting seminars and counseling. He eventually co-founded the Tayba Foundation, which is currently the only organization offering a distance learning program in Islamic Education to incarcerated men and women. In addition to traditional teaching licenses (ijazah), Rami holds a B.A. in Human Development with a focus on Early Childhood and a M.A. in Educational Psychology. Rami resides in the San Francisco Bay Area, is married and has two children.

Isa Abdullah, Office Manager & Teacher

"Whoever knows God is only made happy by Him" Junaid, d.909ce

Isa Abdullah Amezquita, a Latino and Oakland California native is the current office manager for the Tayba Foundation. He converted to Islam over 20 years ago. During his early adulthood he was a manager for a Fortune 500 Sports and Entertainment Company. His entrepreneurial spirit led him to own and manage businesses in music, clothing and a custom wheel and tire shop.

While incarcerated in the California prison system, Isa became affiliated with the Tayba Foundation. It was there that he met one of Tayba's long time and most successful students who encouraged Isa to study traditional Islam through the Madhara system. Isa continues to study and memorize classical texts in Fiqh and Aqida. He is currently working on a book entitled "1001 Questions with the Sheikh" which will address the most extensive concerns of the incarcerated Muslim's day-to- day life.

Nabil Afifi, Fundraising Manager & Teacher

Working closely with the Tayba's staff and volunteers, Nabil helps Tayba succeed by implementing and improving existing programs as well as new ones. He also helps develop fundraising activity plans and strategies to increase contributions. Nabil holds a Masters in Public Administration from CSUEB with many years of experience in both business and nonprofit settings. Also, he studied sacred knowledge for 4 years in the seminary of Murabit al Hajj in Mauritania.

Nabil is originally from Morocco, is married and has 3 children. About working in Tayba he enjoys supporting Muslim inmates and their spiritual needs and says "I pray to Allah that He accepts our work…Ameen…At the end that is all what matters." Nabil is the Co-Founder of Tayba Foundation.

Michelle Harmer (Khadija), Academy Administrator

Michelle's role as Academy Administrator involves managing the development of the unique Islamic studies curriculum that Tayba offers to incarcerated men and women. As a part of helping students attain success with Tayba, Michelle is working on developing student tracking, and implementing best practice in all aspects of Tayba's courses. Michelle also lends a hand in other Tayba projects including development and outreach.

Michelle holds a BA (Hons) in Retail Marketing and a Professional Diploma in Marketing from the Chartered Institute of Marketing (UK). As a retail marketing graduate, Michelle has five years experience in both business-to-business and consumer marketing and PR. She brings an additional six years experience from the nonprofit sector.

Michelle is originally from Britain and embraced Islam in 2004. She is married, has one child and currently lives in Toronto, Canada. About working with Tayba she says, "Personally, the work is a means through which I hope to please Allah's beloved (Allah bless him and grant him peace), and thus have him acknowledge me, insha Allah. I support the work Tayba does as I believe it is a sincere effort to improve the lives of our students, those around them, and their communities. Tayba is delivering to these students what they need, that is reliable, practical education in a highly accessible form."

Waleed Rajabally, Office Administrator

Waleed provides administrative support, maintains student records, handles correspondence and assists with publicity. In college he was heavily involved in various forms of community service. He served as a tutor and teacher's assistant at educational programs in San Francisco, Oakland, and Woodland, catering to at-risk children. He also founded a social justice organization on campus called Student Activists United and interned for the Sacramento Green Party of CA.

After graduating he entered into the public health field, working for 2 1/2 years, most notably at the Haight-Ashbury Free Clinic. In addition to working at the Tayba Foundation, he is currently a research assistant at Cal State East Bay. Waleed enjoys reading, soccer, and boxing.

About the work at Tayba he says, "The Tayba Foundation is unique in that it is a service that has a broad scope of influence in the greater community. As someone who advocates for social justice issues, I find this aspect of Tayba very appealing. The Tayba Foundation uses sacred knowledge as a means of transformation for individuals who impart a positive influence on their respective communities."

Sr Marianne Hogan (Umm Faisal), Teacher

Marianne Hogan Nsour was born and reared in Mississippi. She participated in the Civil Rights Movement in the 1970's while a college student including the Salad Bowl Boycott in support of the United Farm Workers where she met her late husband, Salameh Abdulhamid Nsour of Salt, Jordan. They lived in Jordan for eleven years and resettled in California in 1991 with their five children. She has worked as an English teacher and real estate agent for many years. Her interests include creative writing and researching the Arabic origins of all languages. She dreams of opening a da'wa center in her hometown of Vicksburg.

Ustadha Fadwa Silmi, Teacher

Fadwa Silmi received her B.A. in Middle Eastern Studies from the University of California in Berkeley in 1997. After teaching in a private elementary school for five years, she returned to academia and received a Master's Degree in Elementary Education as well as her teaching credential from San Francisco State University in 2004. Fadwa has studied basic and intermediate Maliki Fiqh, Aqeedah, Seerah, Purification of the Heart, Prohibitions of the Tongue, Arabic as well as other courses in Islamic adab at the Zaytuna Institute in Hayward, California from 1997-2005. She has been blessed to study with Shaykh Hamza Yusuf, Shaykh Khatri ould Bauba, Shaykh Saleck Ould Sidine as well as other visiting scholars to the Bay Area. Fadwa previously served as the Program Director for the Children's Quran School at the Zaytuna Institute in Hayward, CA and is a co-founder and board member of The Rahmah Foundation, a non-profit dedicated to serving the Islamic educational needs of women and girls. She currently teaches math and science at Northstar School, and acts as an educational consultant to both schools and homeschooling families. Fadwa has taught various Islamic sciences privately and in small class settings. She currently resides in Hayward, California with her husband and three children.

Jawad Piorek, Social Media Manager

Jawad develops and maintains several media outlets for Tayba including the Facebook page and website. He has built several blogs and maintains several Facebook pages. Jawad holds a degree in IT from France and his professional background is in IT and has worked in this field for the past 10 years, in Europe and Canada.

He has extensive experience in translating Islamic educational material from English to French including several articles for dawa purpose and legal answers. He has worked with a charity association in Montreal and has translated some parts of their website into French. He has also organized educational programs for fiqh in Montreal, Canada.

Born and raised in France to a Catholic family, he converted to Islam in 2004, after spending several months in Morocco, searching for the true path. He enjoys spending time with family, studying the Islamic sciences, learning the Arabic language, reading, blogging, technologies and travelling.

About his work Tayba Jawad says, "Working with Tayba Foundation give me the possibility to serve an amazing cause. In fact, helping the Muslims inmates, motivated (unfortunately more motivated than the vast majority of Muslims living in freedom) to learn the traditional Islamic sciences in jail, are examples for me. I'm very impressed by them. Even if they are struggling out there and are often forsaken by our community, they have still this deep desire to learn their deen. One of reason why I became muslim was because of Malcolm X and I know for sure that behind all these bars there are new Malcolm ready to get out of these jail, to spread the true message of Islam like Malcolm did it in America."

Educational Program

Our curriculum is designed to ensure that all the course work fits into a specific theme of character reformation. We believe that character reformation is the key to not only working with current or formerly incarcerated men and women, but also to their eventual release and reintegration into the greater society.

Our curriculum incorporates a significant amount of spiritual and behavioral modification geared towards developing qualities which increase accountability for actions. These components of our curriculum are thoroughly reinforced throughout all the courses.

The three core components of the program are:

1) Sound Islamic knowledge
2) Realization of the prisoner's experience
3) Recognition of prison guidelines

Key Highlights of the Curriculum:

• Emphasis on character development influences our choice of texts
• Students learn the essentials of their faith (fard 'ayn)
• An opportunity to learn the Arabic Language

- Emphasis on recognizing and respecting differences of opinion
- Students are required to write an essay that speaks about how the course affected them at the personal, familial and communal level
- Students have a base for meaningful reflection and spiritual development
- Draws upon methodology and texts used in many Islamic centers of higher learning.

Current courses offered

Beliefs of a Muslim	IMAN 100
Islamic Theology Part 2	IMAN 201
How to Study	ADAB 100
Prayer and Purification (Maliki option)	FIQH 101
Five Pillars (Maliki Option)	FIQH 102
Prayer and Purification (Hanafi option)	FIQH 111
Rights of Parents	ADAB 101
Prohibitions of the Tongue	ADAB 102
Intro to Purification of the Heart 101	IHSN101
Purification of the Heart Part 1	IHSN201
Medina Arabic Book 1	ARBC 101

Upcoming courses

Islamic Theology Part 1	IMAN 101
Purification of the Heart Part 2	IHSN 202

Five Pillars (Hanafi Option)	FIQH 112
Prayer and Purification (Shafi'i option)	FIQH 121
Five Pillars (Shafi'i Option)	FIQH 122
Fiqh Marriage/Divorce 1	FAML 201
Fiqh Marriage/Divorce 2	FAML 202
Fiqh Transactions 1	BUSN 201
Fiqh Transactions 2	BUSN 202
Astronomy	ASTR 101
Islam in West Africa	HIST 101
Introduction to Hadith	HDTH 101
Introduction to Quran	QRAN 101
Introduction to Usul	USUL 101
Life of the Prophet	SIRA 101
Introduction to Recitation of the Quran	TJWD 101
Medina Arabic Book 2	ARBC 102
Medina Arabic Book 3	ARBC 103

TAYBA FOUNDATION
IMAN 100 Exam Fall 2016
100 Questions

Remember:
- NEVER GUESS. If you are not sure, then leave it <u>blank</u>, which indicates "<u>I don't know</u>."
- All questions relate to the text, commentary or any supplementary material. These questions are not testing or referring to "general" knowledge that you may have acquired. Make sure to base your answers on the terminology you used in the text. An example would be "sunna" in the general sense as opposed to the classification used by the text, as opposed to "mandub."
- If you believe, a question is incorrectly worded or confusing, please include a written explanation on a SEPARATE piece of paper and submit it along with the test sheet.
- Mark the correct answer on the test sheet with a pen or pencil. Failure to submit the test sheet in a timely manner could result in a failing grade. We advise that you keep a copy of the test sheet for yourself before mailing the original.
- Keep this Exam and only submit the test sheet along with your essay.
- Make sure to write the following on your test sheet: Your name, your ID number, the course title, and the Exam title (for this one it would be "ADAB 100 Exam".

1. Why is knowledge virtuous?
    a) Knowledge provides the seeker with a profession
    b) Knowledge is the means by which taqwa is achieved
    c) Knowledge improves marriageability

2. Doubt is caused by
    a) humility
    b) laziness
    c) wittiness
    d) fortitude

3. The best way to increase memory is to
    a) be serious all the time
    b) be consistent in studying
    c) eat less food than needed
    d) read Quran while looking at it

4. Which one of these is *not* a part of piety?
   a) Avoiding sleeping too much
   b) Avoiding satiation
   c) Avoiding speaking too much about unbeneficial matters
   d) Avoiding eating at someone's home where there are wealthy people present

5. How old was Hasan ibn Ziyad when he began studying fiqh?
   a) 8 years old
   b) 18 years old
   c) 38 years old
   d) 80 years old

6. Once you have taken a lesson, you should:
   a) repeat it, take a new lesson and review again
   b) take a new lesson and then review the old lesson
   c) review, repeat and then take a new lesson
   d) repeat the lesson and then take a new lesson

7. Which of these is *not* among those things that cause forgetfulness?
   a) Disobedience
   b) Using a notebook to write things down
   c) Anxiety and depression about matters of this worldly life
   d) Excessive sins

8. According to the text, knowledge will be gained by honoring and respecting one's
   a) children
   b) teacher
   c) wealth
   d) parents

9. Debate is better than review only if
   a) you are very argumentative
   b) the one you are debating has a fair disposition
   c) you know that you will win
   d) none of the above

10. Too much food and drink cause
    a) laziness
    b) forgetfulness
    c) wittiness
    d) humility

11. Which characteristic is specific to humans?
    a) compassion
    b) knowledge
    c) generosity
    d) strength

12. When striving to seek knowledge, the student should
    a) strive until they feel overburdened
    b) seek gentleness while striving
    c) more at a comfortable pace
    d) none of the above

13. Initially, a student should study
    a) tawheed
    b) seerah
    c) grammar
    d) logic

14. Why must one have an intention while learning?
    a) to maintain their focus
    b) intention is the root of all actions
    c) to achieve their goal
    d) intentions allow one to begin with purpose

15. Lessons should be reviewed
    a) quietly and calmly
    b) quietly and energetically
    c) energetically and powerfully
    d) powerfully and repeatedly

16. Why is it an obligation to have knowledge of matters such as arrogance, greed, cowardice and waste?
    a) It is not an obligation, it is merely a good thing to have
    b) We cannot advise others in these matters if we do not have adequate knowledge
    c) Without knowledge of them, one cannot get rid of them

17. It is obligatory to seek knowledge that is
    a) preserved
    b) relevant
    c) all encompassing
    d) complete

18. Why should a student avoid reading argumentation that appeared after the passing of the scholars?
    a) it is a waste of a life
    b) causes solitude and enmity
    c) distances one from fiqh
    d) all of the above

19. According to the text, the main factors in achieving one's goals are
    a) seriousness, persistence and high aspirations
    b) dedication, hardwork and patience
    c) sacrifice, loyalty and seriousness
    d) persistence, dedication and sacrifice

20. The more pious a seeker of knowledge is
    a) the more beneficial they will be
    b) the easier studying will be for them
    c) the more benefit they will gain
    d) all of the above

21. Part of respecting a teacher is to do the following except:
    a) avoid walking in front of them
    b) talk in their presence without permission
    c) honor their children
    d) ask to extend the lesson past the allotted time

22. The amount of a lesson for a beginner should be such that it can be retained by repeating it
    a) 100 times
    b) 10 times
    c) 5 times
    d) 2 times

23. All of the following improve memory except
    a) using a siwak
    b) drinking honey
    c) eating dates
    d) eating frankincense with sugar

24. Fiqh means
    a) knowledge
    b) learning
    c) rules
    d) knowledge with understanding

25. How many lessons should the student review each day?
    a) two
    b) three
    c) four
    d) five

26. True or False: A person will not gain or benefit from knowledge unless they honor knowledge and the people of knowledge.
    a) True
    b) False

27. Why is seeking counsel regarding one's seeking of knowledge so important?
    a) So we may have a good opinion of the person after they give us advice
    b) Because seeking knowledge is one of the most notable and difficult of matters
    c) To let others know that you will soon be a scholar
    d) To give ourselves time to think over whether we should seek knowledge

28. What reason does the author mention for astrology not being permitted?
    a) It only harms and does not benefit
    b) We are not to study the stars for any reason
    c) There is some benefit, but there is more harm
    d) There is benefit, but only of a worldly nature

29. A person of knowledge should be patient in all of the following except
   a) sticking to one teacher
   b) sticking to one subject
   c) sticking to one book
   d) sticking to one language of study

30. A student who has been blessed with wealth should
   a) save it so they do not have to worry about seeking provision while they study
   b) seek refuge in Allah from miserliness and spend it on the path for knowledge
   c) rely on others to support them on their path for knowledge
   d) none of the above

31. It has been said that the one who memorizes something will lose it, and the one that writes it down will
   a) preserve it
   b) forget it
   c) seek it
   d) share it

32. Which of the following is a fard kifaya (communal obligation)?
   a) paying zakat
   b) getting married
   c) burying the dead

33. The text says that each student should learn the best area of each subject. What does this mean?
   a) the highest level of each subject
   b) the area where most people have written on the subject
   c) the area one would need to learn applicable to one's current state
   d) the area most interesting to one's interests

34. When is the best time to review the lesson?
    a) after fajr
    b) between maghreb and isha
    c) before dhuhr
    d) after asr

35. Knowledge is greater than
    a) Work
    b) Jihad
    c) Family
    d) Action

36. The seeker should always carry
    a) an inkpot and notebook
    b) a book that they are studying
    c) prayer beads to make dhikr
    d) money so that they are able to purchase what they want

37. Which prayer is well known to increase sustenance?
    a) maghrib prayer
    b) duha prayer
    c) eid prayer
    d) taraweh prayer

38. In order to grasp and understand a lesson, it should be
    a) short
    b) repeated often
    c) reflected upon
    d) all of the above

39. Complete the following sentence from the text: "Everyone takes steps towards great intentions but what is rare in people is _____"
    a) Growth
    b) Perseverance
    c) Participation
    d) Hope

40. In seeking knowledge, it is necessary for a seeker of knowledge to have
    a) seriousness
    b) persistence
    c) aspiration
    d) all of the above

41. It is obligatory to know
    a) anything needed to perform an obligation
    b) matters related to rectifying the heart
    c) matters related to staying away from the prohibited
    d) all of the above

42. Muhammad ibn al-Hasan would say, "sleep is from heat, one must fight it with
    a) a cool breezy walk
    b) prayer
    c) cold water
    d) a short nap

43. If an action is obligatory, learning to perform that action is:
    a) obligatory
    b) recommended
    c) praiseworthy

44. The definition of knowledge given by the author is:
    a) a person knowing their responsibilities
    b) knowing many facts about the world we live in
    c) a person knowing their rights
    d) A characteristic that allows its possessor to know something

45. When choosing a study partner, choose someone who:
    a) talks a lot
    b) is lazy
    c) has a good temperament
    d) you have known since childhood

46. A person of knowledge should
    a) avoid that which belittles knowledge or the people of knowledge
    b) be humble
    c) avoid self degradation
    d) all of the above

47. The seeker should do the following to maximize the benefit of knowledge except
    a) keep to oneself
    b) face qibla while studying
    c) avoid store bought prepared foods
    d) request the prayers of the righteous

48. Imam Fakhr al-Islam Qadikhan would say, "One seeking fiqh must always have one book of fiqh memorized so that later it will be easy for him to:
    a) review wherever they are
    b) memorize other fiqh rulings when he hears him
    c) cite the text
    d) look up a ruling

49. When choosing a teacher, the student should choose:
    a) the most popular teacher
    b) the oldest, most knowledgeable teacher
    c) the teacher closest to their home
    d) all of the above

50. How is speech made like an arrow?
    a) By choosing the right words
    b) by reflection
    c) by aiming them in the right direction
    d) none of the above

51. Which of the following is not a reason that the author wrote the text?
    a) to aid the seeker in attaining knowledge
    b) to clarify the methodology for seeking knowledge
    c) to obtain the prayers of those who benefit from the text
    d) to evaluate the learning methods practiced in the region

52. A person can be described as the full type if they
    a) have a good opinion but do not seek counsel
    b) seeks counsel but does not have a good opinion
    c) have a good opinion yet seeks counsel
    d) does not have a good opinion and does not seek counsel

53. Committing a sin will prevent sustenance, especially
    a) cheating
    b) backbiting
    c) lying
    d) stealing

54. A seeker of knowledge must discuss, review and debate with others with
    a) argumentation, loud voices and harshness
    b) fairness, patience and reflection
    c) deliberation, argumentation and logic
    d) Fairness, argumentation and clarity

55. A seeker of knowledge must have the following qualities except
    a) compassion
    b) jealousy
    c) good intentions
    d) intelligence

56. If one is obliged to seek provision for one's family, they should
    a) leave their studies until they secure enough wealth
    b) find a sponsor so that they can continue to study
    c) he should do so and study and review as well
    d) he should continue studying and leave seeking provision

57. The seeker of knowledge should be
    a) modest in what they take on in their studies
    b) look to others to fund their pursuit of knowledge
    c) one of high aspirations and not covet the wealth of others
    d) one of high aspirations and use the wealth of others to avoid working themselves

58. Complete the sentence as stated in the text "the one who concerns himself with that which _____ concern him will _____ that which does concern him".
    a) Should, be overwhelmed by
    b) Does not, miss
    c) should lightly, forget
    d) often, focus

59. A sign that a student will reach his intended goals as they relate to acquiring knowledge is
    a) being persistent when faced with hardship
    b) sleeping well at night to recharge for the next day's lessons
    c) learning the lesson quickly
    d) all of the above

60. The best day to begin a lesson is on
 a) Monday
 b) Tuesday
 c) Wednesday
 d) Friday

61. The Messenger of God said, "seek sustenance by
 a) increasing your night prayers
 b) giving charity
 c) fasting on Mondays
 d) making umrah

62. The benefits to reducing food include
 a) better health
 b) modesty
 c) giving preference to others
 d) all of the above

63. What should the seeker do when they become weary of the subject that they are studying?
 a) switch to another subject
 b) review the previous lesson
 c) take a nap
 d) have a nice meal

64. In seeking knowledge, one should not:
 a) learn to benefit himself and others
 b) seek to gain the pleasure of people
 c) intend to remove ignorance from themselves and others
 d) seek to revive the deen (religion)

65. Respecting books is demonstrated in the following ways except
 a) being in a state of wudu whenever one touches a book of knowledge
 b) never facing their feet towards a book
 c) never placing anything on top of a book except another book
 d) writing the manuscript in small print

66. In balancing our hope and fear of Allah, one should
    a) avoid disobedience because they fear disobeying creation and getting in trouble
    — b) avoid disobedience and maintain the boundaries set by Allah
    c) maintain the boundaries set by Allah to prevent others from hearing of your sins
    d) maintain the boundaries set by Allah to avoid others hearing about their sins

67. It is blameworthy to engage in flattery except
    a) for the merchant trying to make a sale
    — b) for the seeker of knowledge with his teacher
    c) for the seeker of knowledge with himself
    d) for the teacher with his students

68. Respect is better than
    a) charity
    — b) obedience
    c) knowledge
    d) light

69. Who said this line 'Go after knowledge; should you become poor, it will be your wealth, and should you become rich, it will be your embellishment'
    a) Al Hassan Basry
    b) Imam Shafi'
    c) Abi Bakr
    d) al-Zubayr ibn-abi-Bakr

70. Why is the learned man like the keeper of Allah's most valuable treasures according to the author?
    a) Because Allah has bestowed upon the heart of the learned man knowledge
    — b) Because He has the keys to success in this life and in the next
    c) Because few men can be trusted with this treasure
    d) None of the above

71. According to Imam Ghazzali, happiness will never be attained except through
    a) Knowledge
    b) Wealth
    c) Works
    d) Knowledge and works

72. On the day of resurrection which of the individuals will intercede [before Allah]?
    a) Prophets
    b) Scholars
    c) Martyrs
    d) All of the above

73. What is the purpose of the last section in this book?
    a) to summarize the previous sections
    b) to define knowledge
    c) to motivate seekers of knowledge
    d) to comprehend the excellence and value of knowledge

74. Why did `Ali ibn-abi-Talib say that "Knowledge is better than riches?"
    a) Because knowledge guardeth thee whereas thou guardest riches
    b) Because knowledge governs while riches are governed
    c) Because riches diminish with spending but knowledge increases therewith
    d) All the above

75. Which of the following did the Prophet mention that Allah will guide onto a path leading to Paradise?
    a) A scholar
    b) A seeker of knowledge
    c) A teacher
    d) A generous Muslim

76. What best exemplifies the following concept, "what is sought for its own [intrinsic value]," mentioned in the book?
    a) Money
    b) Health
    c) Knowledge
    d) Work

77. What is the main purpose of the section of the text "evidence (for the excellence of knowledge) from reason"?
   a) To comprehend the excellence and value of knowledge
   b) To show us how to come up with our conclusions
   c) To define the term excellence
   d) To understand which types of knowledge are valued

78. According to the author, what is the foundation of this religion (Islam)?
   a) Sincerity
   b) Compassion
   c) Jurisprudence
   d) Brotherhood

79. On the day of resurrection the ink of the learned men will be likened to:
   a) A just judge's ink
   b) A single mother's sweat working hard to raise her child
   c) Tears of repentance from a sincere servant
   d) The blood of the martyrs

80. In the Hadith, envy is unlawful except:
   a) Regarding two categories of persons
   b) When no one gets hurt
   c) When you can ask for forgiveness
   d) There is no exception

81. The Prophet mentioned that when a man dies all except three of his works perish: a permanent endowment for charity, a righteous progeny. Which of the following is the third action?
   a) A good reputation
   b) An invention
   c) A poem
   d) Useful knowledge

82. Why did Sufyan al-Thawri want to leave 'Asqalan without delay?
   a) He was overwhelmed by the number of students
   b) There were enough scholars in town
   c) He was ordered to leave by the ruler
   d) No man questioned him

83. What did Solomon, the son of David, choose when given the choice ?
   a) Knowledge
   b) Power
   c) Wealth
   d) long life

84. Who said the following, "While I sought knowledge, I was abased, but when I was sought for it, I was exalted."
   a) The son of Abbas
   b) The prophet
   c) David, son of Solomon
   d) Imam Malik

85. Who owns this saying: "The learned have more compassion for the followers of Muhammad than either their fathers or mothers?"
   a) 'Ikrimah
   b) Yahya ibn-Mu'adh
   c) The Prophet
   d) Al Ghazzali

86. According to Al-Hasan what does this Ayah mean: "Give us good in this world and good in the next," (2:197)?
   a) good in this world meant knowledge and worship while that of the next signified paradise
   b) Make it easy for us in this world and in the next
   c) Plenty of wealth in this world and paradise in the next
   d) Contentment in this world and good companionship in the next

87. Which of these groups did the Prophet chose to sit with when given the choice?
   a) A group making remembrance
   b) A group studying knowledge
   c) A group reading Quran
   d) A group distributing charity

88. The excellence of learning is attested to in the:
   a) Sunnah
   b) Quran
   c) companions' sayings
   d) All the above

89. What does the nourishment of the heart consist of?
    a) Knowledge
    b) Calories
    c) Protons
    d) Wisdom and knowledge

90. In a prophetic narration mentioned in the book, why would Allah forgive the learned men on the day of resurrection?
    a) because they are special
    b) because they deserve it
    c) because they made an effort to study and teach the commands of Allah
    d) because He did not imbue them with His Knowledge in order to torment them

91. Complete the following Hadith; "To rise up before daybreak and learn but a section of knowledge is ..
    a) Better than the entire life."
    b) Better than prostrating yourself in prayer a hundred times."
    c) Better than the moon and stars all together."
    d) Better than charity."

92. Why shouldn't one conceal knowledge?
    a) Because it is not nice to do so
    b) Because that is the norm among learned men
    c) Because it is recommended to do so
    d) It is forbidden to conceal knowledge

93. What distinguishes man from the other animals?
    a) Curiosity
    b) Virility
    c) Sentiments
    d) Intellect

94. According to ibn-`Abbas, how much higher is the learned man's rank above the believers?
    a) Higher that the distance between the earth and the higher sky
    b) Seven hundred grades higher
    c) If he learns all sciences then he is as high as the Uhud mountain
    d) There is no difference, and they are in the same rank

95. Why are the learned men the heirs of the prophets?
    a) Because they inherited the prophet's' knowledge
    b) Because they relate to them in their mission
    c) They aren't prophets inheritors
    d) Because they receive revelation

96. According to the author, which of the following do human interests extend to?
    a) Material
    b) Spiritual
    c) Essentials
    d) Material and spiritual

97. According to Ata', attending an assembly of learning removes:
    a) The evil of attending seventy places of entertainment
    b) The evil of a yearlong of backbiting
    c) The evil of missed prayers
    d) None of the above

98. The author refers to politics as a fundamental activity. What kind of politics does he mean?
    a) The one that gives you power over people
    b) Politics on how to deal with governors and people as a scholar
    c) Attributed to a political party which pursues followers and a political agenda
    d) Politics that is made to guide people to the straight path and insures salvation in this world and the next

99. In this Ayah, "We have sent down to you raiments wherewith to cover your nakedness," (7:25) what does Allah refer to by raiment?
    a) Jewels
    b) Modesty
    c) Garments
    d) Knowledge

100. How many sections comprise the Book of Knowledge By Imam al Ghazzali?
    a) Two sections
    b) Four sections
    c) Seven sections
    d) Nine sections

Instruction of the Student

By Imam al-Zarnuji

Translation and Notes by Rami Nsour

All Praise be to Allāh ﷻ who made the children of Ādam (alayhis salam) more virtuous than all of creation by giving them knowledge and implementation of that knowledge. May prayers and peace be sent upon Muḥammad, the master of the Arabs and non-Arabs. And may prayers and peace be sent upon his family and companions, the springs of knowledge and wisdom.

To commence, I have witnessed many seekers of knowledge striving to gain knowledge, yet they do not achieve what they desire. They are also prevented from gaining the benefits and fruits of knowledge which is to implement it and spread it. The reason for this is that they did not follow the correct methods of learning and did not fulfill the preconditions of knowledge. Everyone who chooses the wrong method will be misguided and will not gain what they are seeking, this is whether what they are seeking is great or small. For these reasons, I wanted to clarify to seekers the method of learning based on what I have read in books and heard from my teachers, the possessors of knowledge and wisdom. It is my hope, in writing this, that those who are sincerely interested in this text pray for my victory and salvation on the Day of Judgment. I wrote this text after praying my *istikhāra*[1] and I have titled it:

"Teaching the Student about the Methods of Learning."

---

[1] Means to seek goodness from Allah. When one intends to do an act, he or she asks Allah to guide them if this task is good for them or not.

I have divided it into the following chapters:

Chapter 1: The definition of knowledge and fiqh[2] (Understanding) and their virtue.
Chapter 2: Intentions while learning.
Chapter 3: Choosing a subject, teacher, study partner and Steadfastness.
Chapter 4: Honoring knowledge and those who carry it.
Chapter 5: Seriousness, perseverance and aspiration.
Chapter 6: Prioritization and the amount to study.
Chapter 7: Depending on Allāh.
Chapter 8: The time of acquirement.
Chapter 9: Compassion and advice.
Chapter 10: Benefit and Procuring Etiquette
Chapter 11: Wara'[3] (scrupulousness) while studying
Chapter 12: That which Increases memory and what causes forgetfulness.
Chapter 13: That which increases sustenance and that which decreases it. That which increases and decreases lifespan.

And my success is only by God, upon him I rely and and it is to Him that I turn.

جعلته فصولا:

1. فصل : فى ماهية العلم، والفقه، وفضله.

2. فصل : فى النية فى حال التعلم.

3. فصل : فى اختيار العلم، والأساتذ، والشريك، والثبات.

4. فصل : فى تعظيم العلم وأهله.

5. فصل : فى الجد والمواظبة والهمة.

6. فصل : فى بداية السبق وقدره وترتيبه.

7. فصل : فى التوكل.

8. فصل : فى وقت التحصيل.

9. فصل : فى الشفقة والنصيحة.

10. فصل : فى الإستفادة واقتباس الأدب.

11. فصل : فى الورع.

12. فصل : فيما يورث الحفظ، وفيما يورث النسيان.

13. فصل : فيما يجلب الرزق، وفيما يمنع، وما يزيد فى العمر، وما ينقص.

وما توفيقى إلا بالله عليه توكلت وإليه أنيب.

---

[2] Referring to the broader meaning of the word which is real understanding & not the science of fiqh
[3] Is to refrain from that which is suspected to be a sin or unsure of its permissibility.

Chapter 1
The definition of knowledge and fiqh and their virtue

The Messenger of Allāh ﷺ said:

"Seeking knowledge is an obligation on every Muslim[4]."

Know that it is not an obligation upon every Muslim to seek every type of knowledge. What is obligatory is that one seeks relevant knowledge[5]. It has been said:
"The best type of knowledge is that which is relevant and the best type of action is preserving one's current state."
It is an obligation for a Muslim to seek whatever is relevant to his state, in whatever state that may be. It is obligatory for him to know the rules of the prayer to the point of properly performing it. It is incumbent to know the amount that it will take to perform whatever is incumbent upon him. This is because anything needed to perform an obligation (farḍ) becomes obligatory farḍ. Whatever is a means to performing something incumbent (wājib), then that matter is incumbent (wājib) as well. The same rule applies to fasting, zakat (if one has wealth), hajj (if it is incumbent upon him), and the rules of transactions, if one is engaged in business.

It was said to Muḥammad ibn al-Ḥasan (may Allah have mercy on him), "Can you write a book about zuhd (renouncing the world)?" He said, "I wrote a book about business transactions." By this, he means that the zāhid (one who renounces the world) is the one who stays clear of the doubtful and the disliked matters in business transactions. The

---

[4] Male & female. Al-Tirmidhi, Hadith 74.
[5] The author is referring to the knowledge one is in need to fulfill the right and responsibility of the situation he or she is in. Example, learning the prayer ruling when becoming legally responsible or learning the marriage rules when getting married.

same applies to all other types of interactions and trades. Everyone who engages in something is obligated to know how to stay away from the prohibited aspects of that matter. It is also obligatory for one to know about the state of the heart, such as dependence (Tawakkul), repentance (Inaba), fear (Khashya) and contentment (Rida). For, the state of the heart is something a person deals with all the time.

The virtue of knowledge is not hidden from anyone, as it is specific to humankind. All characteristics, other than knowledge, are equally shared by humans and animals. Examples are courage, boldness, strength, generosity, compassion and everything else other than knowledge. Allāh ﷻ distinguished Ādam ☐ from the angels through knowledge and then ordered them to prostrate to him. The virtue of knowledge is due to the fact that it is a means to achieving *taqwā*[6]. It is by *taqwā* that one will achieve honor and everlasting happiness from Allāh ﷻ. It is as was said to Muḥammad ibn al-Hasan ibn Abdullah:

"Learn! For knowledge is an adornment to those who have it.
It is a virtue and sign for all praiseworthy things.

Everyday, be one who gains an increase
In knowledge and swim in the ocean of beneficial things."

---

[6] Taqwa is a state of vigilance against falling into sin in negligence. Scholars have defined 5 levels of Taqwa, the least is to avoid disbelief and the highest is being vigilant of letting anything enter the heart save Allah. This is discussed in detail in Tayba's course IHSN 101 (Introduction to The Purification of the Heart). Ibn Ashir, in his book, "The Helpful Guide," defines taqwa as fulfilling the commands outwardly and inwardly and avoiding the prohibitions outwardly and inwardly. Outwardly means on the limbs and inwardly means in the heart.

Learn fiqh! For fiqh is the best guide *To righteousness and taqwā. It is also the straightest of paths.*	تفقه فإن الفقه أفضل قائد الى البر والتقوى وأعدل قاصد
It is knowledge which will lead to the traditions of guidance. *Knowledge is a fortress which will save you from all calamities.*	هو العلم الهادى الى سنن الهدى هو الحصن ينجى من جميع الشدائد
For verily one faqīh (jurist) who has waraʾ (scrupulousness) *Is harder on the devil than 1000 worshippers."*	فإن فقيها واحدا متورعا أشد على الشيطان من ألف عابد
Knowledge is also the means to know about all other characteristics such as generosity, greed, cowardice, foolishness, arrogance, humility, modesty, waste, stinginess, etc. Verily arrogance, greed, cowardice and waste are prohibited. **One cannot avoid those matters without knowledge of them and how to get rid of them. So it is an obligation for everyone to have knowledge of those matters.**	(والعلم وسيلة إلى معرفة: الكبر، والتواضع، والألفة، والعفة، والأسراف، والتقتير، وغيرها) ، وكذلك فى سائر الأخلاق نحو الجود، والبخل، والجبن، والجراءة.فإن الكبر، والبخل، والجبن، والإسراف حرام، ولايمكن التحرز عنها إلا بعلمها، وعلم ما يضادها، فيفترض على كل إنسان علمها.
The master, great Imam, teacher and martyr Nāṣir al-Dīn Abū al-Qāsim wrote a book about Akhlaq (good character), and what a great book that is. Every Muslim should memorize it[7].	وقد صنف السيد الإمام الأجل الأستاذ الشهيد ناصر الدين أبو القاسم كتابا فى الأخلاق ونعم ما صنف، فيجب على كل مسلم حفظها.

---

[7] Kitab Al-Dhariʾah ila Makarim Al-Shariah (The Path to the Honorable Traits of the Shariah) by al-Raghib al-Isfahani. It is an early work on the subject of character and ethics that influenced later works and authors, including Ghazzali. One of Tayba's faculty, Rami Nsour, has read through much of the book to review it for our students. It is an early work on the subject (the author died in 501 Hijra/ 1108 or 1109 CE) and thus the style, vocabulary, and Hadith references make it a difficult book to read for a beginner student. The author's intent was to train the student on the subject of character, which was then refined greatly in the style of Ghazzali and other authors. This work was then refined even further in the works of Shaykh Muhammad Mawlud, making it much easier for the beginner to go through and memorize the subject and get exactly what he or she needs to know about the subject. The heart of the book can be found in Tayba's courses of ADAB 101, ADAB 102, IHSN 101, and IHSN 201. For those who would like to look into the book of Al-Raghib, it was translated by Mohammed Yassin Alli under the title "The Path to Virtue: The Ethical Philosophy of Al-Raghib Al-Esfahani. An Annotated Translation with Critical Introduction of Kitab Al-Dhariʾah ila Makarim Al-Shariah" (Published by International Institute of Islamic Thought and Civilization in 2006 with the ISBN 9839379402).

As for those matters that happen once in awhile, knowing the rules is a collective obligation (farḍ kifāya). If a portion of the people of a locale learn those matters, then it is not an obligation for the rest of the community. If no one fulfills the obligation of the farḍ kifāya, then the entire community equally share the sin. It is incumbent upon the ruler to order that community to fulfill that duty and he can force them to do so. It has been said, *"knowledge that will be relevant to a person at all times is like food, in that every person needs it. Knowledge of things that do not happen regularly is like medicine, in that a person only needs it when they are sick."*

As for astrology[8], it is like a disease and so to learn it is prohibited since it only harms and does not benefit. Fleeing from the order of Allāh ﷺ and His decree is not possible. It is befitting that every Muslim spend all his other time in remembering Allāh, supplications, being humble before Him, reciting Quran and giving charity to repel tribulations[9]. One should ask Allāh ﷺ for forgiveness and well-being in this life to gain protection from tribulations and calamities. Whoever is given the ability to supplicate will not be prevented from having those prayers answered. If the tribulation was divinely decreed, then it will happen no matter what. But in that case, Allāh ﷺ will make it easy[10] for him and give him patience all through by the blessing of the supplication. If a person is studying the stars to learn how to determine

---

[8] Astrology is different than astronomy. It is lawful (halal) to study astronomy as it is useful in predicting the beginning of months and seasons, determining the direction of Qibla.
[9] Abu Umamah *narrated that the* the Messenger of Allah -sallAllahu alayhi wa sallam- said, "Treat your sick by giving *Sadaqah* (charity)" (Narrated in the Jami). Ubadah bin Samit said, "I heard the Messenger of Allah -sallAllahu alayhi wa sallam-saying, 'There is no person who is afflicted with a wound on his body, and he gives charity due to that, then Allah expiates from him the like of what he gave in charity" (Narrate by Ahmad)
[10] "O you who have believed, seek help through patience and prayer. Indeed, Allah is with the patient." (Qur'an, 2:153)

the *qibla* and the prayer times, then it would be permissible. As for the study of medicine, it is permissible[11]. Medicine is a cause from amongst the causative matters[12] and so learning it is permissible just like learning any other category of causative matters. The Prophet ﷺ at times sought treatment. It has been mentioned that Imam Shafiʿī said: *"Knowledge is of two types: knowledge of fiqh for religion and knowledge of medicine for bodies. Everything else is just conversational material."*[13] The definition of knowledge (*ʿilm*) is a characteristic that allows its possessor to know something. *Fiqh* is knowing the details of knowledge with a type of understanding. Abū Ḥanīfa said: *"Fiqh is a person knowing their rights and responsibilities."*	عليه ويرزقه الصبر ببركة الدعاء. اللهم إذا تعلم من النجوم قدرما يعرف به القبلة، وأوقات الصلاة فيجوز ذلك وأما تعلم علم الطب فيجوز، لأنه سبب من الأسباب فيجوز تعلمه كسائر الأسباب وقد تداوى النبى عليه السلام، وقد حكى عن الشافعى رحمة الله عليه أنه قال: العلم علمان: علم الفقه للأديان، وعلم الطب للأبدان، وما وراء ذلك بلغة مجلس. وأما تفسير العلم: فهو صفة يتجلى بها المذكور لمن قامت هى به كما هو. والفقه: معرفة دقائق العلم مع نوع علاج. قال أبو حنيفة رحمة الله عليه: الفقه معرفة النفس ما لها وما عليها.

---

[11] It is indeed a fard kifaya meaning that if no one knows then the community is at sin, and everyone qualified needs to seek that knowledge.

[12] What the author is referring to here is the concept of the *sabab*, or cause (pl. *asbab*). We know that Allah is in control of everything and has power over all things. So when we look at the world around us and see things happen, how do we join between the idea that Allah is in control and that certain things cause things to happen? Take for example fire, which can burn. But who really is causing the burning? Is it Allah or the fire? When we say, "la hawla wa la quwwata illa billahi (There is no power or might except with Allah)," we mean it to be total. So if we say the fire has the inherent ability to burn, then we have associated a power of Allah with a created thing, which cannot be. Rather, we say that Allah is the one who ultimately is in control of the burning and has just made fire a "sabab" or "cause" for His power to be shown. It is for this reason that if he takes away the power of burning, like in the case of when Ibrahim alayhis salam was thrown into the fire, we find that the sabab/cause is gone and that the fire does not burn. Going back to the text, medicine is a sabab/cause in that we know that Allah is the one who grants healing, but He has chosen to do so through the sabab/cause of medicine.

[13] The author means here that any science that doesn't get you close to Allah is only good to embellish gatherings.

He also said:

> "Knowledge is for nothing more than to implement it. That implementation is to give up this life for the next."

Therefore, one must acquire that which is beneficial and avoid that which is harmful in his early or later age. So he does what is needed to bring benefit and he stays away from that which causes harm. This is so that his intellect and knowledge are not a proof against him and then his punishment is worse. We seek refuge in Allāh ﷺ from His anger and His punishment.

There has been much mentioned about the virtue of knowledge and these are found in verses of the Quran and sound and famous sayings. We will not go into these so that the book does not become drawn out[14].

---

[14] A number of these verses have been mentioned in the section on knowledge by Ghazzali.

Chapter 2: Intentions While Learning

فصل

فى النية فى حال التعلم

It is a must that one have a proper intention while learning. For verily the intention is the root of all actions. This is taken from the Sahih (sound) Ḥadīth of the Messenger of Allāh ﷺ:

"Actions are by their intentions."

Also related from the Messenger of Allāh ﷺ is the saying:

"How many actions will outwardly be in the form of worldly acts and through a good intention it will become from the actions of the next life? And how many actions will outwardly be in the form of the actions of the next life and it will become from the actions of the worldly life because of a bad intention?"

The seeker of knowledge should intend to:

- Seek the pleasure of Allāh
- Gain the afterlife
- Remove ignorance from oneself
- Remove ignorance from all other ignorant people
- Revive the dīn (religion of Islam)
- Preserve Islam, as Islam will only be preserved through knowledge[15].

There can be no renouncing of the world (zuhd)[16] or taqwa if they are coupled with ignorance.

ثم لابد له من النية فى زمان تعلم العلم، إذ النية هى الأصل فى جميع الأفعال لقوله عليه السلام:

إنما الأعمال بالنيات. حديث صحيح.

روى عن رسول الله صلى الله عليه وسلم:

كم من عمل يتصور بصورة عمل الدنيا، ثم يصير بحسن النية من أعمال الآخرة، وكم من عمل يتصور بصورة عمل الآخرة ثم يصير من أعمال الدنيا بسوء النية.

وينبغى أن ينوى المتعلم بطلب العلم رضاء الله والدار الآخرة، وإزالة الجهل عن نفسه، وعن سائر الجهال، وإحياء الدين وإبقاء الإسلام، فإن بقاء الإسلام بالعلم، ولايصح الزهد والتقوى مع الجهل.

---

[15] In reality it is Allah who is preserving the Din (religion).
[16] Zuhd entails abandoning the matters of this dunya in exchange for better in the hereafter.

My teacher, the Shaykh and Imām, Burhān al-Dīn[17] (the author of al-Hidāya) recited some poetry:

> "An immoral scholar is a huge corruption
> And greater than him is the ignorant worshipper
> Both are a huge tribulation amongst the creation
> For those who follow their lead in the religion."

The student should also intend to be thankful for the blessing of intellect and a healthy body. He should not intend to gain:

- Acceptance from people,
- To gather some of the scraps of this worldly life, or
- Honor from the ruler

Muḥammad ibn al-Ḥasan said:

> "If all of humanity were my slaves, I would have freed them and absolved myself of their connection to me."

This is because the one who finds the sweetness of knowledge and implementation of that knowledge will rarely be desirous of what people have. The Shaykh, great Imam and teacher Qawām al-Dīn Ḥammad ibn Ibrāhīm ibn Ismāʿīl al-Saffār al-Anṣārī[18] recited to us some poetry of Abū Ḥanīfa:

> "Whoever seeks knowledge for the next life
>   Will gain a bounty of guidance
> Oh what a loss for the seekers of knowledge

---

[17] Burhān al-Dīn Abu'l-Ḥasan ʿAlī bin Abī Bakr bin ʿAbd al-Jalīl al-Farghānī al-Marghīnānī (Arabic: برهان الدين المرغيناني) was an Islamic scholar of the Hanafi school of jurisprudence. He was born in Marghinan near Farghana in 530/1135 (in Present Day Uzbekistan). He died in 593/1197.

[18] Owner of much praise, Imam of his time and shaikh of Islam, he studied under his father and focused in religious sciences until he became the authoritative interpreter of the religious law of Islam (*mujtahid*) of his time.

Who seek a bounty from the slaves!"

An exception to this rule would be if one sought prestige so to:

- Enjoin righteousness and forbid evil
- Establish rights
- Strengthen the religion

But this would not be allowed for selfish reasons or to seek his desires. It would only be allowed in the amount that it would take to perform the enjoining of righteousness and forbidding of evil. A seeker of knowledge should reflect on this as he is spending a great amount of energy in gaining knowledge. So he should not spend it to get a paltry, worthless, and finite portion of this *dunya* (worldly life). The Prophet ﷺ said:

"Beware of the dunyā for by the One Who holds the soul of Muhammad, it is more magical than Hārūt and Mārūt."[19]

[A Poet has said]

"It is the dunya and it is less than the paltry
The one who is in love with it is lower than the low
With its magic, the dunya deafens and blinds many people
So they become confused and are without a guide."

A person of knowledge should not degrade himself by coveting things that should not be covetted. He should avoid anything that belittles knowledge and the people of

---

[19] Some printed versions of this book do not contain this Hadith reference.

knowledge. He should be humble: humility is a station between arrogance and being abject, and modesty is the same (in that it is the middle path). The details of this can be found in the Book of Character[20]. The Shaykh, great Imam and teacher Rukn al-Islām (who is well known as Al-Adīb al-Mukhtār[21]) recited some of his own poetry to me:

"Verily humility is a quality of one with taqwā
And by it the one with taqwā ascends high stations
One of the wondrous things is the vanity of the ignorant
whether his state is one of the blessed ones or the wretched[22]
Or that he does not know how his life or soul will be sealed
On the day of destruction, whether it will be lowly or high
Majesty belongs to our Lord and it is a characteristic
That is specific to Him, so stay away from it and have taqwā."

Abū Ḥanīfa said to his companions:

"Make your turbans big and your sleeves wide."

He said this is so that people would not belittle knowledge and the people of knowledge[23].

---

[20] See footnote #7.
[21] The pillar of the Din, Abu Abd Allah Mohammed ibn abi Bakr al-Farghany wrote many books among them: "البيان", "مفاتيح الاخبار" و, "هدية الاصدقاء" and "في غريب القران". He died in the year 594.
[22] In a Hadith narrated by Bukhari, it is reported that the Messenger of Allah, the truthful and truly-inspired, said, "Each one of you collected in the womb of his mother for forty days, and then turns into a clot for an equal period (of forty days) and turns into a piece of flesh for a similar period (of forty days) and then Allah sends an angel and orders him to write four things, i.e., his provision, his age, and whether he will be of the wretched (*shaqiyy*) or the blessed (*sa'eed*) (in the Hereafter). Then the soul is breathed into him."
[23] To help the general public know who they are and avoid messing with them. Also, to easily identify scholars and be able to ask for fatwa and questions, and other support if needed.

It is a must for every student to acquire the Book of Advice that Abū Ḥanīfa wrote to Yūsef ibn Khālid al-Samti when he returned to his family. The one who seeks out this book will find it.	وينبغى لطالب العلم أن يحصل كتاب الوصية التى كتبها أبو حنيفة رضى الله عليه ليوسف بن خالد السمتى عند الرجوع إلى أهله، يجده من يطلب العلم
My teacher the Shaykh al-Islam and proof of the Imams, 'Ali ibn Abu Bakr (may Allāh sanctify his spirit) ordered me to transcribe it when I returned to my family and I did so. The teacher and the mufti need that book to properly deal with people[24]. And success is only by Allah.	وقد كان أستاذنا شيخ الإسلام برهان الدين على بن أبو بكر قدس الله روحه العزيز أمرنى بكتابته عند الرجوع إلى بلدى فكتبته، ولابد للمدرس والمفتى فى معاملات الناس منه، وبالله التوفيق.

---

[24] The text of this advice is: "Know that if you harm ten people, you will have enemies, even if they are your mothers and fathers, but if you do good to ten people who are not your relatives, they will become like mothers and fathers to you. If you enter Basra and oppose its people, elevate yourself over them, vaunt your knowledge among them, and hold yourself aloof from their company, you will shun them and they will shun you; you will curse them and they will curse you; you will consider them misguided and they will think you misguided and an innovator. Ignominy will attach itself to you and us, and you will have to flee from them. This is not an option. It is not an intelligent person who is unsociable to the one who is unsociable until Allah shows him a way out.

When you go to Basra, the people will receive you, visit you and acknowledge your due, so put each person in his proper position. Honour the people of honour, esteem the people of knowledge and respect the shaykhs. Be kind to the young and draw near to the common people. Be courteous to the impious but keep the company of the good. Do not disregard the authorities or demean anyone. Do not fall short in your chivalry and do not disclose your secrets to anyone or trust them until you have tested them. Do not socialise with the base or the weak. Do not accustom yourself to what you disapprove of outwardly. Beware of speaking freely with fools.

You must have courtesy, patience, endurance, good character and forbearance. Renew your clothing regularly, have a good mount and use a lot of what is good. Offer your food to people: a miser never prevails. You should have as your confidants those you know to be the best of people. When you discern corruption, you should immediately rectify it. When you discern righteousness, you should increase your attention to it.

Act on behalf of those who visit you and those who do not. Be good to those who are good to you and those who are bad to you. Adopt pardon and command the correct. Ignore what does not concern you. Leave all that will harm you. Hasten to establish people's rights. If any of your brethren is ill, visit him yourself and send your messengers. Inquire after those who are absent. If any of them holds back from you do not hold back from him.

Show affection to people as much as possible and greet even blameworthy. When you meet others in a gathering or join them in a mosque and questions are discussed in a way different to your position, do not rush to disagree. If you are asked, tell the people what you know and then say, "There is another position on it which is such-and-such, and the evidence is such-and-such." If they listen to you, they will recognise your worth and the worth of what you have. If they ask, "Whose position is that?" reply, "One of the fuqaha".

Give everyone who frequents you some of the knowledge they are expecting. Be friendly with them and joke with them sometimes and chat with them. Love encourages people to persevere in knowledge. Feed them sometimes and fulfil their needs. Acknowledge their worth and overlook their faults. Be kind to them and tolerant of them. Do not show them annoyance or vexation. Be like one of them. Do not burden people with what they cannot do."

Chapter 3

Choosing a Subject, Teacher, Study Partner and Having Steadfastness

A student must seek the best area of each subject. This would include what one needs to know about the *dīn* applicable to his current state and then what he needs to know for the future. So what should be given priority is knowledge of *tawhīd* and *m'arifa*. One should know Allāh ﷻ through proof because although the faith of the *muqallid* is sound according to us, he would be sinning by not seeking proofs[25]. One should choose what is older rather than new matters[26]. Some have said:

> "Hold fast to what is old and beware of new things!"

---

[25] What the author is referring to here is a discussion amongst the scholars of theology about taqlid (following without seeking proof) in the matter of faith (iman). In other words, if someone says that they are Muslim and believe in Allah but when asked what is their proof for their being One God, they say, "I don't know" or they say, "I heard people say they believe in One God so I followed them." About this person there is a difference of opinion on whether or not it is considered actual faith (iman) or whether the person is still a non-believer (kafir). Some of the scholars said the person is a believer but has sinned for not seeking proofs, some said he is a non-believer (kafir), some said he is a sinner only if he has the intellectual ability to seek proofs, and others have said that he is a Muslim in any case and this is considered by some to be the strongest opinion. The author is mentioning the opinion that according the "us" (meaning the Hanafi Maturidi scholars) the person has sinned. If one were to ask why this is such a matter of contention, we would point them to the many verses in the Quran that discuss the "proofs" of the Oneness of Allah and thus seeking proofs for each person is a very important matter. Some of these verses are 10:101, 12:105, 17:42, 21:22, 23:91, 30:30. Another very famous story of proving the existence of Allah through proofs is the story of Ibrahim alayhis salam with Nimrod (Quran 2:258). This topic of seeking proofs is covered further in IMAN 100. In any case, the point of this discussion is to encourage us to strengthen our faith through proofs and not to accuse anyone of not fulfilling this duty of seeking proofs for our faith. -rsn

[26] If the intent was to innovate! "Beware of newly invented matters, for every invented matter is an innovation and every innovation is a going astray, and every going astray is in Hell-fire." But if the intent is to reform knowledge for some benefit while preserving the sound foundations then it is a great endeavour.

Beware of studying the argumentation that has appeared after the passing of the great scholars[27]. It will distance a student from *fiqh*, waste his life, cause solitude and enmity. It is also from amongst the signs of the Final Hour and the removal of knowledge and fiqh. This has been narrated in a Ḥadīth[28].

As for choosing a teacher, a student must choose the most knowledgeable, most pious and the oldest. Just as Abū Ḥanīfa chose Hammad ibn Abi Sulayman[29] (RAH) after deliberation and reflection. Abū Ḥanīfa said:

"I found him to be a dignified, gentle and patient shaykh."

He also said:

"I stood fast with Hammad ibn Abi Sulayman and so I sprouted."

He also said:

"I heard one of the wise men of Samarqand say:

One of the seekers of knowledge sought counsel from me about seeking knowledge and he already made up his mind about traveling to Bukhara to seek knowledge."

وإياك أن تشتغل بهذا الجدال الذى ظهر بعد انقراض الأكابر من العلماء، فإنه يبعد عن الفقه ويضيع العمر ويورث الوحشة والعداوة، وهو من أشراط الساعة وارتفاع العلم والفقه، كذا ورد فى الحديث.

أما اختيار الأستاذ: فينبغى أن يختار الأعلم والأورع والأسن، كما اختار أبو حنيفة، رحمة الله عليه، حماد بن سليمان، بعد التأمل والتفكير، قال:

وجدته شيخا وقورا حليما صبورا فى الأمور.

وقال:

ثبت عند حماد بن سليمان فنبت

وقال أبو حنيفة رحمة الله عليه:

سمعت حكيما من حكماء سمرقند قال:

إن واحدا من طلبة العلم شاورنى فى طلب العلم، وكان قد عزم على الذهاب إلى بخارى لطلب العلم.

---

[27] The Prophet said: "No people go astray after being guided except that they indulge in arguments." Ahmad and Al-Tirmidhi, sound hadith

[28] The Prophet said: "Near the establishment of the Hour (religious) knowledge will be taken away (vanish) and general ignorance will spread." Bukhari.

[29] He is the Imam from among the generation after the companions of the Prophet known as the التابعين. He is Abu Ismail Hamad ibn Muslim Abu Sulaiman al Asha'ary Al Kufi from among the Imams of jurisprudence and Hadith science. He narrated on Anas ibn Malik, Annakhi', Hassan al Basry, and Ikrimah. Among those who narrated on him are Abu Hanifa, Jurayr ibn Abdullah, Hamad ibn Salamah, and Al-Thawry. He was known to be generous, and he was give the position of magistrate. He died 127 Hijrah.

This is how the student should be in seeking counsel about everything. For Allāh has ordered His Messenger to seek counsel about all things. There is no one more intelligent than the Messenger of Allāh, and even at that, he was ordered to seek counsel from others[30]. He used to seek counsel from his companions all things, even matters of the house. ʿAli, may Allāh ennoble his face said:

"*No one who seeks counsel will be destroyed.*"

It has been said that people are of three types; full, half, and one that is nothing. As for the full one, he is the one who has a good opinion yet seeks counsel. Half a man is the one who has a good opinion but does not seek counsel. Or the person who seeks counsel but does not have a good opinion. The one who is nothing is the one that does not have an opinion and does not seek counsel. Jaʿfar al-Sadiq said to Sufyan al-Thawrī:

"*Seek counsel from those who fear Allāh.*"

Seeking knowledge is one of the most notable as well as most difficult matters, so seeking counsel about it is even more important and necessary.
The wise man said:

"*When you go to Bukhara, do not be quick to go to the scholars. Spend two months so that you can deliberate and choose a teacher. This is because, if you go to a scholar and begin studying*

---

[30] The concept of Mushawara or Consultation. In the Qur'an, Allah (swt) orders the Prophet to:
"[…] consult them [i.e. the Muslims] in the matter. And when you have decided, then rely upon Allah. Indeed, Allah loves those who rely [upon Him]."(Qur'an 3:159).

with him, you may not like his lesson and so you will leave him and go to another. Thus, you will not get blessing in your studies. So deliberate two months when choosing a teacher and seek counsel so that you do not have to leave and turn away from him. This way, you will stick to your teacher so that your studies will be blessed and you benefit a lot from your knowledge."

Know that patience and perseverance are an important foundation in all matters. It has been said:

"Everyone takes steps towards great intentions
But what is rare in people is perseverance."

It was asked, *"What is courage?"* An answer was given that *"Courage is having patience in the moment."*

So a seeker of knowledge must be perseverant and patient in sticking to one:

- teacher
- book, so that he does not leave it cut short[31]
- subject, so that he does not begin another subject before grasping the first
- place, so that he does not travel to another place without a need to do so.[32]

عنده فربما لا يعجبك درسه فتتركه فتذهب إلى آخر، فلا يبارك لك فى التعلم. فتأمل فى شهرين فى اختيار الأستاذ، وشاور حتى لا تحتاج إلى تركه والاعراض عنه فتثبت عنده حتى يكون تعلمك مباركا وتنتفع بعلمك كثيرا.

واعلم أن الصبر والثبات أصل كبير فى جميع الأمور ولكنه عزيز، كما قيل:

لكل إلى شأو العلا حركات   ولكن عزيز فى الرجال ثبات

قيل: ما الشجاعة؟

قيل: الشجاعة صبر ساعة.

فينبغى أن يثبت ويصير على أستاذ وعلى كتاب حتى لا يتركه أبتر، وعلى فن حتى لا يشتغل بفن آخر قبل أن يتقن الأول، وعلى بلد حتى لا ينتقل إلى بلد آخر من غير ضرورة،

---

[31] By not completing it.
[32] Once at the school of Murabit al Hajj an old man pulled a student to the side and pointed out a huge tree and asked him what makes the tree so strong and unshakable. The student stayed quiet then the old man told him it was because it did not move to many places by being transplanted. The same goes for a student he need to remain in an area until he acquires the knowledge of the place.

The reason for this is that all these matters will cause disarray in everything, preoccupy the heart, waste time, and bother the teacher. The student must be patient in refusing the wants of the self (nafs) and desire (hawa).

One of the poets said:

"Desire is nothing other than disgrace itself.
The victim of desire is a victim of disgrace.
Every one who wrestles a desire will be out-wrestled."

The student must be patient during trials and tribulations. There is a saying that says: "*The storehouses of what is sought are gained after numerous tribulations.*" Some lines of poetry were recited to me, and it has been said that they are by ʿAlī ibn Abi Talib:

"Verily you will not gain knowledge except by having six things
I will tell you about them all with clarity:

Intelligence, avidity, patience, sufficient means,
the guidance of a teacher and a long time."

فإن ذلك كله يفرق الأمور ويشغل القلوب ويضيع الأوقات ويؤذي المعلم. وينبغي أن يصبر عما تريده نفسه وهواه.

قال الشاعر:

إن الهوى لهو الهوان بعينه
وصريع كل هوى صريع هوان

ويصبر على المحن والبليات.

قيل: خزائن المنن، على قناطير المحن.

ولقد أنشدت، وقيل إنه لعلي بن أبي طالب كرم الله وجهه شعرا:

ألا لن تنال العلم إلا بستة
سأنبيك عن مجموعها ببيان
ذكاء وحرص واصطبار وبلغة
وإرشاد أستاذ وطول زمان

65

[33]Choosing a Study Partner

As for choosing a study partner, a student must choose someone who is serious, pious, and has a good temperament. The student should stay clear of one who is lazy, wastes times, talks a lot, is corrupt or a trouble-maker. One of the poets has said:

"About a man do not ask but look to his friend
For everyone will follow whom they befriend,

If that friend is an evil person, then get away from him quickly
And if he is a good person, then stick to him and you will be guided."

The following lines were recited to me:

"Do not befriend a lazy person in any of his states
For how many righteous people have been corrupted by the corruption of another?
The illness of a foolish one is quick to spread to the intelligent one
Like the ember placed in ash that quickly is extinguished."

The Messenger of Allāh ﷺ said:

"Every person is born in the original state of Islam. It is just that the child's parents make him a Jew, Christian or Zoroastrian."

There is a wise saying in the Persian language that states:

وأما اختيار الشريك، فينبغى أن يختار المجد والورع وصاحب الطبع المستقيم المتفهم، ويفر من الكسلان والمعطل والمكثار والمفسد والفتان.

قال الشاعر:

عن المرء لا تسل وأبصر قرينه
فإن القرين بالمقارن يقتدى
فإن كان ذا شر فجنبه سرعة
وإن كان ذا خير فقارنه تهتدى

وأنشدت شعرا آخر:

لا تصحب الكسلان فى حالته
كم صالح بفساد آخر يفسد
عدوى البليد إلى الجليد سريعة
كالجمر يوضع فى الرماد فيخمد

قال النبى صلى الله عليه وسلم: كل مولود يولد على فطرة الإسلام، إلا أن أبواه يهودانه وينصرانه ويمجسانه. الحديث.

ويقال فى الحكمة بالفارسية:

باريد بدتر بود ازماربد بحق ذات باك الله الصمد

---

[33] It is still common practice in schools in Mauritania for students to start books and have lessons at the same time so they can review and compete each other. It is called *dawla* in local Mauritanian dialect. In English this would be like the cohort system.

باربد ازدترا سوی حجیم بار نیکــوکــیر نابی نعـیم	"A bad companion is worse than a black snake and more harmful About this I swear by the Purity of Allāh ﷺ the Everlasting A bad companion will bring you to the edge of Hell So take good companion and through him you will find Paradise."

وقیل:
إن كنت تبغى العلم وأهله أو شـاهدا يخـبر عن غائب
فاعتبر الأرض بأسمائها واعتبر الصاحب بالصاحب
	It has been said:
	    "If you desire knowledge from the scholars
	    Or a witness to describe an unseen land to you
	    Then know the lands by their names
	    And know a friend through friends."

Chapter 4: Honoring Knowledge and Scholars

Know that a seeker of knowledge will not gain or benefit from knowledge except by honoring knowledge and the people of knowledge. Knowledge will be gained by honoring and respecting one's teacher. It has been said:

"No one that achieved[34] did so except by respect. And no one who failed did so except through disrespect."

There is a saying that, *"Respect is better than obedience."* Consider that a person does not fall into disbelief through disobedience alone? A person disbelieves by making light of the act of disobedience and not respecting the prohibition[35].

One of the ways of honoring knowledge is by honoring the teacher. 'Ali, may Allāh ennoble his countenance, said:

"I am the slave of the one who teaches me one letter. If he wants, he can sell me, free me or keep me as a slave."

The following lines of poetry were recited to me about this subject:

*"I consider the greatest right is that of the teacher[36]
It is the most incumbent matter upon every Muslim to preserve*

فصل

فى تعظيم العلم وأهله

اعلم أن طالب العلم لا ينال العلم ولا ينتفع به إلا بتعظيم العلم وأهله، وتعظيم الأستاذ وتوقيره.

قيل:

ما وصل من وصل إلا بالحرمة، وما سقط من سقط إلا بترك الحرمة.

وقيل: الحرمة خير من الطاعة، ألا ترى أن الإنسان لا يكفر بالمعصية، وإنما يكفر باستخفافها، وبترك الحرمة.

ومن تعظيم العلم تعظيم الأستاذ، قال على رضى الله عنه:

أنا عبد من علمنى حرفا واحدا، إن شاء باع، وإن شاء استرق.

وقد أنشدت فى ذلك:

رأيت أحق الحق حق المعلم

---

[34] Here he means attained knowledge or high states of piety

[35] Meaning if someone commits a sin knowing it is a sin, they are better off someone who is challenging the ruling of Allah.

[36] This is an exaggeration from the author since according to the scholars, after Allah and His Messenger, there is no higher right than one's parents. This point, and the proof that the highest right is that of the parents, is discussed at length in ADAB 101 (The Rights of Parents). In any case, the only situation where this would even be applicable is in the case where the parents brought the child into the world and did not teach the child about faith (*iman*). The teacher who taught the child about faith first would be the one who the author must be referring to. Whereas if a parent taught the child faith and allowed the child to be raised with the *shahadatayn*, then there is no greater teacher in that child's life, as iman is the greatest lesson that can be give.

The teacher has gained the right to be honored with a gift
Of 1,000 dirhams for one letter that he taught"
[37]

He who teaches you one letter of some religious matter that you are in need of, is your father in the religion[38].
Our teacher, the Shaykh and Imam Sadid al-Dīn al-Shirazi (RAH), used to say that the scholars mention that:

"Whoever wants his child to be a scholar should search for the unknown jurists (fuqaha) by being generous to them, feeding them, honoring them and giving them something. If his child does not become a scholar, then his grandchild will."

Part of respecting a teacher is to;

- not walking in front of him
- not sitting in his place
- not speaking in his presence without his permission
- not to speak too much in his presence without his permission
- not to ask a question when he is weary
- be punctual in the lesson
- not knock on his door; rather wait until he comes out of his home

In general, the student should seek the pleasure of the teacher and avoid making him angry. He should[39] obey his order in anything that is not a disobedience of Allāh as "There is no obedience to a creature in that which is disobedience to the Creator." As the Prophet ﷺ said;

وأوجبه حفظا على كل مسلم

لقد حق أن يهدى إليه كرامة

لتعليم حرف واحد ألف درهم

فإن من علمك حرفا واحدا مما تحتاج إليه فى الدين فهو أبوك فى الدين.

وكان أستاذنا الشيخ الإمام سديد الدين الشيرازى يقول: قال مشايخنا: من أراد أن يكون ابنه عالما ينبغى أن يراعى الغرباء من الفقهاء، ويكرمهم ويطعمهم ويطيعهم شيئا، وإن لم يكن ابنه عالما يكون حفيده عالما.

ومن توقير المعلم أن لايمشى أمامه، ولا يجلس مكانه، ولا يبتدئ بالكلام عنده إلا بإذنه، ولا يكثر الكلام عنده، ولا يسأل شيئا عند ملالته ويراعى الوقت، ولا يدق الباب بل يصبر حتى يخرج الأستاذ.

فالحاصل: أنه يطلب رضاه، ويجتنب سخطه، ويمتثل أمره فى غير معصية الله تعالى، فإنه لا طاعة للمخلوق فى معصية الخالق كما قال النبى صلى الله عليه وسلم:

---

[37] The poet's intent is to say that there is no price for the knowledge we gain. There is no price tag.
[38] Because his teaching will get you to the pathway of paradise.
[39] Or something that may upset his parents.

> "The worst of people are those who lose their religion for worldly things through disobedience."

Part of honoring a teacher is to honor his children and those who are close to him. Our teacher, the shaykh of Islam Buran al-Dīn (the author of al-Hidaya) used to mention the following account:

> "One of the great scholars of Bukhara used to sit in the place where he would teach from and would frequently stand up. People asked him about that and he said, 'My teacher's son is playing with the other children in the street and he sometimes comes to the door of the masjid. When I see him, I stand up for him out of respect for my teacher.'"

The Qadi and Imam Fakhr al-Dīn al-Irsabandi[40] was the head of the scholars of Maru and the ruler used to respect him greatly. He would say:

> "I was given this rank through service of a teacher. I used to serve the teacher, Qadi and Imam Abu Zayd al-Dabbusi. I would serve him and cook his food for thirty years and I would never eat any of what I cooked."
> [41]

إن شر الناس من يذهب دينه لدنيا بمعصية الخالق.

ومن توقيره: توقير أولاده ومن يتعلق به.

وكان أستاذنا شيخ الإسلام برهان الدين صاحب الهداية رحمة الله عليه حكى: أن واحدا من أكابر الأئمة بخارى كان يجلس مجلس الدرس، وكان يقوم فى خلال الدرس أحيانا فسألوا عنه, فقال: إن ابن أستاذى يلعب مع الصبيان فى السكة، ويجيئ أحيانا إلى باب المسجد، فإذا رأيته أقوم له تعظيما لأستاذى.

والقاضى الإمام فخر الدين الأرسابندى كان رئيس الأئمة فى مرو وكان السلطان يحترمه غاية الاحترام وكان يقول: إنما وجدت بهذا المنصب بخدمة الأستاذ فإنى كنت أخدم الأستاذ القاضى الإمام أبا زيد الدبوسى وكنت أخدمه وأطبخ طعامه ثلاثين سنة ولا آكل منه شيئا.

---

[40] Fakhruddin Abu Bakr Muhammad ibn Al Husayn al Arsbandi. He was a well versed Faqih and brilliant in the science of Usul, he was ahead of his peers, and he was giving the magistrate position. He died 512.

[41] There is an amazing story about serving one's teacher that I heard of when studying the Mukhtasar of Khalil, which is written by Khalil ibn Ishaq. The Mukhtasar is the foremost references in the Maliki school. Ahmed Baba Al Timbukti narrates that Ibn Ghazi said, "It has been narrated that one day he [meaning Khalil] came to the house of one of his shuyukh. He found that the toilet in the house was open and he did not find the shaykh in the house. Khalil asked about this was told, 'The matter of this toilet is bothering him and so he went to hire someone to clean it.' Khalil said, 'I should be the one to clean it.' He then proceeded to roll up his sleeves and went down into the toilet area to clean it. The shaykh returned and saw him in that state and the people were all around him looking at him in amazement of what he was doing. The shaykh said, 'Who is this?' To which they replied, 'Khalil.' The shaykh was very impressed by that and spent a lot of time making du'a for him because of his talent and sincere intention. Khalil gained the blessing of that du'a and Allah placed blessing in his life."

The great shaykh and Imam Shams al-A'imma al-Halwani left Bukhara and lived in a village for a few days due to something that happened to him. All his students visited him except the shaykh and Imam Shams al-A'imma Abu Bakr al-Zaranjari. When al-Halwani saw him he said, "Why didn't you visit me?" He said, "I was busy taking care of my mother." He said, "You will be given a long life, but you will not be given the splendor of classes." It ended up being just as he said. Al-Zaranjari spent most of his time in the villages and was never able to establish a class.[42]

Whoever bothers his teacher will be prevented from the blessing of knowledge and will only benefit a little from him.

"Verily the teacher and the doctor
Will not give advice if they are not honored
So have patience with your sickness if you bothered the one who is treating it
And be content with your ignorance if you did not honor the teacher."

It has been narrated that Harun al-Rashid sent his son to al-Asma'i to be taught knowledge and good manners. One day, Harun al-Rashid saw al-Asma'i performing wudu, washing his foot and the son of the khalifa pouring the water on that foot. Al-Rashid rebuked al-Asma'i for that and said:

I sent my son to you to teach him and instill in him good manners. So why didn't you order him to pour the water with one hand and wash your foot with the other?

---

[42] A right of a mother is higher than that of a teacher no matter how high his rank.

Respecting Books

One aspect of respecting the teacher is to respect books. So a student of knowledge should not pick up a book unless he is in a state of tahara. It has been mentioned that Shaykh Shams al-A'imma al-Halwani (RAH) said, "I gained this knowledge through honoring it. I never picked up a piece of paper except that I had tahara." The Shaykh and Imam Shams al-A'imma al-Sarakhsi (RAH) had a stomach issue. One night, he was studying and he performed wudu 17 times because he would only study if he was in a state of wudu. This is because knowledge is light, and wudu is light as well, and that increases the light of knowledge.

Part of respect is that one should not extend their feet towards a book. One should place the books[43] of tafsir above all other books out of respect. One should not place on top of a book something other than books.

Our teacher, Shaykh al-Islam Burhan al-Dīn used to relate a story from one of the teachers:

> There was a faqih who had placed an inkpot on top of a book and so the teacher said to him, 'You will not attain the fruit of knowledge!'

Our teacher, the Qāḍī and great Imam Fakhr al-Islām who is better known as 'Qāḍī khan' (RAH) used to say:

> If one does not intend disrespect by doing that (inkpot on a book), then

---

[43] Quran and tafseer should be on top followed by hadith books then fiqh and seerah then grammar..etc

there is no harm in it, but the best thing would be to avoid it.

Part of the necessary respect is that one writes nicely, avoids writing in fine(very small) print, and avoids writing in the margins unless needed. Abū Ḥanīfa saw someone writing very finely and said:

> Why are you writing so small? If you live you will be regretful and if you die you will be cursed[44].

This means that if you grow old and your eyesight becomes weak, then you will be regretful for doing that. It has been mentioned that the Shaykh and Imam Majd al-Dīn al-Surkhakti said;

> We never wrote in small print except that we regretted it. We never abridged anything except that we regretted it. We never left comparing manuscripts except that we regretted it.

The shape of books should be square[45], as that is the way that Abū Ḥanīfa used to make them. It is also the easiest shape to hold, put down and look through. There should not be any red ink in books as that is the custom of the philosophers and not the custom of the pious predecessors (*salaf*). Some of our teachers disliked using red ink[46].

ومن التعظيم: أن يجود كتابة الكتاب ولا يقرمط ويترك الحاشية إى عند الضرورة.

ورأى أبو حنيفة رحمه الله تعالى كتابا يقرمط فى الكتابة فقال: لا تقرمط خطك، إن عشت تندم وإن مت تشتم. يعنى إذا شخت وضعف نور بصرك ندمت على ذلك.

وحكى عن الشيخ الإمام مجد الدين الصرخكى، حكى أنه قال:

ما قرمطنا ندمنا، وما انتخبنا ندمنا، وما لم نقابل ندمنا.

وينبغى أن يكون تقطيع الكتاب مربعا، فإنه تقطيع أبى حنيفة رحمه الله تعالى، وهو أيسر على الرفع والوضع والمطالعة.

وينبغى أن لا يكون فى الكتابة شيئ من الحمرة، فإنه من صنيع الفلاسفة لا صنيع السلف، ومن مشايخنا كرهوا استعمال المركب الأحمر.

---

[44] When old, your eyesight weakens and you won't be able to read if not clearly written. When you pass away, others will curse you because they won't be able to benefit from the book and its content.
[45] Or rectangular.
[46] It is permissible but not in conformity with the tradition of Islamic scholars unless the red ink is used to highlight the text (*nass*) and then write the commentary (*sharh*) in black ink.

Part of respecting knowledge is to honor your fellow seekers of knowledge, fellow students of a particular class, and the students of who you study with. Flattery is blameworthy except in seeking knowledge. So it should be done when dealing with one's teacher and study partners to gain benefit from them[47].

A seeker of knowledge should listen to knowledge or wisdom with respect and sanctity, even if he heard a matter or a word one thousand times. It has been said that "whoever's respect of knowledge after the thousandth time is not like the first time is not from the people of knowledge."

A seeker of knowledge should not choose a subject on his own. Rather, he should give that decision to the teacher. This is because the teacher has a lot of experience in choosing subjects, and he knows what is best for every person and what best suits that person's disposition. The shaykh, great Imam and teacher Burhan al-Dīn used to say:

> *"In the early days, seekers of knowledge would turn the decision about what to study over to their teacher. For that reason, they used to reach their goals and what they wanted. **Now, they choose for themselves and so they don't***

---

[47] This topic of praise and when it is prohibited and when it is permissible is discussed at length in the ADAB 102 course which you will cover in sha Allah. The idea the author is referring to here is that we should normally not be overly praising those around us in life, especially if we are trying to get wealth or prestige. This causes a type of insincerity when a person praises others to get something. At the same time, by praising others, you can draw closer to them and they open up to you. When trying to gain knowledge, it is important to get close to your teachers and fellow students and thus praising often is something which is good in this situation. An example of flattery would be to give the teacher a title, like "shaykh" or "shaykhna/our shaykh" or any other title. Normally, we don't use titles with other people unless we want to flatter them. Take for example going to a medical doctor. If you were to speak with him or her using a first name, the person may not feel as respected and this may affect the attention he or she gives you. So, you call them "Dr." Another way to get close to them is to give gifts. I know of one student who used to give our teacher Murabit al Hajj gifts all the time, even when he could only afford to give very paltry things. One time he brought him a sour berry (tugga berry) from a tree that grows wild. Murabit al Hajj was impressed more of the thought of his gift, and really appreciated the gift.

achieve their goals in fiqh and knowledge.

It has been mentioned that Muḥammad ibn Ismail al-Bukhari [48](RAH) began studying the Chapter of Prayer with Muḥammad ibn al-Hasan. Muḥammad said to him, "Go and study the science of Ḥadīth." This was because he saw that science was more suited for his disposition. He then sought the science of Ḥadīth and surpassed all the Imams of Ḥadīth.

A seeker of knowledge should not sit close to his teacher during the lesson without a necessity. Rather, there should be between him and the teacher the distance of a bow as this is nearer to respect[49].

A seeker of knowledge should avoid bad characteristics, for they are metaphorical dogs. The Messenger of Allāh ﷺ said:

The angels will not enter a house that has a dog or pictures in it.

A person only learns by way of an angel[50]. Bad characteristics can be learned by studying the Book of Character[51]. Clarifying good and bad character is beyond the scope of this book. Be especially careful of

---

[48] Commonly referred to as Imam al-Bukhari, he was a Persian Islamic scholar who was born in Bukhara (the capital of the Bukhara Region (viloyat) of Uzbekistan). He authored the hadith collection known as Sahih al-Bukhari, regarded by Sunni Muslims as the most sahih (authentic) of all hadith compilations.

[49] It was narrated on the authority of Umar (may Allah be pleased with him), who said, "While we were one day sitting with the Messenger of Allah (peace be upon him), there appeared before us a man dressed in extremely white clothes and with very black hair. No traces of journeying were visible on him, and none of us knew him. He sat down close by the Prophet (peace be upon him), **rested his knee against his thighs**, and said, "O Muhammad! Inform me about Islam…"

[50] The author means here a good companion.

[51] Again, as mentioned before, the core of this book can be achieved through the ADAB AND IHSN courses in Tayba (ADAB 101, ADAB 102, IHSN 101, IHSN 201)

arrogance, with it one will not gain knowledge. It has been said:

> Knowledge is an enemy to the arrogant young man
> Just as the flood is an enemy to high ground.

It has also been said:

> It is by striving, not by luck, that all glory is attained
> And is striving without luck glorious?
> How many slaves are at the rank of the free?
> And how many free are at the rank of the slave?

والأخلاق الذميمة تعرف فى كتاب الأخلاق وكتابنا هذا لا يحتمل بيانها. وليحترز خصوصا عن التكبر ومع التكبر لا يحصل العلم.

قيل:

العلم حرب للفتى المتعالى كالسيل حرب للمكان العالى

(Arabic missing)

Chapter 5 on Seriousness, Persistence and Aspiration

Next, it is necessary for a seeker of knowledge to have seriousness, persistence and aspiration in seeking knowledge. This is referred to in the Quran by the saying of Allāh ﷺ:

And for those that struggle for Our sake, we will guide them to Our paths.

And the saying of Allāh ﷺ:

O Yaḥyā! Take the Book with strength[52]!

It has been said:

Through seriousness, not your grandfathers, is the attainment of every high rank
For is a grandfather without seriousness a noble person?
For how many slaves have the rank of a free man?
And how many free men have the rank of slaves?

It has been said:

Whoever seeks something and is serious will find it. Whoever knocks on the door and is persistent will enter.

It has also been said:

Based on how much you exert yourself will gain you what you desire.

It has been said:

There are three types of people that are in need of seriousness: A student,

---

[52] Here it means "take it seriously" not meaning "snatch." The verse of the Quran here is 19:12.

teacher as well as a father if he is living.

The shaykh, Imam and teacher Sadid al-Dīn al-Shirazi recited to me some poetry of al-Shafi'i;

Seriousness brings near every distant matter
Seriousness opens every closed door.

The creature of Allāh that is in most need of seriousness is a person
Who has aspiration but has been given the tribulation of constricted circumstances.

One of the proofs of Divine Ordainment and its Judgment
Is the hard life of an intelligent person and the easy life of a fool[53]

But the one who is given intelligence is prevented from wealth
They are two opposites that differ in many ways.

The following, from someone other than al-Shafi'i, was told to me:

You wish to become a competitive jurist Without dedication? Surely the types of insanity are many.

Wealth is not gained without hardship that is endured. So how do you expect knowledge to be?

---

[53] The author is asking us to reflect on the nature of this life (dunya) and how it is not always logical. The example he gives is of rizq or "sustenance." If we were to use our logic, we would say that an intelligent person who knows how sustenance should be gained would be the person most likely to get sustenance, whether in the form of money, jobs, land, wealth, etc. But the reality is that sometimes we see an ignorant fool making more money than an intelligent person, even if they are both trying the same things and giving the same level of work and attention. That is just the nature of the dunya. It is for this reason that we sometimes see a lowly dog getting all the food it needs plus more, while the noble lion may day of hunger. This should be a lesson for us to know that Allah is in control of everything and He gives to whoever He pleases. Also, it is a reminder that we should not put our hopes in this dunya. The Abode of True Compensation, where everyone gets what is deserving of their level, is in the Afterlife.

Abu al-Tayyib[54] said: I have not seen a fault amongst people like the fault Of not completing something for the one who is able to complete it. It is like the poet[55] said: Achievement of high stations depends on how much hardship there was And he who seeks high stations will stay awake during the nights You seek honor and then you sleep at night? The one who seeks pearls dives into the ocean! The elevation of glory is through high aspirations The honor of a person is in staying awake during the nights. The one who seeks glory without hardship Has wasted his life in seeking the impossible. O my Lord, I have left sleep during the nights To seek your approval, Oh Owner of the slaves, So grant me success in gaining knowledge And make me reach the limits of glory. It has been said: *"Take the night as a camel to reach what you wish for."* I was able to write some poetry along these same lines:	قال أبو الطيب المتنبي: ولم أرى في عيوب الناس عيبا كنقص القادرين على التمام ولا بد لطالب العلم من سهر الليالي كما قال الشاعر: بقدر الكد تكتسب المعالي ومن طلب العلى سهر الليالي تروم العز ثم تنام ليلا يغوص في البحر من طلب اللآلي علو الكعب بالهمم العوالي وعن المرء في سهر الليالي تركت النوم ربي في الليالي لأجل رضاك يامولى الموالي ومن رام العلى من غير كد أضاع العمر في طلب المحال فوفقني إلى تحصيل علم وبلغني إلى أقصى المعالي قيل: اتخذ الليل جملا تدرك به أملا. وقد اتفق لي نظم في هذا المعنى شعر:

---

[54] Ibn al-Ḥusayn al-Mutanabbī al-Kindī (915 – 23 September 965) was an Arab poet. He is considered as one of the greatest poets in the Arabic language. Much of his poetry revolves around praising the kings he visited during his lifetime.

[55] Abū ʿAbdullāh Muḥammad ibn Idrīs al-Shāfiʿī is a Muslim jurist, who lived from (767 — 820 CE / 150 — 204 AH). Al-Shāfiʿī was one of the four great Imams, whose legacy on juridical matters and teaching eventually led to the Shafi'i school of fiqh (Madh'hab).

Whoever desires to gain all of his wishes Should take his night as his camel to achieve them. Reduce your food so that you can attain the ability to stay awake at night[56]. This is if you desire to reach completeness my friend.	من شاء أن يحتوي آماله جملا فليتخذ ليله في دركها جملا إقلل طعامك كي تحظى به سهرا إن شئت يا صاحبي أن تبلغ الكملا
It has been said that whoever keeps himself awake at night, his heart will rejoice during the daytime. The seeker of knowledge must be persistent in taking lessons and reviewing during the first part of the night and the last part. Between Maghrib and 'Isha, as well as the end of the night, is a blessed time[57]. About this matter the following has been said: O seeker of knowledge embrace piousness Stay away from sleep and leave satiation. Be constant in the lesson and do not leave it[58]. Through lessons knowledge has been established and raised. So one should seize the days of youthfulness [59] and the prime of youth as was said: Based on your struggle you will be given what you desire, So whoever seeks their desire will get up in the night,	وقيل: من أسهر نفسه بالليل، فقد فرح قلبه بالنهار. ولا بد لطالب العلم من المواظبة على الدرس والتكرار في أول الليل وآخره، فإن ما بين العشائين، ووقت السحر، وقت مبارك. قيل في هذا المعنى: يا طالب العلم باشر الورعا وجانب النوم واترك الشبعا وداوم على الدرس لا تفارقه فإن العلم بالدرس قام وارتفعا فيغتنم أيام الحداثة وعنفوان الشباب، كما قيل:

---

[56] Also the sunnah of napping helps in reducing the amount one needs to sleep during the night.

[57] It is still common, in traditional islamic schools, for students to work their study schedules around these blessed times. Students will usually get in groups to encourage and motivate themselves to study especially during difficult times like during the last third of the night.

[58] Make it a habit of studying and do not be like a camel who is trained to drink every other day or every few days to get ready for long trips

[59] In this hadith the Prophet sal Allaahu alayhi wa sallam said to a man while he was advising him:
"Take advantage of five matters before five other matters: **your youth, before you become old**; and your health, before you fall sick; and your richness, before you become poor; and your free time before you become busy; and your life, before your death."

And seize the days of youth! Verily the days of youth do not last. The student should not burden himself with hardship nor become weakened to where he stops doing things. Rather, he should use gentleness when striving. Gentleness is a core foundation for many things. The Messenger of Allāh ﷺ said: Verily this religion is weighty, so traverse in it with gentleness. Do not make yourself hate the worship of Allāh. The *munbattu*[60] does cut across land and does not have a ride. The Messenger of Allāh ﷺ said: Your body is your ride so be gentle with it. The seeker of knowledge must have high aspirations for knowledge. For a person will fly with his aspiration just as a bird will fly with its wings. Abu al-Tayyib said: Great things will come based on how much resolution people have. Generosity will come based on the level of the generous ones. Small matters will become grand in the eyes of the small person And grand matters will become small in the eyes of the grand.	بقدر الكد تعطى ما تروم فمن رام المنى ليلا يقوم وأيام الحداثة فاغتنمها ألا إن الحداثة لا تدوم قال رسول الله صلى الله عليه وسلم: ألا إن هذا الدين متين فأوغل فيه برفق، ولا تبغض نفسك فى عبادة الله تعالى فإن المنبت لا أرضا قطع ولا ظهرا أبقى. وقال عليه السلام: نفسك مطيتك فارفق بها. فلا بد لطالب العلم من الهمة العالية فى العمل، فإن المرء يطير بهمته كالطير يطير بجناحيه. وقال أبو الطيب رحمه الله: على قدر أهل العزم تأتى العزائم وتأتى على قدر الكرام المكارم وتعظم فى عين الصغير صغارها وتصغر فى عين العظيم العظائم

---

[60] The *munbatt* is the Arabic term used in Hadith to refer to a riding animal which has been driven into the ground. If one is not gentle in the pace a horse or camel, and rather chooses to beat the animal to go as fast as it can, the animal will respond and keep going until it dies and thus is "driven into the ground." The result is that you have not reached your destination and you do not have an animal to ride. The same is true for the way we force ourselves to do things in that if we don't pace ourselves we can "burn ourselves out."

The main factor in achieving things is seriousness and high aspiration. So whoever has the aspiration to memorize all the books of Muḥammad ibn al-Hasan (RAH) and he couples that with seriousness and consistency, then he will likely memorize most or half of them. Whereas if he has high aspiration is not serious, or he is serious but does not have a high aspiration, then he will only attain a small amount of that knowledge.

In his book, Makarim al-Akhlaq, the great shaykh Imam and teacher Radiy al-Dīn al-Naysaburi (RAH) mentioned that:

> When Dhul Qarnayn wanted to travel to conquer the East and the West he sought the counsel of the wise men. He said, 'How can I travel for this much dominion? This worldly life is little and finite, and ownership of it is paltry? This is not part of having a high aspiration!' The wise men said, 'Travel so that you gain dominion of the *dunya* and *akhira*.' He said, 'This is better.'

The Messenger of Allāh ﷺ said:

> "Allāh loves high matters and dislikes the lowly ones."[61]

It has been said:

> Do not be hasty in your matter but be consistent.
> You will not get a straightening of your staff like with the consistent one.[62]

---

[61] Al-Tabarani

[62] Do not try straightening your staff by bending it with excessive force as it may break, rather bend it slowly after making it soft with heat then it will become straight and stronger. The same analogy goes for other matters, so take your time and prepare the transition.

Abū Ḥanīfa said to Abu Yusuf:

You used to be dull-witted, but consistency took you out of that. Beware of laziness for it is a misfortune and a great calamity.

The shaykh and Imam Abu Nasr al-Saffar al-Ansari (RAH) said:

O self! O self! Do not become lazy in doing deeds of righteousness,
justice and good (iḥsān) performed while being calm.

Everyone who does works of goodness is envied.
In tribulation and calamity you will find every lazy person.

I was able to write some poetry in line with this idea:

O self! Leave laziness and procrastination. Otherwise, remain in shame.
I have not seen that the lazy ones are given things
Other than remorse and prevention of what they desire

It has been said:

How much shame, incapacity and remorse
Befalls a person due to laziness?

Beware of laziness when researching something that is unclear
In what you have learned. Your doubt is caused by laziness.

قيل:

قال أبو حنيفة رضى الله لأبى يوسف: كنت بليدا أخرجتك المواظبة، وإياك والكسل فإنه شؤم وآفة عظيمة.

قال الشيخ الإمام أبو نصر الصفار الأنصارى:

يا نفس يا نفس لا ترخى عن العمل
فى البر والعدل والإحسان فى مهل
فكل ذى عمل فى الخير مغتبط
وفى بلاء وشؤم كل ذى كسل

وقد اتفق لى فى هذا المعنى شعر:

دعى نفسى التكاسل والتوانى
وإلا فاثبتى فى ذا الهوان
فلم أر للكسالى الحظ يعطى
سوى ندم وحرمان الأمانى

وقيل:

كم من حياء وكم عجز وكم ندم
جم تولد للإنسان من كسل
إياك عن كسل فى البحث عن شبه
فما علمت وما قد شذ عنك سل

There is a saying that laziness is from not giving much thought to the status of knowledge and its virtue. So, a seeker of knowledge must motivate himself to gain knowledge, be serious and consistent by reflecting on the virtues of knowledge. [63]

Knowledge remains with the retention of the information and wealth vanishes, as the Commander of the Believers 'Ali ibn Abi Talib said:

> We are content with the decree of the Almighty.
> We have knowledge and the enemies have wealth. [64]
>
> For wealth will soon perish.
> And knowledge will remain forever.

Beneficial knowledge will cause a person to have a good reputation, and that will remain after his death, as knowledge is everlasting life. The shaykh, great Imam Dhahir al-Dīn, the Mufti of the Imams, Ḥasan ibn 'Alī who is known as al-Marghnani (RAH) recited to me the following lines:

> The ignorant ones are dead before they die.
> The knowledgeable ones, even when they die, are living. [65]

The Shaykh of Islam, Burhan al-Dīn, recited to us the following lines:

> Ignorance, for its people, is death before death
> Their bodies are graves prior to the graves.
>
> For if a person does not get life through knowledge then he is dead,

---

[63] Review chapter on the virtues of knowledge.
[64] It has been said that knowledge protects you while you need to protect wealth
[65] By keeping behind beneficial knowledge others will read and benefit from. They and their work will be mentioned like living people.

And there is no resurrection for him during the Resurrection.	وإن امرؤ لم يحيى بالعلم ميت فليس له حين النشور نشور
Another poet said:	وقال غيره:
The possessor of knowledge is living infinitely after his death, And his bones crumble under the dirt.	أخو العلم حي خالد بعد موته وأوصاله تحت التراب رميم
The ignorant one is dead as he walks upon the earth. It is believed that he is from the living yet he is non-existent.	وذو الجهل ميت وهو يمشى على الثرى يظهر من الأحياء وهو عديم
Someone else said:	وقال آخر:
The heart's life is through knowledge so seize it! The death of the heart is by ignorance, so stay away from it!	حياة القلب علم فاغتنمه وموت القلب جهل فاجتنبه
The Shaykh of Islam, Burhan al-Dīn, recited to us the following lines:	وأنشدنى أستاذنا شيخ الإسلام برهان الدين رحمة الله عليه شعرا:
Knowledge is the highest of stations. Beneath it is the honor of all people.	ذا العلم أعلى رتبة فى المراتب ومن دونه عز العلى فى المواكب
The knowledgeable one's honor remains multiplied While the ignorant one is under the dirt after his death.	فذو العلم يبقى عزه متضاعفا وذو الجهل بعد الموت فى الترائب
It is far-fetched and hopeless for one to reach the limits of knowledge's glory By ascending the position of power and leading armies.	فهيات لا يرجو مداه من ارتقى رقى ولى الملك والى الكتائب
I will relate to you some things about knowledge so listen, And I am unable to mention all of the virtues of knowledge.	سأملى عليكم بعض ما فيه فاسمعوا فبى حصر عن ذكر كل المناقب
It is every light that can be, and it guides the blind one Whilst the ignorant one goes through life in severe darkness.	هو النور كل النور يهدى عن العمى وذو الجهل مر الدهر بين الغياهب؛ هو الذروة الشماء تحمى من التجا إليها ويمشى آمنا فى النوائب به ينتجى والناس فى غفلاتهم

Knowledge is the high mountain that protects he who seeks refuge On it, and he will walk safely during calamities.	به يرتجـــى والـروح بين الترائب
With it, one will be saved while people are in their heedlessness With it one has hope while the soul is in the chest	به يشفع الإنسان مـن راح عاصـيا
With it, a person will intercede[66] for another that went in a state of disobedience Towards the levels of Hell, which is the worst of punishments	إلى درك النيران شـر العــواقب
Whoever desires knowledge desires all that can be wanted. Whoever attains it has attained all that is sought.	فمن رامه رام المآرب كلـــها ومــن حازه قد حاز كل المطالب
It is the high position, Oh[67] intelligent one, So if you gain it, take it easy when you lose other positions.	هو المنصب العالي يا صاحب الحجا إذا نلته هون بفــــوت المـناصب
So if this world and all its pleasure passes you by, Turn a blind eye to it, for knowledge is the best of gifts.	فإن فاتك الدنيا وطيب نعيمـــها فغمض فإن العلم خير المواهب
Someone recited to me the following:	وقيل فى هذا المعنى:
If the learned one is proud of his knowledge Then the knowledge of *fiqh* is more worthy to cause pride.	إذا مـــا اعتز ذو علم بعـــلم فعلم الفقــه أولـــى باعتزاز
The aromas of perfume are many but they are not like musk,	فكـــم طيب يفوح ولا كـمسك وكـــم طير يطير ولا كبازى

---

[66] There are a number of Hadiths narrated about certain categories of people interceding on behalf of others on the Day of Judgement. One of those people will be the one who memorizes the Quran. Others include the scholars and the martyrs.

[67] The poet means that if you achieve a higher state of knowledge then don't worry about other matters like wealth ..etc as they are guaranteed afterwards.

And there are many birds that fly but not like the falcon.[68] I was also told: *Fiqh* is the most valuable thing you will store. Whoever studies knowledge will not have his glorious deeds wiped out. So attain for yourself what you wake up not knowing. For the beginning and end of knowledge is happiness. The pleasure gained through knowledge, *fiqh* and understanding[69] should be enough of a cause to motivate one to study. Laziness may be caused by too much phlegm and moisture. The way to reduce that is by reducing food. It has been said that seventy doctors are in agreement that most forgetfulness is caused by too much food. Too much phlegm is from drinking too much and that is caused by eating too much. Dry bread will prevent phlegm as well as eating raisins on an empty stomach. One should not eat a lot of raisins so that he won't have to drink water and cause the phlegm to increase. Using a toothbrush (*miswāk*) will also reduce phlegm and increase memory and eloquence, as it is a grand *sunna*. It	وأنشدت أيضا لبعضهم: الفقه أنفس كل شيئ أنت ذا خـــــره مــن يدرس العلم لم تدرس مفاخره فاكسب لنفسك ما أصبحت تجهــــله فأول العلم إقبال وآخــــــــــره وكفى بلذة العلم والفقه والفهم داعيا وباعثا للعاقل على تحصيل العلم. وقد يتولد الكسل من كثرة البلغم والرطوبات، وطريق تقليله، تقليل الطعام. قيل: اتفق سبعون طبيبا على أن النسيان من كثرة البلغم، وكثرة البلغم من كثرة شرب الماء، وكثرة شرب الماء من كثرة الأكل، والخبز اليابس يقطع البلغم، وكذلك أكل الزبيب على الريق، ولا يكثر منه، حتى

---

[68] The comparison of fiqh vis a vis other sciences is like Musk to other scents and like a falcon to other birds. He is saying here that the grade of fiqh in comparison to other sciences is that it is a higher grade. This should be noted because oftentimes people discredit the study of fiqh, calling it dry and other terms which should not be used. The reality is that not a day goes by that we don't need to know the ruling of something in our lives, and the answer is in fiqh.

[69] One of the scholars used to say, "If the son of rulers know the pleasure we experience from knowledge they would fight us for it." In other words, the sons of the rulers are fighting each other for power, wealth, prestige, land etc. and they are not fighting and vying with the scholars to take what they have. Through all of this fighting, they are looking for pleasures of this world. But if they knew the pleasure found in knowledge, they would have fought the scholars to take it from them in the same way they fight for worldly things. But the pleasure of knowledge is hidden, and only the students and scholars experience it. One of our teachers, Murabit Haddameen said once that the pleasure of not knowing something, then coming across the answer in a book is incomparable to any pleasure of this world. We found this to be true and we pray that you, the reader and aspiring student, find that same pleasure in knowledge.

increases the reward of the prayer and recitation of Quran.[70] Regurgitation also reduces phlegm and moistures[71].	لايحتاج إلى شرب الماء فيزيد البلغم. والسواك يقلل البلغم، ويزيد الحفظ والفصاحة، فإنه سنة سنية، تزيد فى ثواب الصلاة، وقراءة القرآن، وكذا القيء يقلل البلغم والرطوبات
The way to reduce food is to reflect on the benefits of eating less. Those benefits are health, modesty[72], and giving preference[73] to others[74]. It has been said: What a disgrace! A disgrace! And Disgrace For one to become wretched over food[75] It has been related that the Prophet ﷺ said: There are three people that Allāh hates without them having committed a crime: The glutton, the miser and the arrogant one.	وطريق تقليل الأكل التأمل فى منافع قلة الأكل هى: الصحة والعفة والإيثار. وقيل فيه شعر: فعار ثم عار ثم عار شقاء المرء من أجل الطعام وعن النبى عليه السلم أنه قال: ثلاثة يبغضهم الله من غير جرم: الأكول والبخيل والمتكبر.

---

[70] In the Hadith " The prayer before which the Miswak is utilized is 70 times more superior to that before which it is not used."- Ahmad.
[71] The idea of reducing phlegm, moistures and other bodily fluids comes from the type of medicine called "humorism" which has its origins in Greco-Roman tradition and was adopted and developed by many Muslims, especially during the "Golden Age of Islam." It is basically made up of four humours of hot, cold, wet and dry and their qualities of yellow bile, blood, black bile, and phlegm. As with all forms of medicine, it should only be practiced by a professional who is trained. Thus, the suggested treatment of regurgitating food should only be done under the care of someone who is trained in medicine.
[72] Is a state of being moderate "*Eat and drink, but not to excess*" Quran *7:31*
[73] The Prophet said : "*He is not a believer who eats to his fill but his neighbor goes without food.*" Sahih Bukhari
[74] If humans enacted this globally, think of how it could solve the crisis of food and water.
[75] This means that a person should consider the causes of what will lead them into wretchedness, which will then cause the person to get punished. I remember once hearing a person reflect on people who abuse donkeys saying, "How humiliating it will be for them on the Day of Judgement to be punished and shamed in front of all over a donkey!?" In the same way, some people will allow their love of food to lead them to disobedience which will then be punished. In other words, "Was that haram food really worth it considering that you will be punished and humiliated in the next life for it?"

There are many things to reflect on as far as the harms of overeating, such as sickness and causing a lazy disposition. There is a saying that satiation removes intelligence. It has been mentioned that Galen[76] said, "All pomegranate is beneficial and all fish is harmful." A little amount of fish is better than a lot of pomegranate.[77] Overeating also wastes wealth. Eating beyond satiation is a clear harm and whoever does so, deserves a punishment in the next life. The glutton is hated by people.[78] The way to reduce food is to eat oily food and start with the finer and more tasty food. Do not eat with hungry people. If one has a proper intention when eating his full, such as gaining strength to fast, pray or do heavy labor, then that would be fine.	وتأمل فى مضار كثرة الأكل وهى: الأمراض وكلالة الطبع، وقيل: البطنة تذهب الفطنة. حكى عن جالينوس أنه قال: الرمان نفع كله، والسمك ضرر كله، وقليل السمك خير من كثرة الرمان. وفيه أيضا: إتلاف المال، والأكل فوق الشبع ضرر محض ويستحق به العقاب في دار الآخرة، والأكول بغيض فى القلوب. وطريق تقليل الأكل: أن يأكل الأطعمة الدسمة ويقدم فى الأكل الألطف والأشهى، ولا يأكل مع الجائع إلا إذا كان له غرض صحيح، بأن يتقوى به على الصيام والصلاة والأعمال الشاقة فله ذلك.

---

[76] Better known as Galen of Pergamon, was a prominent Greek physician, surgeon and philosopher in the Roman empire.
[77] He means that overeating from anything is bad, even healthy foods.
[78] Except for those who needs it because of the type of work or activities they are engaged in

Chapter 6 On Starting a Lesson, The Amount Studied and the Lesson Plan

Our teacher, the shaykh of Islam, Burhan al-Dīn (RAH) used to begin his lessons on Wednesday. He would narrate a Ḥadīth related to that[79] and would say that the Messenger of Allāh ﷺ said:

There is nothing that begins on a Wednesday except that it is completed.[80]

This is what Burhan al-Din used to do, may Allāh have mercy on his soul. He used to narrate this Ḥadīth on the authority of his teacher, the shaykh and great Imam Qiwam al-Dīn Ahmed ibn Abdul Rashid (RAH). I heard from a source I trust that Shaykh Yusuf al-Hamdani (RAH) used to begin all his good deeds on a Wednesday. This is because Wednesday is the day that light was created on. It is also a day of misfortune for the disbelievers, thus it is a blessed day for the believers.

As for the amount that one should make the lesson, my father (RAH) used to mention that the shaykh, *qadi* (judge) and Imam 'Umar ibn Imam Bakr al-Zaranjari (RAH) used to say:

Our teachers have told us that the amount of the lesson for the beginner should be an amount that he can retain by repeating it twice at a moderate pace.

---

[79] Although a weak hadith, the Ulama allow the use of weak hadiths for implementing extra righteous acts (*fada'il al-a'mal*). In the traditional schools or Mahdara in Mauritania students are encourage to do their first class of a new book on Wednesday. The rulings of implementing weak hadiths will be discussed in Tayba's HDTH 101 course.

[80] Two meanings; physical completion of a book or getting the blessings and understanding of what is studied.

Then he adds one word everyday until he is able to retain the lesson by repeating it twice, whether it was a short or long lesson. He should gently and moderately add to the lesson's amount. If the lesson is so long that it takes him in the beginning ten times to retain it, then at the advanced level it will take him ten times as well. This is because that will become a habit and he will not leave his habit except by great difficulty. It has been said that the lesson should be one letter and the review 1000 times.

The student should start with a subject that he can easily comprehend. The shaykh, Imam and teacher Sharaf al-Dīn al-'Aqili (RAH) used to say:

> I hold that the correct manner in this is what our teachers used to do. They would choose for the beginners very basic books, since it is easier to understand and retain. Those books are also less likely to cause boredom as well as being more accepted by people.

After gaining command of a lesson and reviewing it a lot, a student should write down notes as this is very beneficial. One should not write down something they do not understand as it will cause a lazy disposition, reduce intellect and waste time. The student must be serious in gaining understanding by means of the teacher, reflection, thinking and numerous repetitions. If the lesson is short, and there is a lot of review and reflection, he will grasp and understand it.

It has been said that memorizing two letters is better than hearing two loads, and understanding two words is better than memorizing two loads[81]. If one neglects comprehending the lesson once or twice, then he will get used to that and not be able to comprehend a simple discussion. So the student must not neglect comprehension. Rather, he should strive to comprehend and humbly pray to Allāh ﷺ, for He will respond to those who call on Him and He will not disappoint those who have hope in Him ﷺ.

The shaykh and great Imam Qawam al-Dīn Hammad ibn Ibrahim ibn Isma'il al-Saffar (RAH) recited to us some poetry of Qadi Khalil ibn Ahmed al-Sijzi that relates to this idea:

Serve knowledge, the service of one who is benefiting
Be continuous in the lesson, in a praiseworthy manner.

If you don't memorize something, repeat it
Then reinforce it a great deal

Take notes on it so that you can come back to it
And forever be able to study it again

Once you are sure that you will not lose the lesson
Then quickly take a new lesson

But review the previous lesson
With the same devotion that you put to this new lesson

Teach[82] people knowledge so that you may become alive.
Do not be far from intelligent people

---

[81] The author here uses heavy load to mean a lot of text.
[82] Teaching others is by far the most efficient tool to stay on top of books studied and explore new meanings. One scholar use to say: " thanks to our teachers and the students"

If you conceal knowledge you will be made to forget it until
You will be seen as nothing other than an ignorant fool

Then on the Resurrection you will be bridled with fire[83]
And burn in the extreme punishment

      A seeker of knowledge must discuss, review and debate with others. It must be with fairness, patience and reflection. He should avoid quarreling and anger, for review and discussion is a type of seeking counsel. Seeking counsel is only done to seek the correct opinion and that can only happen with reflection, patience and fairness. It will not be achieved with anger and quarrelling. If his intention is to defeat the opponent, then it is not permissible to debate. It is only permissible to clarify truth and falsehood. Using deception in debate is not permissible unless the opponent is stubborn and not trying to seek the truth. If a question was brought to Muḥammad ibn Yaḥya (RAH) and he did not have an answer, he would say, "What I have decided on the matter stands, I will look into the matter and above every knowledgeable one is one more knowledgeable."

Debate and discussion has a stronger benefit than mere review. In debate is a review and more. It has been said that one hour of debate is better than one month of review. This is only if the debate is with someone who is fair and has a fair disposition. Beware of debating one who is obstinate and does not have a sound disposition. This is because

---

[83] In the Hadith: "Whoever is asked about [sacred] knowledge and withholds it will have a bridle of fire placed on him on the Day of Judgment." Tirmidhi.

dispositions take over, manners are contagious, and proximity will influence.[84] In the poetry mentioned by Khalil ibn Ahmed (RAH) are many benefits. It has been said:

One of the necessary things about knowledge, for the one who serves it,
Is that it will make all people servants to him[85]

The seeker of knowledge must always reflect on the finer points of knowledge and he should make this a habit. The finer points of knowledge will only be attained through reflection, and for this reason it has been said reflect and you will acquire. Reflection is a must before speaking, so that what is said is correct. Speech is like an arrow; it must be made straight through reflection before shooting it so that it hits the target. It was stated in a book of uṣūl al-fiqh[86] that "a great foundation is that a faqih's words in discussion have been pondered on." It has been said that the root of intellect is speech made with dignified patience and pondering. One of the poets said:

---

[84] Any debate or discussion among students of knowledge shouldn't be based on challenge or position gain rather on checking information and increase in knowledge.

[85] This brings up a very important point, which is service to our teachers. One of the important aspects of Islam is to be good to those who have done good for you. One of the greatest good that we get is from our teachers. One of the things that has been a traditional practice is for students to offer some sort of service to the teachers. This is fine as long as it is not impeding the student's ability to learn. Secondly, if their teacher is expecting this type of service, then it should be clear between the teacher and the student what the exchange is. In this way, it is an exchange of services; the student does some work for the teacher to free up his or her time so as to allow the teacher the time to teach and guide the student. So here the author is saying that knowledge has this aspect of causing people to do service to you if you teach them. I must highlight an important point about service to the teacher which Sidi Ahmad Zarruq makes which is that a person should not gain or give knowledge for the sake of gaining prestige or to gain some worldly benefit. The other aspect of teaching, which is something I reflected on, is that just as the students can become servants of the one giving knowledge, the teacher in a way becomes a servant of the people, by teaching them, advising them, guiding them and answering their questions. And more often than not, teachers give out more service to others than they receive from their students.

[86] Of Muhammad b. Ahmad b. Abi Sahl Abu Bakr al-Sarakhsi was a Persian jurist, or Islamic scholar of the Hanafi school. He died sometime around 490/1096. His main works are the Usul al-Fiqh, the Kitab al-Mabsut, and the Sharh al-Siyar al-Kabir.

I will give you five points of advice about speaking, If you obey the compassionate advisor; Do not be heedless about the reason of speech,[87] it's proper time, How to speak, how much to say and the place of it[88]	أوصيك فى نظم الكلام بخمسة إن كنت للموصى الشفيق مطيعا لا تغفلن سبب الكلام ووقته والكيف والكم والمكان جميعا
The seeker of knowledge should seek benefit at all places and times and from all people[89]. The Messenger of Allāh ﷺ said: "*Wisdom is the lost animal of the believer. Wherever he finds it he takes it*".[90] It has been said, "Take what is clear and leave that which is obscure[91]." I heard the shaykh, Imam and teacher Fakh al-Dīn al-Kashani (RAH) say: The slave girl of Abu Yusuf (RAH) was in the trust of Muḥammad (RAH)[92]. Muḥammad said to her, 'Do you currently remember any of the fiqh discussions of Abu Yusuf?' She said, "No, other than something he used to repeat and say 'the revolving share is	ويكون مستفيدا فى جميع الأوقات والأحوال من جميع الأشخاص قال رسول الله صلى الله عليه وسلم: الحكمة ضالة المؤمن أينما وجدها اخذها. وقيل: خذ ما صفا، ودع ما كدر. وسمعت الشيخ الإمام الأجل الأستاذ فخر الدين الكاشانى يقول: كانت جارية أبى يوسف أمانة عند محمد بن الحسن فقال لها: هل تحفظين أنت فى هذا الوقت عن أبى يوسف فى الفقه شيئا؟ فقالت:

---

[87] As for reasons: one should speak to answer a question, guide a student or advise a seeker. Other than this being silent is safer.

[88] As for the time: it should be when listening and after the person talking has finished. As for the how, it depends on the audience and the speech method or communication style that would work for them. As for the amount, it would only depend on the audience and how much attention they can pay. As for the place it follows the audience.

[89] People of knowledge are those who follow the sunnah of the Messenger and warn against innovation

[90] Tirmidhi

[91] The one with intellect absorbs what is sound knowledge and leaves what is doubtful or unclear. On the authority of Abu 'Abdullah al-Nu'man bin Bashir (ra) who said: I heard the Messenger of Allah ﷺ say:"The halal is clear and the haram is clear, and between them are matters unclear that are unknown to most people. Whoever is wary of these unclear matters has absolved his religion and honor. And whoever indulges in them has indulged in the haram. It is like a shepherd who herds his sheep too close to preserved sanctuary, and they will eventually graze in it. Every king has a sanctuary, and the sanctuary of Allah is what He has made haram. There lies within the body a piece of flesh. If it is sound, the whole body is sound; and if it is corrupted, the whole body is corrupted. Verily this piece is the heart."(Bukhari & Muslim)

[92] Abu Yusuf and Muhammad were the two main students of Abu Hanifa.

dropped." So he learned this from her and it was an unsolved issue for Muḥammad and the obscurity was removed for him[93].

So we see that benefiting is possible from everyone.

It is for this reason that Abu Yusuf answered the question that was asked of him, "How did you gain this knowledge?" by answering, "I was never arrogant about gaining benefit, and I was never miserly about benefiting others[94]." It was said to Ibn Abbas, "How did you gain this knowledge?" He said, "With an inquisitive tongue and an intelligent heart." The seeker of knowledge was called, "What is your opinion?[95]" for no reason other than that in the early days, they used to often ask, "What is your opinion in this matter?"

Abū Ḥanīfa gained knowledge of *fiqh* through a lot of discussion and review while he was in his store during the time he was a silk merchant[96]. By this, we see that gaining knowledge and *fiqh* can be attained while one seeks a livelihood. Abu Hafs al-Kabir used to work for a living and review his lessons. If the student must seek a livelihood for his family and others, then he should do so and continue reviewing and studying[97]. He should not become lazy and there is no excuse for a person with a healthy body and mind to not study and learn *fiqh*. One cannot be more poverty stricken than Abu Yusuf, and his

---

[93] There is a saying that the one who befriends a perfumer will always smell good. Same goes for those who are around scholars; they will benefit from their knowledge. In Mauritania many kids memorise a good portion of books just by overhearing other students reciting or learning them.
[94] Some scholars have said that teaching how to remove arrogance from a student's heart should be the the first task.
[95] Or what do you say about such situation?
[96] Abu Hanifa used to be a fabric merchant and used to hold great discussions with scholars and intellectuals in his store
[97] One should always have intention of being a student of knowledge even if he only can study one sentence a day because of the higher state of students of knowledge.

poverty did not prevent him from learning *fiqh*.

For the one that has a lot of wealth, then "How wonderful is righteous wealth for a righteous person" and that is spent in the path of knowledge. A scholar was asked, "How did you gain knowledge?" He said, "By having a wealthy father who used his wealth to honor scholars and righteous people." This is because honoring those people is a cause to increase knowledge, as it is being thankful for the blessing of intellect and knowledge. That thankfulness is the cause of the increase. Abū Ḥanīfa (RAH) said:

I only gained knowledge through praise and thanks. Every time that I understood some aspect of knowledge or was given success in acquiring *fiqh* or wisdom, I would say 'al-ḥamdulillāh.'

This is the way a seeker of knowledge must be and thank Allāh[98] in his words, heart, limbs and wealth. He should recognize that understanding, knowledge and success is from Allāh[99]. He should pray for guidance from Allāh by supplicating and turning humbly to Him. Verily Allāh guides whoever seeks His guidance.

The people of truth, and they are People of the Sunna and Congregation, sought truth from the AL-Ḥaqq, Al-Mubīn, Al-Hādī, and Al-ʿĀṣim[100]. So, He protected them from misguidance. So, Allāh ﷺ guided them and protected them from being misguided.

---

[98] Shukr is the ability to use the blessing ones have from Allah in His pleasure. It is higher than Hamd because it is unique to the tongue.
[99] These are blessings and forms of sustenance from Allah. Attributing any of these achievements to one's self is a type of vanity
[100] Names of Allah. Al Haqq (The Truth), Al Mubin (The Clarifier), Al Hadi (The Guide), Al Asim (The Protector)

The misguided people were impressed by their own opinions[101] and intellect, so sought truth from the incapable creation. That incapable creation is the intellect, because it cannot comprehend all things, just like human sight. Because sight does not see all things. So they were veiled, powerless, and then were misguided[102] and they misguided others.

The Messenger of Allāh ﷺ said, "Whoever knows himself will know his Lord." So, if he comprehends the incapacity of the human, he will realize the Power of Allāh ﷻ. The seeker should not depend on himself and his intellect; rather he should depend on Allāh ﷻ and seek the truth from Him. Whoever depends on Allāh ﷻ, He will be sufficient for him and guide him to the straight path[103].

The one who has lawful wealth should not be miserly and should seek refuge in Allāh from miserliness. The Prophet ﷺ said, "Which disease is worse than miserliness[104]?" The father of the shaykh and great Imam Shams al-A'imma al-Halwani was poor and he used to sell sweets. He would give some of the sweets to the jurists and say, "Pray for my son." So, by the grace of his generosity, firm

---

[101] Like many people who think they don't have to follow a madhhab and can look into Hadith and Quran without going back to the scholars opinions and understanding of the Quran and sunnah.

[102] This is common trick satan would mislead muslims while letting them think they are on the right path

[103] It has been narrated that the Noble Prophet (S) said: I asked Jibrail: "What is 'tawakkul'?" He replied: "Cognizance (of the fact) that the creation (of Allah) can neither cause harm nor yield benefit; neither can it grant nor withhold (a bounty); (one must) sever all expectations from the creation (of Allah). When a person becomes such, he shall never work for anyone other than Allah (s.w.t.) and shall never hope and expect from anyone other than Him, and this is the reality of 'tawakkul'

[104] This is a figure of speech meaning "There is nothing worse than miserliness!"

belief and humility, his son attained a high station.

A student should also purchase books and hire scribes[105] to copy out books, for that will aid in studying and learning *fiqh*. Muḥammad ibn al-Hasan used to have a large amount of wealth to the point that he had 300 people appointed to supervise his wealth. He spent all his wealth in the pursuit of knowledge until he did not have a single fancy garment. Abu Yusuf once saw him wearing a tattered garment and sent him a number of fancy garments. He refused and said, "Yours has been expedited and ours has been delayed[106]." Even though it is *sunna* to accept gifts, maybe the reason he refused was because he considered that to be a detraction from his status[107]. The Prophet ﷺ said, "A believer is not allowed to degrade himself."

It has been mentioned that Shaykh Fakhr al-Islam al-Arsadabndi (RAH) once gathered watermelon rinds, washed them and then ate them. A bondswoman saw him and informed her master of the incident. The master prepared a meal and invited Shaykh Fakhr to it but he declined to attend. This is how a seeker of knowledge should be. He should

---

[105] The author talks about a time when printing did not exist. Copies of books could only be acquired by copying them or paying someone to do so.
[106] Meaning he rather have these gifts in store for him in Paradise
[107] This brings up a very important principle which is avoiding the lesser of two harms. Since refusing a gift is against the sunnah, that is a type of harm to do so. At the same time, doing something that will take away from your status and dignity is also a harm. So if accepting a gift will lead to detracting from one's dignity, then one may refuse the gift to preserve self-dignity. A harm that would come out of accepting a gift is maybe the person later doing mann, which is reminding the receiver of the favor bestowed upon them with comments like, "I did such and such for you" or "I gave you such and such." The giver may even come back and expect something from the person and that could cause a predicament of having to repay a favor to someone you don't want to associate with or to do something you do not want to do.

have high aspirations and not covet people's wealth. The Messenger of Allāh ﷺ said, "Beware of greed, for verily it is immediate poverty."

The seeker should not be miserly[108] with his wealth. He should spend it on himself and others.

The Prophet ﷺ said, "All people are in poverty[109] because of the fear of poverty." In the early generations, people used to learn a trade and then seek knowledge so that they would not have to seek the wealth of others.

There is a wisdom that states, "The one who becomes wealthy through the wealth of others has become poor." If a scholar is greedy, he will lose the sanctity of knowledge and will not speak the truth. It is for this reason that the Giver of the Law[110] ﷺ used to seek refuge from greed that draws faults near.

A believer should only desire things from Allāh ﷺ and should only be afraid of Him. This will become apparent in transgressing the boundaries of the Law or not doing so. So, whoever disobeys Allāh ﷺ out of fear of a creature has feared other than Allāh ﷺ. But, if one does not disobey Allāh ﷺ out of fear of a creature, and has observed the boundaries of the Law, then he has not feared other than Allāh, ﷺ rather he has feared Allāh. This goes the same for hope.

---

[108] Miserliness (*bukhl*) is denying those in need an established right they have in one's wealth, or earnings.
[109] Because they are in that state of mind. A muslim should trust what is in the hands of Allah more than what he has with him.
[110] The Prophet Muhammad, peace be upon him

A seeker of knowledge must count and measure for himself a specific review, for the lesson will not stick until he reaches that amount. He should review the previous day's lesson five times, and the lesson from the day before that, four times, and the one before that three times, the one before that twice and the one before that once[111]. This manner will more likely cause one to memorize. He should not get used to reviewing silently[112], because the lesson and the review should be done with power and energy. He should not raise his voice in a way that makes him struggle. This is so that he will not stop his review, and "the best of matters is the middle ground[113]."

It has been mentioned that Abū Yūsuf (RAH) was once powerfully and energetically reviewing *fiqh* with the jurists. His in-law who was with him was amazed at his state and said, "I personally know that he has been hungry for the last five days, and even at that he is discussing with power and energy!" A seeker of knowledge must not have a time without studies, for verily that will be his demise. The teacher, Shaykh al-Islam

---

[111] An example of a study pattern would be:

	Day 1	Day 2	Day 3	Day 4	Day 5
Lesson 1	100	50	25	15	10
Lesson 2		100	50	25	15
Lesson 3			100	50	25
Lesson 4				100	50
Lesson 5					100

[112] Still common today in traditional Islamic schools, students will raise their voices while memorizing or reviewing their lessons. You can also notice different rhythms and tones as each student will make up his own to help in his memorization.

[113] This quote is a Hadith.

وينبغي أن لا يكون لطالب العلم فترة فإنها آفة، وكان أستاذنا شيخ الإسلام برهان الدين رحمه الله يقول: إنما غلبت شركائي بأني لا تقع لي الفترة في التحصيل.

وكان يحكى عن الشيخ الأسبيجابي أنه وقع في زمان تحصيله وتعلمه فترة اثنتي عشرة سنة بانقلاب الملك، فخرج مع شريكه في المناظرة إلى حيث يمكنهما الإستمرار في طلب العلم وظلا يدرسانه معا ولم يتركا الجلوس للمناظرة اثنتي عشرة سنة. فصار شريكه شيخ الإسلام للشافعيين وكان هو شافعيا.

وكان أستاذنا الشيخ القاضي الإمام فخر الإسلام قاضي خان يقول: ينبغي للمتفقه أن يحفظ كتابا واحدا من كتب الفقه دائما فيتيسر له بعد ذلك حفظ ما سمع من الفقه.

Burhan al-Dīn (RAH), used to say, "I surpassed my colleagues because I never had a time without studying." He also mentioned that Shaykh al-Islam al-Isbijabi had an interruption in his studies of twelve years due the changes in political power. So he and his study partner went to review in a place where they could continue their studies. They spent twelve years studying and his study partner became Shaykh al-Islam for the Shafi'is as he was a Shafi'i.

Our teacher the shaykh, qadi and Imam Fakhr al-Islam Qadikhan would say, "One seeking *fiqh* must always have one book of *fiqh* memorized so that later it will be easy for him to memorize any *fiqh* ruling that he hears.

Chapter 7 Depending on Allāh

The seeker of knowledge must depend on Allāh ﷻ while seeking knowledge. He should not concern himself with provision and not preoccupy his heart with that. Abū Ḥanīfa (RAH) narrated that Abdullah ibn al-Hasan al-Zabidi (RAD), a companion of the Messenger of Allāh ﷺ said, "Whoever gains understanding (fiqh) of the dīn of Allāh ﷻ, Allāh will take care of his concern and his provision will come from where he does not even know." The one who preoccupies his heart with the matter of provision, such as food and clothing, will rarely have the chance to gain good manners and high stations.

It has been said [sarcastically]:

Forego great the finer things and don't travel to gain them
Just stay put and focus on getting food and clothing.

Some said to Mansur al-Hallaj, "Advise me." He said, "The advice is in regards to yourself. If you don't occupy it, it will occupy you." Everyone must be occupied with doing good actions, so that the self will not occupy them with desire[114].

The intelligent one should not be worried about matters of the *dunyā*, as worry and depression will not benefit or repel tribulation. Rather, worry and depression will harm the heart, intellect and body. It will also cause flaws in good deeds[115]. One should be worried about the afterlife, as that worry will be beneficial.

---

[114] "And your self (desires) is like a child (infant), if you let him keep on drinking milk he will come of age with the habit of drinking (milk). And if you wean it, it will stop." Imam Busayri

[115] By not performing the acts of worship in the best complete manner or with an insincere intention

As for the Prophetic saying, "There are sins that will not be expiated except by worrying about livelihood," this refers to the amount of worry that will not cause flaws in good deeds. Additionally, it should not be worry that would occupy the heart in a way that disrupts the heart's concentration while in prayer. That small amount of worry is what is considered to be from the deeds of the afterlife. *What small amount*

A seeker of knowledge should reduce *dunyā* associated matters, and it is for this reason that people chose to leave their homeland [for study][116]. Hardship must be endured while traveling to seek knowledge[117]. This, as Musa, upon him and our Prophet be the prayers and peace of Allāh ﷺ, said while traveling to seek knowledge, "We have found hardship in this travel of ours[118]." This was to show the journey to seek knowledge will never be without hardship. Knowledge is a grand thing, and according to most scholars, it is better than *jihād*[119]. Reward is commensurate to the amount of hardship endured. Whoever has patience in that situation will find a pleasure that exceeds all the pleasures of the *dunyā*. It is for this reason that when Muḥammad ibn al-Hasan would stay up at night and figure out a difficult issue, he would say, "Where are the princes when it comes to these pleasures[120]?"

---

[116] And even when far from their homeland some preferred not to be communication to avoid getting some news that may influence their decision on studying.
[117] This hardship is what makes you appreciate knowledge and its people
[118] Quran 18:62 Surah Al Kahf
[119] Unless the physical jihad becomes a personal obligation. Otherwise seeking knowledge is much higher.
[120] Princes and people of wealth experience the material short pleasures of this life, but people of knowledge experience spiritual growth which has long lasting pleasure.

ولهذا كان محمد بن الحسن إذا سهر الليالى وانحلت له المشكلات يقول: أين أبناء الملوك من هذه اللذات؟.

وينبغى لطالب العلم ألا يشتغل بشيئ آخر غير العلم ولا يعرض عن الفقه.

قال محمد بن الحسن رحمه الله: صناعتنا هذه من المهد إلى اللحد فمن أراد أن يترك علمنا هذا ساعة فليتركه الساعة.

ودخل فقيه، وهو إبراهيم بن الجراح، على أبى يوسف يعوده فى مرض موته وهو يجود بنفسه، فقال أبو يوسف: رمي الجمار راكبا أفضل أم راجلا؟ فلم يعرف الجواب، فأجاب بنفسه.

وهكذا ينبغى للفقيه أن يشتغل به فى جميع أوقاته فحينئذ يجد لذة عظيمة فى ذلك.

وقيل: رؤي محمد بن الحسن فى المنام بعد وفاته فقيل له: كيف كنت فى حال النزع؟ فقال: كنت متأملا فى مسألة من مسائل المكاتب، فلم أشعر بخروج روحى.

وقيل إنه قال فى آخر عمره: شغلتنى مسائل المكاتب عن الإستعداد لهذا اليوم، وإنما قال ذلك تواضعا.

A student must not engage in anything other than knowledge, and he should not disregard *fiqh*[121].

Muḥammad ibn al-Ḥasan (RAH) said, "This profession of ours is from the cradle to the grave. Whoever wants to leave this knowledge of ours for one hour, then he should leave it now!" A faqih named Ibrahim ibn al-Jarrah visited Abu Yusuf when the latter was terminally ill and was close to death. Abu Yusuf said, "Is casting the stones of the Jimar better while one is on foot or riding?" The faqih did not know the answer and so Abu Yusuf answered it himself saying, "Casting the stones during the first two while on foot is better." This is how the faqih should be at all times, and in this he will experience a great pleasure. It is said that after Muḥammad's death, he was seen by someone in a dream, and that person said to him, "How were you while your soul was being taken?" He said, "I was reflecting on the matter of the *mukatab*[122] and so I did not feel my soul being taken." It has also been said that at the end of his life, he said, "Thinking about the rulings related to the *mukatab* has distracted me from preparing for my death." He only said that out of humility.

---

[121] Because fiqh has no limit and new questions and situations always emerge.
[122] The *mukatab* is the slave who has made a contract with his owner to purchase his own freedom.

Chapter 8 The Times of Study

It is said that the time of seeking knowledge is from the cradle to the grave[123]. Al-Hasan ibn Ziyad began studying *fiqh* when he was 80 years old. He did not lie on his mattress for 40 years, and then, he issued fatwa for 40 years. The best time to study is during the early part of youth, the end of the night, and between the prayers of Maghrib and 'Isha. The seeker of knowledge should use all of his time, and so if he grows weary with one subject then he should move to another. When Ibn 'Abbas would grow weary with the subject of *aqidah*, he would say, "Bring us the collections of poetry[124]." Muḥammad ibn al-Hasan would not sleep at night and would keep near him. If he grew weary of one, he would move to the next. He used to keep water nearby and would fight drowsiness with it[125]. He would say, "Sleep is from heat, and one must fight it with cold water."

---

[123] Age can not be an excuse for one to stop seeking knowledge.
[124] Or any other subject to change focus and refresh the brain.
[125] By sprinkling water on him so he doesn't fall to sleep. Or simply making wudu with cold water.

Chapter 9
On Compassion and Advice

A knowledgeable person should be compassionate and should benefit others. A person of knowledge should not be a jealous [126] person, as jealousy harms and does not benefit. Our teacher, Shaykh al-Islam Burhan al-Dīn, used to say:

> The son of a teacher will become a scholar because the teacher wants his students to become scholars. So, because of the grace of his belief and compassion, his son will become a scholar[127].

He used to also mention that Sadr al-Ajal set the time of the lesson for his two sons, Sadr al-Shaheed Husam al-Dīn and Sadr al-Sa'id Taj al-Dīn, during the late morning after all the other lessons. They used to say, "We become tired and bored at that time." Their father said, "The travelers and the children of the elders come to me from all edges of the earth and so I must begin with their lessons." So, by the grace of his compassion, his children surpassed most of the great jurists in the world at that time in the subject of *fiqh*.

---

[126] Jealousy or hasad in Arabic is a disease of the heart by which a person wishes for the deprivation of a blessing, talent or merit, real or imagined, possessed by another person. And, if he had the capability to take it away from him he would do it.

[127] What the author is referring to here is the idea that caring for others will allow that same benefit to come back to you. So by a teacher sincerely desiring and helping others to become scholars, Allah will bless him by making his children scholars. To change the phrase "Do unto others..." a bit I would say, "Do unto others, as you would have Allah do unto your family."

The student should never contend or argue with another, as it will waste time. It is said that a doer of good will be rewarded with his goodness and the doer of evil will be sufficed by his actions. The shaykh and Imam, Rukun al-Islam Muḥammad ibn Abi Bakr (better known as Imam Khawahir Zadah al-Mufti) (RAH) recited some poetry to me that was recited to him by Sultan al-Shari'ah Yusuf al Hamdani (RAH):

> Do not punish a person who did evil
> What is in it will suffice him as well as what he is doing.

It is said that whoever wants to spite his enemy should recite the above poetry.

The following was also recited to me:

> If you would like to defeat your enemy,
> As well as kill and burn him with grief[128]
>
> Then seek a high station and increase your knowledge. For
> The one who increases in knowledge will increase the grief of the jealous one!

You should be occupied with things that benefit you[129] and not defeat your enemy. If you do things that benefit yourself then you are sure to defeat your enemy. Beware of enmities, for they will cause you shame and waste your time. You must be forbearing, especially with the fools. 'Isa, the son of Mary, ☐ said, "Bear one thing from the fool so that you gain ten[130]."

---

[128] Obviously the author isn't recommending such actions but is letting us know about the nature of such behavior.
[129] As mentioned above one should not look to crush his opponents rather have the best intentions towards them
[130] Because by trying to return their enmities you invite him to increase and be more aggressive towards you.

وأنشدت لبعضهم شعرا:

بلوت الناس قرنا بعد قرن
ولــــم أر غير ختال وقالي
ولم أر في الخطوب أشد وقعا
وأصعب من معاداة الرجال
وذقت مرارة الأشياء طـــرا
وما ذقت أمر مـــن السؤال

وإياك أن تظن بالمؤمن سوءا فإنه منشأ العداوة ولا يحل ذلك، لقوله عليه الصلاة والسلام: ظنوا بالمؤمنين خيرا. وإنما ينشأ ذلك من خبث النية وسوء السريرة، كما قال أبو الطيب:

إذا ساء فعل المرء ساءت ظنونه
وصدق ما يعتاده مـــن توهم
وعادى محبيه بقول عداتــــــه
وأصبح في ليل من الشك مظلم

وأنشدت لبعضهم:

تنح عن القبيح ولا تــرده
ومن أوليته حسنا فزده
ستكفى من عدوك كل كيد
إذا كــاد العدو فلا تكده

The following was recited to me:

> I have tested people time after time
> And I have not seen other than cheaters and haters.
> I have not seen a matter worse
> Than enmity between men.
> I have tasted the bitterness of all things
> And there is nothing more bitter than asking things from others.

Beware of having a bad opinion about the Believers, for it is the root of enmity. Having a bad opinion is not permissible[131] based on the Ḥadīth of the Prophet ﷺ, "Have a good opinion of the Believers." Bad opinions are caused by having a disgusting intention and an evil inward state as Abu al-Tayyib said:

> If a person's actions are bad, then his opinions of others will be bad
> And he will believe all the thoughts that he has.
> He will turn on his beloved ones based on what his enemies say
> And will travel in a dark night of doubt.

The following lines were recited to me:

> Stay away from bad things and do not desire them
> And whomever you did good to, increase that goodness

---

[131] Nevertheless one should take his or her precautions when dealing with others especially in things related to his Dīn, wealth and family like Imam Zarruq mentioned.

You will be protected from every plot of your enemy 　　If your enemy plots against you, do not plot against him[132]. The following lines of Shaykh al-Ma'ed Abu al-Fath al-Busti were recited to me: 　　The intelligent one will never be safe from the ignorant one 　　The ignorant one will burden the intelligent one with oppression and endless problems. 　　So the intelligent one should choose peace over warring with him 　　And always be silent when he screams[133].	وأنشدت للشيخ العميد أبى الفتح البستى: ذو العقل لا يسلم مــــن جاهل يسومـــــــه ظلما وإعناتا فليختر السلم على حربـــــه ولـــــيلزم الإنصات إنصاتا

---

[132] Allah has praised those who respond to evil with good deeds. Those who repel evil with good will find that their enemies will become their friends. "Not equal are the good deed and the bad deed. Repel evil by that which is better, and then the one who is hostile to you will become as a devoted friend." (Surah Fussilat 41:34-35)

[133] Abu Hurairah narrates that Rasulullah, peace be upon him, said: *"The strong man is not the one who is strong in wrestling, but the one who controls himself in anger."* (Bukhari, Muslim)

Chapter 10 On Benefitting

The seeker of knowledge must be gaining benefit at all times so that he may attain virtue. The way to gain benefit is to always have an inkpot[134] so that one may write down beneficial things that one hears. It has been said that whoever memorizes something will lose it, and whoever writes something down will preserve it. It has also been said that knowledge is that which has been taken from the mouths of men, since they have memorized the best of what they have heard and only say the best of what they have memorized[135].

I heard the teacher, shaykh, Imam and Adib, Zayn al-Islam, who is well known as 'al-Adib al-Mukhtar' say that Hilal ibn Yasar said:

> I saw the Prophet ﷺ telling his companions some knowledge and wisdom and so I said, 'Oh Messenger of Allāh, repeat to me what you said to them.' He said, 'Do you have an inkpot?' So I said, 'I do not have an inkpot.' He said, 'Oh Hilal, always have an inkpot, for goodness is contained in it and in those who carry it until the day of judgment[136].'

Al-Sadr al-Shaheed Husam al-Dīn advised his son to memorize a small amount of

---

[134] Have a pen handy. This become even easier with all technology we have at our service.
[135] Referring here to the scholars. They are the people whom Allah chooses to preserve this Din by giving them the gift of a good memory.
[136] Seeking Allah through sound knowledge is the safest path to Him. Other paths can also take you there but they are less traveled and perilous.

knowledge and wisdom every day for soon it will become a lot.	ووصى الصدر الشهيد حسام الدين إبنه شمس الدين أن يحفظ كل يوم شيئا من العلم والحكمة فإنه يسير، وعن قريب يكون كثيرا.
'Isam ibn Yusuf purchased a pen for one dinar[137] to write down what he heard.	واشترى عصام بن يوسف قلما بدينار ليكتب ما يسمعه فى الحال، فالعمر قصير والعلم كثير.
Life is short and knowledge is vast[138], so the seeker[139] must not waste time and should seize nights and solitude. Yahya ibn Mu'adh al-Razi said:	فينبغى أن لا يضيع طالب العلم الأوقات والساعات ويغتنم الليالى والخلوات. يحكى عن يحيى بن معاذ الرازى أنه قال الليل طويل فلا تقصره بمنامك، والنهار مضيئ فلا تكدره بآثامك.
The night is long, so do not shorten it with your sleep. The day is bright, so do not soil it with your sins.	
The seeker should seize shuyukh and benefit from them. Not everything that is missed can be regained[140]. As our teacher, Shaykh al-Islam said, "How many great teachers have I met but did not seek benefit from?" I have authored this line of poetry about this loss:	وينبغى أن يغتنم الشيوخ ويستفيد منهم، وليس كل ما فات يدرك، كما قال أستاذنا شيخ الإسلام فى مشيخته: كم من شيخ كبير أدركته وما استخبرته. وأقول على هذا الفوت منشئا هذا البيت:
O what a pity for not meeting, what a pity! Not everything that is missed or finished can be regained!	لهفا على فوت التلاقى لهفا ما كل ما فات ويفنى يلفى

---

[137] Which was a lot of money for a pen but generally people who love knowledge can spend a lot of money because they understand the priceless value of it.
[138] Contradict with life is short, play hard
[139] The student of knowledge.
[140] It is a rare opportunity for someone to have the right conditions for studying so if one feels blessing in that way he/she should take advantage of every minute or he will be regretting it for the rest of his life.

'Ali (KA) said:

> If you are engaged in a matter then be present. It is enough of a disgrace and a loss to turn away from the knowledge of Allāh ﷻ during your days and nights. So seek refuge in Allāh ﷻ from that.

The seeker of knowledge must endure hardship and abasement when seeking knowledge. Flattery is blameworthy except when seeking knowledge. This is because one must flatter his teacher, study partners and others to gain benefit from them. It is said that knowledge is glory that has no abasement, but it will only be attained with abasement with no glory. One of the poets has said:

> I see that you have a self that you want to glorify
> You will not gain glory until you abase it

Chapter on Piety While Seeking Knowledge

Some of the scholars have narrated a Ḥadīth on this topic that says:

Whoever does not have piety[141] during his time of study, Allāh ﷺ will give him a tribulation in one of three things: Either He will cause him to die in his youth, exile him to remote villages, or will test him with having to serve the ruler.

The more pious a seeker of knowledge is, the more beneficial his knowledge will be[142], the easier the studying will be and the benefits will be more.

Part of piety is to avoid satiation, sleeping too much and speaking too much about unbeneficial matters.

He should also avoid eating the food of the marketplace if he is able. This is because the food of the marketplace is more likely to have filth and cheating in it[143]. It is also farther from the remembrance of Allāh ﷺ and closer to heedlessness. Also because the poor people will lay their eyes on that food and not be able to purchase it so they will be hurt by that and the blessing of the food will be taken away[144].

---

[141] Wara' is to refrain from that which is suspected to be a sin or unsure of its permissibility.
[142] "The likeness of those who were entrusted with the (obligation of the) Tawraat (Torah) (i.e. to obey its commandments and to practise its laws), but who subsequently failed in those (obligations), is as the likeness of a donkey which carries huge burdens of books (but understands nothing from them). How bad is the example of people who deny the signs (proofs, evidences, verses, signs, revelations, etc.) of Allaah. And Allaah guides not the people who are oppressors (polytheists, wrongdoers, disbelievers)." [al-Jumu'ah 62:5]
[143] A sound mind is in a sound body. "O mankind, eat from whatever is on earth [that is] lawful and good and do not follow the footsteps of Satan. Indeed, he is to you a clear enemy." Baqara 2:168
[144] Reflect on how there is a food and water crisis in the world today. How much of that could be solved if we worked on spiritual solutions in addition to environmental protection programs?

It has been mentioned that the shaykh and great imam Muḥammad ibn al-Faḍl (RAH) would never eat food from the marketplace during the time he was studying. His father lived in the village and would prepare food for him and bring it to him on Friday. He came to the house of his son one day and saw some bread that was purchased from the market. He did not speak to him out of anger for him. His son apologized himself and said, "I did not buy it nor was I happy with it, but my study partner brought it." He said, "If you were careful and piously avoided these types of things, your study partner would not have dared to buy it!"

This is how pious they were, and so they were successful in learning and spreading knowledge and their names have been preserved until the Day of Resurrection[145].

One of the ascetic jurists advised a seeker of knowledge by saying, "You must avoid backbiting and sitting with people who talk a lot." He also said, "The one who speaks much will steal your life and waste your time."

Part of *wara'* is to stay away from the people of corruption, sinning, and who waste time. The seeker should be around righteous people, for proximity will no doubt have an affect[146]. The seeker should sit facing the *qibla* and implement the *sunna* of the Prophet ﷺ. He should seize the prayers of the righteous and beware of the supplications of oppressed people.

It has been mentioned that two men left their homeland to seek knowledge. They were study partners while on their quest and after many years they returned home. One of

---

[145] Through the books and stories they left us behind.
[146] Being in the company of a perfumer will affect the way you smell. The same goes for befriending a blacksmith; your clothes will have burn marks and dirt.

them gained *fiqh* while the other did not. The jurists of that area reflected on this and asked about how they reviewed and sat. They were told that the one who gained *fiqh* would, while reviewing, face the *qibla* and the city where he gained his knowledge. The other student, while reviewing, would have his back to the *qibla* and did not have his face to the city.

The scholars and the jurists were unanimous that the jurist gained his knowledge of *fiqh* by the blessing of facing the *qibla*. This is because facing the *qibla* is the *sunna* while sitting, except when there is an excuse. This was also due to the blessing of the supplication of the Muslims, for cities are never empty of righteous servants and good people. It seems that one of the righteous servants prayed for him during the night.

So, a seeker of knowledge must not belittle etiquette and *sunna*. Verily the one who neglects etiquette will be prevented from the *sunna* and the one who neglects the *sunna* will be prevented from the obligatory acts[147]. The one who neglects the obligatory acts will be prevented from the Afterlife.

The seeker of knowledge must send many prayers upon the Prophet ﷺ and he should pray in the way of the humble, for that will assist him in gaining knowledge. I was told the following poetry written by the great shaykh and zahid, al-Hajj Najm al-Dīn 'Umar ibn Muḥammad al-Nasafī:

Be one who keeps the orders and the prohibitions

---

[147] Because each of the mentioned strengthens the one after it and acts as a safeguard.

And be constant in performing the prayer.

    Seek the knowledge of the Sharīʿa and struggle in that.
    Seek assistance through pure things. You will become a jurist who preserves.

    Ask your God to preserve your preservation in hopes of
    Gaining His bounty, for Allāh ﷻ is the Best Preserver.

كـــــن للأوامر والنواهى حافظا

وعلى الصلاة مواظبا ومحافظا

واطلب علوم الشرع واجهد واستعن

بالطيبات تصر فقيها حافـــــظا

واسئل إلهك حفــــظ حفظك راغبا

مــــــن فضله فالله خير حافظا

كـــــن للأوامر والنواهى حافظا

وعلى الصلاة مواظبا ومحافظا

واطلب علوم الشرع واجهد واستعن

بالطيبات تصر فقيها حافـــــظا

واسئل إلهك حفــــظ حفظك راغبا

مــــــن فضله فالله خير حافظا

He also said:

Obey, be serious and don't be lazy
    And you are returning to your Lord
Do not sleep, for the best of the creation
    Slept a small portion of the night.

وقال رحمة الله عليه:

أطيعوا وجدوا ولا تكسلوا

وأنتم إلـــى ربكم ترجعون

ولا تهجعوا فخيار الورى

قليلا من الليل ما يهجعون

The seeker must have a notebook to accompany him at all times so that he can read it. It has been said that whoever does not have a notebook in his sleeve, wisdom will not settle in his heart. The notebook should have some blank space to write down whatever is heard from the mouths of people. One should have an inkpot[148] to accompany him to write what one hears, and we mentioned earlier the Ḥadīth of Hilal ibn Yasir.

وينبغى أن يستصحب دفترا على كل حال ليطالعه. وقيل: من لم يكن الدفتر فى كمه لم تثبت الحكمة فى قلبه.

وينبغى أن يكون فى الدفتر بياض ويستصحب المحبرة ليكتب ما يسمع من العلماء. وقد ذكرنا حديث هلال بن يسار.

---

[148] Or a pen.

Chapter 11 On What Increases Memory[149]

The strongest causes for increasing memory is seriousness, consistency, reducing food, and praying at night. Reciting the Quran is also a factor in increasing memory. It has been said that there is nothing that increases memory more than reciting Quran while looking at it. Reciting Quran while looking at it is better because of the saying of the Prophet:

> The best action from my nation is reciting Quran while looking at it[150].

Shada ibn Hakim saw one of his brothers in a dream after the brother's passing, and he said to him, "What thing did you find most beneficial?" He said, "Reciting Quran while looking at it."

When picking up a book, a person should say:

> In the name of Allāh. Glory be to Allāh. Praise be to Allāh. There is no god save Allāh. Allāh is greater. There is no power or might except with Allāh, the High, Great, Glorious, and Knowledgeable. May this be for the number of every word that has been written or will be written forever and throughout time.

After writing anything, a person should say:

> I believe in Allāh, the One and Only. The Truthful One who is alone without any partners. I have disbelieved in all other than Him.

---

[149] Based on experience (*tajriba*).
[150] Meaning reading from the mushaf "the book of Quran".

English	Arabic

The seeker should increase prayers upon the Prophet ﷺ, for he is a mercy to creation. Imam al-Shafi'i said:
 	
    I complained to Waki' about my bad memory
    So he advised me to leave sinning.
 	
    Memory is a bounty from Allāh
    And the bounty of Allāh ﷻ is not given to a sinner.
 	
Siwak, drinking honey, and eating frankincense with sugar all increase memory. Eating 21 red raisins every day on an empty stomach will increase memory and heal many illnesses and diseases[151]. Eating things that reduce phlegm and moisture increases memory.
 	
As for the things that cause forgetfulness, included is disobedience, excessive sins, anxiety and depression about matters of this worldly life, and excessive work and associations. Everything that increases phlegm causes forgetfulness. We previously mentioned that it is not befitting of the intelligent person to be concerned about the matters of this worldly life, because it is harmful and is not beneficial. Anxiety about the worldly life always brings darkness to the heart. Anxiety about the afterlife always brings light to the heart. The traces of anxiety are then present in the prayer. Anxiety about the worldly life prevents one from doing good. Anxiety about the afterlife forces one to do good, to work towards having humble presence in prayer as well as to gain knowledge. This is like what the shaykh and
	شكوت إلى وكيع سوء حفظى
	فأرشدنى إلى ترك المعاصى
	فإن الحفظ فضل مــــــــن الله
	وفضل الله لا يعطى لعاصــــــى.
	
	والسواك وشرب العسل وأكل الكندر مع السكر وأكل إحدى وعشرين زبيبة حمراء كل يوم على الريق يورث الحفظ ويشفى من كثير من الأمراض والأسقام، وكل ما يقلل البلغم والرطوبات يزيد فى الحفظ، وكل ما يزيد فى البلغم يورث النسيان.
	
	وأما ما يورث النسيان فهو: المعاصى وكثرة الذنوب والهموم والأحزان فى أمور الدنيا، وكثرة الإشتغال والعلائق، وقد ذكرنا أنه لا ينبغى للعاقل أن يهتم لأمر الدنيا لأنه يضر ولا ينفع، وهموم الدنيا لا تخلو عن الظلمة فى القلب، وهموم الآخرة لا تخلو عن النور فى القلب، ويظهر أثره فى الصلاة، فهم الدنيا يمنعه من الخيرات، وهم الآخرة يحمله عليه، والإشتغال بالصلاة على الخشوع وتحصيل

---

[151] Ibn Al-Qayyim said in "The Prophetic Medicine": "Az-Zuhri said: "Whoever wants to memorize the Hadith, let him eat raisins.

imam Nasr ibn al-Hasan al-Mirghani said in a poem he wrote to himself:
 	
    Seek assistance Nasr ibn Hasan
    For all knowledge that is to be preserved
 	
    That will dispel depression
    And everything else is not to be trusted
 	
The great shaykh and imam Najm al-Dīn ʿUmar ibn Muḥammad al-Nasafi said to a bondswoman that bore his child[152]:
 	
    Peace be upon the one who has subdued me with her elegance,
    The glistening of her cheeks, and the blinking of her eyes.
 	
    I was taken as a prisoner and made to incline towards a beautiful maiden;
    Minds are bewildered in trying to describe her.
 	
    So I said, "Leave me and excuse me, for I
    Have been enamored by seeking knowledge and uncovering it."
 	
    In seeking knowledge, virtue and piety, I have
    No need for the song of the beautiful women and their scent[153].
 	
As for the things that cause forgetfulness, included is eating fresh coriander, sour apples, looking at the crucified one, reading tombstones, going in between camels, discarding a live louse onto the ground, and cupping on the nape of the neck.
	العلم ينفى الهم والحزن، كما قال الشيخ نصر بن الحسن المرغيناني في قصيدة له:
	
	استعن نصر بن الحسن
	فـــى كل علم يحتزن
	ذاك الذى ينفى الحـزن وما سواه
	باطل لا يؤتمن
	
	والشيخ الإمام الأجل نجم الدين عمر بن محمد النسفي قال في أم ولد له:
	
	سلام على مـــن تيمتنى بظرفها
	ولمعة خـــدها ولمحة طرفها
	سبتنى وأصبتنى فـــتاة مليحة
	تحيرت الأوهام في كنه وصفها
	فقلت: ذرينى واعذرينــى فإنني
	شغفت بتحصيل العلوم وكشفها
	ولى في طلاب الفضل والعلم والتقى
	غنى عن غناء الغانيات وعرفها
	
	وأما أسباب نسيان العلم:
	
	فأكل الكزبرة الرطبة، والتفاح الحامض، والنظر إلى المصلوب، وقراءة الخط المكتوب على حجارة القبور، والمرور بين قطار الجمال، وإلقاء القمل الحي على الأرض، والحجامة على نقرة القفا، كلها يورث النسيان.

---

[152] Umm Walad is a slave girl that give birth to her master's child. She gets this title because her status changes and she can no longer be sold.

[153] Indeed the pleasure of seeking knowledge and gaining wisdom surpasses any other worldly pleasures.

Chapter 12 On What Increases Sustenance

A seeker of knowledge must have nourishment and knowledge of what increases nourishment, longevity, and health. This is so that the seeker of knowledge can have the freedom to gain what he wants. Books have been written about each of those matters and in this text I will briefly mention some of those points. The Messenger of Allāh ﷺ said:

> Divine decree is not stopped except by supplication[154], life is not prolonged except through righteousness and verily one will be prevented from his sustenance due to a sin afflicting him.

This Ḥadīth is a proof that committing a sin will be a cause to prevent sustenance. This is especially true about lying, as it will cause poverty and a Ḥadīth has been narrated specifically about this.

Sustenance is also reduced by sleeping in the morning. Sleeping too much will cause poverty and a loss of knowledge. One of the poets said:

> The happiness of people is in wearing clothes
> Gaining knowledge is by not dozing

---

[154] This must be understood in context. We know that nothing can repel the decree of Allah. Once He makes a decree, it will happen. But what is being spoken about here is the concept of things which seem to change the decree of Allah, which including supplication (dua). There may be things which were decreed to occur in a certain way, unless the person makes du'a. If that du'a is made, then the conditional decree will be affected. As an example, maybe it is written that a person will live to be 70 years old unless he or she makes du'a for a longer life. If the du'a is made, the longer life is given. So it seems like the du'a stopped the decree of Allah, but in reality, the decree of Allah was also that "If the du'a is made, then the life will be longer."

Another person said:

> Is it not a loss that nights
>   Pass by without benefit
> and they are counted from my life?

Someone else said:

> Hey you! Stand in the night so that you may be guided
>   How long will you sleep in the night while your life is dwindling?

The following things also reduce sustenance:

- Sleeping in the nude
- Urinating in the nude
- Eating while in state of *janaba*
- Eating while lying on one's side
- Being careless about the crumbs on the table
- Burning onion and garlic skins
- Sweeping with a cloth
- Sweeping at night
- Leaving garbage in the house
- Walking in front of teachers
- Calling out to parents by their names
- Cleaning between the teeth with any type of wood[155]
- Washing hands with dirt or clay
- Sitting on the doorstep
- Leaning on one of the door panels
- Performing wudu in the bathroom
- Mending clothes while wearing them
- Drying the face with clothing
- Leaving a spider's web in a house
- Being careless about the prayer
- Leaving the masjid quickly after the morning prayer
- Going to the marketplace early
- Returning late from the marketplace

---

[155] One should floss his teeth with known materials that do not cause damage or harm to his teeth and gums.

- Buying bread crumbs from poor people
- Supplicating for something bad to happen to one's child
- Not covering containers
- Blowing out a candle

All these things cause poverty and this has been known through narrations.

The following are also included:

- Writing with a mended pen
- Combing hair with a broken comb
- Not making good supplication for one's parents
- Putting on a turban while seated
- Putting on pants while standing[156]
- Miserliness
- Being stingy in spending
- Wastefulness
- Laziness
- Weakness
- Carelessness

The Messenger of Allāh ﷺ said:

Seek sustenance by giving charity[157].

Getting up early is blessed and increases all blessings especially sustenance. Having good handwriting is one of the ways to gain sustenance. Having a cheerful face and good words increases memory and sustenance. It has been narrated that Hasan ibn 'Ali said, "Cleaning yards and washing dishes increases sustenance." The greatest source of increasing sustenance is establishing the prayer with respect, humility, and properly performing its pillars, obligations, sunnas and

---

[156] One should wear his pants while sitting. It is helpful to not expose nakedness.
[157] It was narrated from Abu Hurayrah (may Allah be pleased with him) that the Prophet (peace and blessings of Allah be upon him) said: "There is no day on which the people get up but two angels come down and one of them says, 'O Allah, give in compensation to the one who spends (in charity),' and the other says, 'O Allah, destroy the one who withholds.' Narrated by al-Bukhari and Muslim.

etiquette. The *duha* prayer is well known to increase sustenance.

- Reciting sura al-Waqi'a in the night, especially before going to sleep
- Reciting sura al-Mulk, al-Muzammil, al-Layl, al-Inshirah
- Coming to the masjid before the adhan
- Constantly being in tahara
- Performing the sunnas of fajr and witr in the house
- Not speaking about worldly things after 'Isha
- Not spending much time with women except when necessary
- Not speaking about things that are useless to one's dīn or dunya

It has been said that the one who concerns himself with that which does not concern him will miss that which does concern him. Buzurjamhir said, "If you see a person speak a lot, then know for sure that he is insane." 'Ali said, "If the intellect is complete, words will decrease." I, the author, say:

If the intellect of a person is complete his words will be few
Be certain about the foolishness of one who speaks a lot

Someone else said:

Speech is adornment and silence is safety
So if you speak, do not be talkative.

I have never regretted silence
But I have regretted speech numerous times

وسائر واجباتها وسننها وآدابها، وصلاة الضحى فى ذلك معروفة، وقراءة سورة الواقعة خصوصا فى الليل وقت النوم، وقراءة الملك، والمزمل، والليل إذا يغشى وألم نشرح لك، وحضور المسجد قبل الأذان، والمداومة على الطهارة، وأداء سنة الفجر والوتر فى البيت. وأن لا يتكلم بكلام الدنيا بعد الوتر ولا يكثر مجالسة النساء إلا عند الحاجة، وأن لا يتكلم بكلام لغو.

وقيل: من اشتغل بما لا يعنيه فاته ما يعنيه. قال بزرجمهر: إذا رأيت الرجل يكثر الكلام فاستيقن بجنونه. وقال على رضى الله عنه: إذا تم العقل نقص الكلام.

قال المصنف رحمه الله: واتفق لى فى هذا المعنى شعرا:

إذا تم عقل المرء قل كلامــــــه
وأيقن بحمق المرء إن كان مكثرا

النطق زين والسكوت سلامة
فإذا نطقت فلا تكون مكــــــــثرا

ما ندمت على سكوت مـــــرة
ولقد ندمت على الكلام مـــــرارا

وأما ما يزيد فى الرزق:

Reciting the following[158] every day after dawn and until the prayer will increase sustenance: "Glory be to Allāh the Great. Glory and praise be to Allāh. I seek forgiveness from Allāh and I repent to him." 100 times

"There is no god except Allāh, the King, Truthful One and Manifest." 100 times every morning and evening.

Say after Fajr and Maghrib every day: "Praise be to Allāh, glory be to Allāh, and there is no god except Allāh." 33 times each.

He should seek forgiveness from Allāh 40 times after Fajr. He should often say, "There is no power or might except with Allāh" and send prayers on the Prophet.

On Friday, he should say the following 70 times: "O Allāh, make content with what You have permitted as opposed to what You have prohibited. And suffice me with your virtue over all others."

He should say this praise every day and night:

> You are Allāh the Glorious, the Wise. You are Allāh the King and Holy One. You are Allāh the Gentle and Generous. You are Allāh the Creator of good and evil. You are Allāh, the Creator of Heaven and Hell. You are the Knower of the hidden and the apparent. You are the knower of the secrets and beyond. You are Allāh the Great and High. You are Allāh the

أن يقول كل يوم بعد انشقاق الفجر إلى وقت الصلاة: سبحان الله العظيم وبحمده، سبحان الله العظيم وبحمده، وأستغفر الله العظيم وأتوب إليه مائة مرة، وأن يقول: لا إله إلا الله الملك الحق المبين كل يوم صباحا ومساء مائة مرة.

وأن يقول بعد صلاة الفجر كل يوم: الحمد لله، وسبحان الله، ولا إله إلا الله، ثلاثا وثلاثين مرة، وبعد صلاة المغرب أيضا، ويستغفر الله تعالى سبعين مرة بعد صلاة الفجر، ويكثر من قول: لا حول ولا قوة إلا بالله العلي العظيم، والصلاة على النبى صلى الله عليه وسلم.

ويقول يوم الجمعة سبعين مرة : اللهم أغننى بحلالك عن حرامك واكفنى بفضلك عمن سواك.

ويقول هذا الثناء كل يوم وليلة : أنت الله العزيز الحكيم, أنت الله الملك القدوس, أنت الله الحكيم الكريم, انت الله خالق الخير والشر, أنت الله خالق الجنة والنار, أنت الله عالم الغيب والشهادة, أنت الله عالم السر وأخفى, أنت الله الكبير المتعال, أنت الله خالق كل شيئ واليه يعود كل شيئ, أنت الله ديان يوم الدين,

---

[158] All prayers and other *wirds* from scholars using the Quran and Sunnah are acceptable as well. The best *wird* is reading Quran unless one is seeking knowledge.

Creator of all things. All things return to You. You are Allāh, the Judge of the Day of Judgment. You have always been and always will be. You are Allāh, there is no god except You. You are Allāh, the One and the Source. He does not beget nor was he begotten, and there is none like unto Him. You are Allāh, the King, Holy One, Complete, Truthful, Watchful One, Glorious, Mighty and High. There is no god except You, the Creator, the Originator, the Fashioner. To Him belong the Highest of Names. All things in the heavens and the earth glorify him, and He is the Glorious and Wise.

Other things that increase sustenance are righteousness, not causing harm, respecting teachers, connecting family bonds and also to say the following every morning and evening three times:

Glory be to Allāh in a way that will fill the scales, gain His pleasure, and be equal in weight to the Throne. Praise be to Allāh, there is no god except Allāh and Allāh is greater and let this saying fill the Scales, reach the limits of knowledge and reach His pleasure and be the weight of the Throne.

The seeker should avoid cutting live trees except out of necessity. He should complete wudu and perform the prayer with reverence. He should perform the hajj and 'umrah together. He should take care of his health. Learning something about medicine is a necessity. He should seek blessings with what has been narrated about medicine that were collected by the shaykh and imam Abu al-'Abbas al-Mustaghfiri (RAH) in his book entitled "Medicine of the Prophet ﷺ." Those who seek it will find it.

Praise be to Allāh for the completion of this text. May the prayers of Allāh be upon our master Muḥammad, the best of the noble messengers. And may the prayers be upon his family and companions, the distinguished leaders. May these prayers go on throughout the ages and as long as the days pass. Amin.	والحمد لله على التمام, وصلى الله على سيدنا محمد أفضل الرسل الكرام, وآله وصحبه الأئمة الاعلام, على ممر الدهور وتعاقب الأيام, آمين.
The first draft of this translation of this text has been completed on the 4th day of Dhul Qa'da in the year 1430 of the blessed Hijra by Rami Nsour, the poor servant in the need of the mercy of his Lord.	

THE BOOK OF KNOWLEDGE

Being a Translation with notes

of

Kitab al-'Ilm

of

Al-Ghazzali's

Ihya' 'Ulum al-Din

by

NABIL AMIN FARIS

CONTENTS

Introduction

BOOK 1: The Book of Knowledge Comprising Seven Sections

SECTION 1 : On the Value of Knowledge, Instruction and Learning together with its evidence in tradition and from reason.
1. ON THE EXCELLENCE OF LEARNING
2. ON THE EXCELLENCE OF TEACHING
3. EVIDENCE [FOR THE EXCELLENCE OF KNOWLEDGE] FROM REASON

Section 2: On praiseworthy and objectionable branches of knowledge

Section 3: On what is popularly considered to be a part of the science of religion, but is (really) not.

Section 4: On the reasons which induced men to pursue the science of polemics, and on revealing the evils of debate and disputation as well as stating the conditions which render them permissible.

Section 5: On the Properties of the Student and the Teacher.

Section 6: On the Evils of Knowledge and on Determining the Distinguishing Features of the Learned People of the Hereafter and those of the Teachers of Falsehood.

SECTION 7: On the Intellect, its Noble Nature, its Definition, and its Divisions

Bibliography

INTRODUCTION

"What the Apostle gives you, take; and

What he forbids, from it desist." (59:7)

In the name of Allah, the Merciful, the Compassionate.

First, I praise Allah, continuously, though the praise of the fervent does not do justice to His glory.

Second, I invoke the blessing of Allah upon His Apostle, the lord of mankind, as well as upon the other messengers.

Third, I ask His help having resolved to write a book on the revival of the religious sciences.

Fourth, I proceed to enlighten you, who are the most self-righteous of those who reject belief, and you, who are the most immoderate of the thoughtless unbelievers.

I am no longer obliged to remain silent, because the responsibility to speak, as well as warn you, has been imposed upon me by your persistent straying from the clear truth, and by your insistence upon fostering evil, flattering ignorance, and stirring up opposition against him who, in order to conform to the dictates of knowledge, deviates from custom and the established practice of men. In doing this he fulfils Allah's prescriptions for purifying the self and reforming the heart, thus somewhat redeeming a life, which has already been dissipated in despair of prevention and remedy, and avoids by it the company of him whom the Lawgiver (Muhammad S.A.W.) described when he said, "The most severely punished of all men on the day of resurrection will be a learned man whom Allah has not blessed with His knowledge."[159] For, by my life, there is no reason for your abiding arrogance except the malady which has become an epidemic among the multitudes. That malady consists in not discerning this matter's importance, the gravity of the problem, and the seriousness of the crisis; in not seeing that life is waning and that what is to come is close at hand, that death is imminent but that the journey is still long, that the provisions are scanty, the dangers great, and the road blocked. The perceptive know that only knowledge and works devoted to Allah avail.

To tread the crowded and dangerous path of the hereafter with neither guide nor companion is difficult, tiring, and strenuous. The guides for the road are the learned men who are the heirs of the Prophet[160], but the times are void of them now and only the superficial are left, most of whom have been lured by iniquity and overcome by Satan. Everyone of them was so wrapped up in his immediate fortune that he came to see good as evil and evil as good, so that the science of religion disappeared and the torch of the true faith was extinguished all over the world. They duped the people into believing that there was no knowledge except such ordinances of government as the judges use to settle disputes when the mob dots; or the type of argument which the vainglorious displays in order to confuse and refute; or the elaborate and flowery language with which the preacher seeks to lure the common folk. They did this, because apart from these three, they could find no other ways to snare illegal profit and gain the riches of the world. On the other hand the science of the path of the hereafter, which our forefathers trod and

---

[159]

[160] Abu al-Darda' (Allah be pleased with him) that the Messenger of Allah (Allah bless him and give him peace) said, "Scholars are the inheritors of the prophets." [Related by Tirmidhi, Abu Dawud, Nasa'i, Ibn Maja, Ahmad, Ibn Hibban, and others] Ibn al-Mulaqqin, Zayla`i, Ibn Hajar, and others seemed it sound (hasan) or rigorously authentic (sahih)]

which includes what Allah in His Book called law, wisdom, knowledge, enlightenment, light, guidance, and righteousness, has vanished from among men and been completely forgotten. Since this is a calamity afflicting religion and a grave crisis overshadowing it, I have therefore deemed it important to engage in the writing of this book; to revive the science of religion, to bring to light the exemplary lives of the departed imams, and to show what branches of knowledge the prophets and the virtuous fathers regarded as useful.

I have divided the work into four parts or quarters. These are: the Acts of Worship, the Usages of Life, the Destructive Matters in Life, and the Saving Matters in Life. I have begun the work with the book of knowledge because it is of the utmost importance to determine first of all the knowledge which Allah has., through His Apostle, ordered the elite to seek. This is shown by the words of the Apostle of Allah when he said, "Seeking knowledge is an ordinance obligatory upon every Muslim."[161] Furthermore, I have begun with the book on knowledge in order to distinguish between useful and harmful knowledge, as the Prophet said, "We seek refuge in Allah from useless knowledge;" and also to show the deviation of the people of this age from right conduct, their delusion as by a glistening mirage, *and* their satisfaction with the husks of knowledge rather than
the pith.

The quarter on the Acts of Worship comprises ten books:

1. The Book of Knowledge
2. The Articles of Faith
3. The Mysteries of Purity
4. The Mysteries of Prayer
5. The Mysteries of Almsgiving
6. The Mysteries of Fasting
7. The Mysteries of the Pilgrimage
8. The Rules of Reading the Qur'an
9. On Invocations and Supplications
10. On the Office of Portions.

The quarter on Usages of Life comprises ten books:

1. The Ethics of Eating
2. The Ethics of Marriage
3. The Ethics of Earning a Livelihood
4. On the Lawful and the Unlawful
5. The Ethics of Companionship and Fellowship with the Various Types of Men
6. On Seclusion
7. The Ethics of Travel
8. On Audition and Grief

161

9. On Enjoining Good and Forbidding Evil
10. The Ethics of Living as Exemplified in the Virtues of the Prophet.

The quarter on the Destructive Matters of Life comprises ten books:
1. On the Wonders of the Heart
2. On the Discipline of the Soul
3. On the Curse of the Two Appetites – The Appetite of the Stomach and the appetite of Sex
4. The Curse of the Tongue
5. The Curse of Anger, Rancour, and Envy
6. The Evil of the World
7. The Evil of Wealth and Avarice
8. The Evil of Pomp and Hypocrisy
9. The Evil of Pride and Conceit
10. The Evils of Vanity.

The quarter on the Saving Matters of Life comprises ten books:
1. On Repentance
2. On Patience and Gratitude
3. On Fear and Hope
4. On Poverty and Asceticism
5. On Divine Unity and Dependence
6. On Love, Longing, Intimacy and Contentment
7. On Intentions, Truthfulness, and Sincerity
8. On Self-Examination and Self-Accounting
9. On Meditation
10. On Death.

In the quarter on the Acts of Worship I shall mention some of the hidden (elements) of its etiquette, the niceties of its rules, and the mysteries of its meanings. (These), the active learned man badly needs; without their knowledge no one will be versed in the science of the hereafter. Most of this information has been neglected in theological studies.

In the quarter on the Usage of Life I shall deal with the rules of practical religion current among men, its deep mysteries, intricate technique, and the piety concealed in its rules of conduct, which no religious man can do without.

In the quarter on the Destructive Matters of Life I shall enumerate every abhorred trait whose exposure the Qur'an has ordered, as well as dealing with the purifying of the soul and the cleansing of the heart therefrom. Under every one of these traits I shall give its definition, the truth about it, its origin, its evil consequences, its symptoms, and finally its treatment. To all this will be added illustrations from the Qur'an tradition, and antiquity.

In the quarter on the Saving Matters of Life, I shall enumerate every praiseworthy trait and every one of the desirable qualities of Allah's favorites *(al-muqarrabun)*[162] and the saints, by means of which the slave seeks to draw near to the Lord of the Universe. Similarly, under every-quality I shall give its definition, the truth about it, its origin, its fruit, the sign by which it is known, its excellence which renders it desirable, together with examples to illustrate it from [the fields of] law and reason.

It is true that men have written several works on some of these aspects, but this one differs from them in five ways:

First, by clarifying what they have obscured and elucidating what they have treated casually.

Second, by arranging what they have disarranged, and organizing what they have scattered.

Third, by condensing what they have elaborated, and correcting what they have approved.

Fourth, by deleting what they have repeated (and verifying what they have set' down).

Fifth, by determining ambiguous matters which have hitherto been unintelligible and never dealt with in any work. For although all have followed one course, there is no reason why one should not proceed independently and bring to light something unknown, paying special attention to what his colleagues have forgotten. It is possible that such obscure things are noticed, but mention of them in writing is overlooked. Or again it may not be a case of overlooking them, but rather one of being prevented from exposing them.

These, therefore, are the characteristics of this work which comprises the aggregate of the (previously enumerated) sciences. Two things have induced me to divide the work into four quarters. The first and original motive is that such an arrangement in research and exposition is imperative because the science by which we approach the hereafter is divided into the science of revelation I mean knowledge and only knowledge. By the science of practical religion I mean knowledge as well as action in accordance with that knowledge. This work will deal only with the science of practical religion, and not with revelation, which one is not permitted to record in writing, although it is the ultimate aim of saints and the desire of the eyes of the *Sincere*. The science of practical religion is merely a path which leads to revelation and only through their path did the prophets of Allah communicate with the people and lead them to Him. Concerning revelation itself, the prophets spoke only figuratively and briefly through signs and symbols, because they realized the inability of man's mind to comprehend. Therefore since the learned men are heirs of the prophets, they cannot but follow in their footsteps and emulate their way.

Furthermore, the science of practical religion is divided into outward science, by which is meant that of the functions of the senses, and inward science, by which is meant that of the functions of the heart The bodily organs perform either acts of worship or usages of life, while the heart, because it is removed from the senses and belongs to the world of dominion, is subject to either praiseworthy or blameworthy [influences]. Inevitably, therefore, this science divides itself into two parts - outward and inward. The outward, which pertains to the senses, is subdivided into acts of worship and usages of life; the inward, which relates to the conditions of the heart and the

---

[162] See Sura 56 for the description of the Close Ones.

qualities of the soul, is subdivided into things which are praiseworthy and things which are objectionable. Together these constitute the four parts of the science of practical religion, a classification objected to by none.

My second motive for adopting this division is that I have noticed that the interests of students in jurisprudence (which has, for the sake of boasting and exploiting its influence and prestige in arguments, become popular among those who do not fear Allah) is genuine. It also is divided into quarters. And since he who dresses as the beloved will also be beloved, I am not far wrong in deeming that the modeling of this book after books of jurisprudence will prove to be a clever move in creating interest in it. For this [same] reason, one of those who wanted to attract the attention of the authorities to [the science of] medicine, modeled it after astronomical lists, arranging it in tables and numbers, and called [his book] Tables of Health. He did this in order that their interest in that [latter] type [of study] might help in drawing them to read it. Ingenuity in drawing hearts to the science which is good for spiritual life is, however, more important than that of interesting them in medicine which benefits nothing but physical health. The fruit of this science is the treatment of the hearts and souls through which is obtained a life that will persist for ever and ever. How inferior, then, is the medicine of the body, which is of necessity destined to decay before long. Therefore we beg Allah for help to [lead us to] the right path and [the way of] truth, verily He is the Generous, the all Bounteous.

BOOK I

THE BOOK OF KNOWLEDGE
COMPRISING SEVEN SECTIONS

The Book of Knowledge comprises seven sections:

1. On the value of knowledge, instruction, and learning.

2. On the branches of knowledge which are *fard'ayn*[163]; on the branches of knowledge which are *fard kifayah*[164]; on the definition of jurisprudence *(fiqh)* and theology *(kalam*[165]*)* [as disciplines] in the science of religion; and on the science of the hereafter and that of this world.

3. On what is popularly considered to be part of the science of religion, but is [really] not, including a discussion on the nature of blameworthy knowledge.

---

[163] An act that is obligatory for Muslims individually.
[164] An act that is obligatory for the Muslim community collectively.
[165] 'Ilm al-kalam is one of the Islamic sciences. It discusses the fundamental Islamic beliefs and doctrines which are necessary for a Muslim to believe in. Other name of f this science is Aqeeda.

4. On the defects of debate and the reasons why people have engaged in dissension and disputation.

5. On the proprieties of the teacher and the student.

6. On the deficiency of knowledge, the [drawbacks] of the learned, and the characteristics distinguishing the scholars of the science of the hereafter from those of the science of this world.

7. On reason, its value, categories and what has been said concerning it [in Tradition].

SECTION I

On the Value of Knowledge, Instruction, and Learning together

with its evidence in tradition and from reason.

The excellence of knowledge The evidence for the excellence of knowledge in the Qur'an [is manifest] in the words of Allah: "Allah bears witness that there is no Allah but He, and the angels, and men endued with knowledge, established in righteousness."(3:16) See, then, how Allah has mentioned Himself first, the angels second, and men endowed with knowledge third. In this you really have honour, excellence, distinction and rank. And again Allah said: "Allah will raise in rank those of you who believe as well as those who are given knowledge." (58:12)

According to ibn-'Abbas[166] the learned men rank seven hundred grades above the believers; between each two of which is a distance five hundred years long. Said Allah. "Say, `shall those who know be deemed equal with those who do not?" (39:12) Allah also said, "None fear Allah but the wise among His servants;" (35:25) and again, "Say, `Allah is witness enough betwixt me and you, and whoever hath the knowledge of The Book!' "(13:43) This I mention to you in order to show that it was possible only through the power of knowledge. Allah also said, "But they to whom knowledge hath been given said, `Woe to you! The reward of Allah is better [for him who believes and does right]," (28:80) showing thereby that the great importance of the hereafter is appreciated through knowledge. And again Allah said, "These parables do we set forth for men: and none understands them save those who know." (29:42) Allah also said, "But if they were to refer it to the Apostle and to those in authority amongst them, those of them who would elicit the information would know it" (4:85) He thus made the knowledge of His will dependent upon their efforts to find it out, and placed them next to the prophets in the [ability] to make it known. It has been said that in the following words of Allah, "O Sons of Adam! We have sent down to you raiments wherewith to cover your nakedness, and splendid garments; but the raiment of piety-this is best," (7:25) the raiments represent knowledge, the splendid garments, truth, and the raiment of piety, modesty. Allah also said, "And We have brought them a book: with knowledge have We explained it;" (7:50) and again, "But it is clear sign in the hearts of those whom the knowledge hath reached;" (29:48) and, "With knowledge will We tell them;"

---

[166] 'Abd Allah ibn al-'Abbas otherwise called (Ibn Abbas; Al-Habr; Al-Bahr; The Doctor; The Sea). He was one of Prophet Muhammad's cousins and one of the early Qur'an scholars.

(7:6) and again, "[He] hath created man, [and] hath taught him articulate speech." (55:2-3) This, however, He said reproachfully.

As to [the evidence of the value of knowledge in] tradition (*al-akhbar*)[167] the Apostle of Allah said, "Whom Allah doth love, He giveth knowledge of religion and guideth him into the straight path;" and again, "The learned men are the heirs of the prophets." It is also well-known that there is no rank above that of prophethood, no honour higher than its inheritance. The Prophet also said, "What is in the heavens and in the earth intercedes for the learned men." And what rank is higher than that of him for whom the angels of the heavens and earth labour interceding with Allah on his behalf, while he is preoccupied with himself. Muhammad also said, "Wisdom adds honour to the noble and exalts the slave until he attains the level of kings." The Prophet pointed this out relating to the benefits of wisdom in this world, since it is well-known that the hereafter is superior and more lasting. Muhammad said again, "Two qualities the hypocrite lacks - good intentions and religious insight." Do not doubt tradition, then, because of the hypocrisy of some contemporary jurisprudents; theirs is not the jurisprudence which the Prophet had in mind. (The definition of jurisprudence will come later). For a jurist to know that the hereafter is better than this world is, after all, the lowest type of knowledge he can possess. Should it prove to be true and prevail, it would clear him of hypocrisy and deceit. The Prophet said, "The best of men is the learned believer who, if he is needed, he will be useful; and if dispensed with, he will be self-sufficient. " And again he said, "Belief is like unto a nude who should be clothed with piety, ornamented with modesty and should have knowledge for progeny[168]." And again, "The nearest people to prophethood are the people of knowledge and the warriors of *jihad*": the former have led men to what the prophets have proclaimed, and the latter have wielded their swords on its behalf. He also said, "The passing away of a whole tribe is more tolerable than the death of one learned man." And again, "Men are like ores of gold and silver, the choicest among them during the *Jahiliyah* days are also the best during the days of Islam, provided they see the light." He also said, "On the day of resurrection the ink of the learned men will be likened to the blood of the martyrs." And again, "Whoever preserves of the law forty Traditions in order to transmit them unto my people, I shall, on the day of resurrection, be an intercessor and a witness on his behalf." Muhammad also said, "Any one of my people who will preserve forty hadiths will on the day of resurrection face Allah as a learned jurist." And again, "Whoever will become versed in the religion of Allah, Allah will relieve him of his worries and will reward him whence he does not reckon" The Prophet also said, "Allah said unto Abraham, `O Abraham! Verily I am knowing and I love every knowing person'." And again, "The learned man is the trustee of Allah on earth." The Prophet said, "There are two groups among my people who when they become righteous the populace becomes righteous, and when they become corrupt the populace becomes corrupt: these are the rulers and the jurisprudents." Again he said, "Should the day come wherein

---

[167] Prophetic tradition. Sayings, acts and approvals of the Prophet peace and prayers be upon him.
[168] Fruit is *thamarah* in arabic

I increase not in knowledge wherewith to draw nearer to Allah, let the dawn of that day be accursed."

Concerning the superiority of knowledge to worship and martyrdom, the Prophet said, "The superior rank the learned man holds in relation to the worshipper is like the superior rank I hold in relation to the best of men." See how he placed knowledge on an equal footing with prophethood and belittled the value of practice without knowledge, despite the fact that the worshipper may not be ignorant of the worship which he observes. Moreover, without this knowledge there would have been no worship. The Prophet also said, "The superior rank the learned man holds over the worshipper is similar to the superiority of the moon when it is full over the other stars." And again, "They will, on the day of resurrection, intercede [before Allah]: the prophets, then the learned, then the martyrs." Great then is the state of knowledge which ranks next to prophethood and stands over martyrdom, the merits of the latter notwithstanding. The Prophet also said, "Allah was not worshipped with anyone better than the learned in religion. Verily a single jurist is more formidable to Satan than a thousand worshippers." For everything has [its] foundation. and the foundations of this religion is jurisprudence. And again, "The best part of your faith is [also] the easiest, and the best form of worship is jurisprudence." The Prophet also said, "The learned believer holds a rank seventy degrees higher than that of the ordinary believer." And again. "Verily you have come upon a time whose jurisprudents are many and Qur'an readers as well as preachers are few, whose beggars are rare and givers numerous, wherein deeds are better than knowledge. But there will come a time when jurisprudents are few and preachers many, whose givers are few and beggars numerous, wherein knowledge is better than works." The Prophet also said, "Between the learned and the worshipper are a hundred degrees, each two of which are separated by the extent of a racing horse's run in seventy years." The Prophet was also asked, "O Apostle of Allah! What works arc best?" To which he replied. "Your knowledge of Allah." He was then asked. "Which knowledge do you mean?" He answered, "Your Knowledge of Allah." Again he was asked, "We enquire about works and you reply concerning knowledge." Muhammad then said, "With your knowledge of Allah, a few works will suffice, but without such knowledge, no works, however numerous, avail." The Prophet also said, "On the day of resurrection Allah will [first] raise the worshippers and then the learned to whom He will say, 'O ye company of the learned, I did not imbue you with My knowledge but for My knowledge of you. Moreover, I did not imbue you with My Knowledge in order to torment you. Go ye, therefore, for verily I have forgiven you'."

As to [the evidence of the value of knowledge in] the sayings of the Companions *(al-athar)*, `Ali ibn-abi-Talib said to Kumayl, "O thou perfect of knowledge ! Knowledge is better than riches; for knowledge guardeth thee whereas thou guardest riches. Knowledge governs while riches are governed. Riches diminish with spending but knowledge increases therewith." And again, "The learned is superior to the fasting, praying and self-mortifying man. Should the learned die, a gap would be created in Islam [by his death] and no one would fill this gap save one of his successors.[169]" `Ali said:

"Learning is the glory of mankind,

The wise are beacons on the road to truth;

Man is worth his knowledge, nothing more –

The fool will be his inveterate foe,

Knowledge is man's hope of life immortal,

Man may die but wisdom liveth ever."

Abu-al-Aswad said, "Nothing is more precious than knowledge; while kings rule over men, they are ruled by the learned." Ibn-`Abbas said, "Solomon the son of David was asked to choose between knowledge, wealth or power, but he chose knowledge and was thereby blessed with wealth and power as well." Ibn-al--Mubarak was asked, "Who constitute humanity?[170]" To which he replied, "The learned". It was then said, "And who are the kings?" He answered, "The ascetics"[171]. And who," he was asked, "constitute the lowest class among men?" "Those," said he, "who, in the name of religion, grow fat in the world." Thus only the learned did [ibn-al--Mubarak] regard as belonging to mankind, because it is knowledge which distinguishes man from the other animals. Furthermore, man is a human being, not because of his physical prowess for physically the camel is his superior; not because of his size for the elephant is larger; not because of his courage for the lion is more courageous; not because of his appetite for the ox has the greater; not because of coitus for the least of the birds is more virile than he, but rather by virtue of his noble aims and ideals. [As a matter of fact] he was only created to know.

One of the wise men said, "Would that I might know what thing was attained by him whom knowledge has escaped, and what thing has escaped him who has attained knowledge." The Prophet said, "Whoever has been given the Qur'an and thinks that anyone has been given something better, he has degraded what Allah has exalted." Fath al-Mawsili said inquiring, "Would not the sick die, if he is given no food or drink or medicine?" They said, "Yes". To which he said, "Similarly the heart will perish if it is cut off from wisdom and knowledge for three days." He did indeed speak the truth, for the nourishment of the heart, on which its life

---

[169] This is a reminder that the greatest resource in terms of knowledge is the human resource. Books, computers, audios and any other form of tool for preserving knowledge is not what preserves knowledge, that is why the statement of the author is that the only one to fill the person of knowledge's place is another person of knowledge. This is what we find foretold in the following Hadith; 'Abdullah bin 'Amr bin Al-'As (May Allah be pleased with them) reported: I heard the Messenger of Allah (ﷺ) saying: "Verily, Allah does not take away knowledge by snatching it from the people, but He takes it away by taking away (the lives of) the religious scholars till none of the scholars stays alive. Then the people will take ignorant ones as their leaders, who, when asked to deliver religious verdicts, will issue them without knowledge, the result being that they will go astray and will lead others astray." [Al- Bukhari and Muslim].

[170] This is a question basically asking, "Who is really a human being?"

[171] Zuhad in Arabic. Even though a Muslim is permitted to enjoy fully whatever unforbidden pleasure God bestows on him, Islam nevertheless encourages and praises those who shun luxury in favour of a simple and pious life.

depends, is knowledge and wisdom, just as the nourishment of the body is food. Whoever lacks knowledge has an ailing heart and his death is certain; yet he is not aware of his doom because the love of this world and his concern therewith have dulled his sense, just as a shock from fright may momentarily do away with the pain of a wound although the wound be real. Thus when death frees him from the burdens of this world he will realize his doom and' will, though to no avail, greatly regret it. This is like the feeling of a person who has attained safety after having been through danger, and like that of a man who has just recovered from his drunkenness. We seek refuge in Allah from the day when all things will be brought to light. Men are asleep but at death they Will awake[172]. Al-Hasan said, "The ink of the learned Will be likened to the blood of the martyrs, and the former will prove superior." Ibn-Mas`ud said, "Seek ye knowledge while it be found; it will be veiled when its narrators pass away. Verily, by Him in whose hand is my life, several men who died martyrs in the cause of Allah would rather that, at resurrection, Allah would raise them up as learned men for what they see of the veneration accorded the learned." No one is born learned, but knowledge is only the result of learning. Ibn-'Abbas said, "I would rather spend a part of the night in learned discussion than in continual prayer." The same was related of abu-Hurayrah and Ahmad ibn-Hanbal. AI-Hasan said that in the words of Allah, "Give us good in this world and good in the next," (2:197) the good in this world meant knowledge and worship while that of the next signified paradise. A wise man was once asked, "What things shall we possess?" He replied, "Those things which you will not lose in the event of shipwreck," meaning thereby knowledge, while by shipwreck, it is said, he meant the decomposition of the body through death. A certain wise man said, "Whoever takes wisdom for his bridle will be acclaimed by men as their leader, and whoever is known for his wisdom will be looked upon with respect." Al-Shaf'i Said "One of the noble things about knowledge is that he who is given a portion of it, no matter how small, rejoices while he who is deprived of it grieves."' Umar said, "O men! Seek ye knowledge. For verily Allah has a mantle of love which He casts upon him who seeks knowledge even of a single section. Should he then commit an offence, Allah will remonstrate with him thrice in order not to rob him of his mantle, even though that offence may persist with him until he dies." Al-Ahnaf said, "The learned men came very near being Allah; and all power which is not supported by knowledge is doomed. Salim ibn-abi-al-Ja'd said, " My master bought me for three hundred dirhams and later set me free. Thereupon I said, 'What shall I take up for livelihood? Finally I took up learning and no sooner had a year passed than the prince of Makkah called upon me but I would not receive him." al-Zubayr ibn-abi-Bakr said, "My father had written me while in al-'Iraq saying. 'Go after knowledge; should you become poor it will be your wealth, and should you become rich it will be your embellishment'." (This has been related among the exhortations of Luqman to his son). He also said, "Sit in the company of the learned and keep close to them; for verily Allah quickens the hearts with the light of wisdom as he refreshes the earth with the rain of heaven." A certain wise man said, "When the learned dies the fish of the sea as well as the fowl of the air will mourn him; while his

---

[172] It is said that this is Ali ibn Abi Talib saying and Allah knows best.

face shall disappear his memory will not be forgotten." Al-Zuhri said, "Knowledge is glorious and is not treasured except by the glorious."

ON THE EXCELLENCE OF LEARNING

The excellence of learning is attested in the Qur'an by the following words of Allah: "And if a party of every band of them march not out. it is that they may instruct themselves in their religion;" (9:123) and again. "Ask of those who have Books of Monition[173] if ye know it not." (16:45)

[As to the evidence of the excellence of learning] in tradition[174], the Prophet of Allah said. "Whoever follows a path in search of knowledge. Allah will guide him into a path leading into Paradise." And again. "Verily the angels will bow low to the seeker after knowledge in approval of what he does." He also said, "To rise up before daybreak and learn but a section of knowledge is better than prostrating yourself in prayer a hundred times." The Apostle again said. "One section of knowledge which a man learns is better for him than all the riches of the world." And again. "Seeking after knowledge is an ordinance obligatory upon every Muslim." He also said, "Seek ye knowledge even [as far as] China[175]." The Prophet further said. "Knowledge is like sealed treasure houses, the keys of which arc inquiry[176]. Inquire. therefore, for therein lies reward for four: the inquirer, the learned, the auditor, and their admirer." He also said, "The ignorant one should not hide his ignorance nor the learned his knowledge." And in a tradition on the authority of abu Dharr, "To be present in the circle of a learned man is better than prostrating oneself in prayer a thousand times. or visiting a thousand sick men. or joining a thousand funerals." It was then said.. "O Apostle of Allah, is it also better than the reading of the Qur'an?" To which he replied, "What good. though. is the Qur'an except through knowledge?" The Prophet also said. "Whoever is overtaken by death while seeking knowledge wherewith to strengthen Islam. between him and the prophets in Paradise is but one grade."

[As to the evidence of the excellence of learning] in the sayings of the Companions, ibn-Abbas said, "While I sought knowledge, I was abased, but when I was sought for it, I was exalted." Similarly, ibn-abi -Mulaykah said, "Never have I seen the like of ibn `Abbas: to behold him is to behold the most handsome man; when he speaks, he is the most eloquent, and when he hands down a judicial opinion, he [reveals himself] as the most learned." Ibn-al-Mubarak said, I wonder how one who sought no knowledge could be moved to any noble deed;" while one of the wise men said, "Verily I pity no one as
I pity the man who seeks knowledge but understands not, and him who understands and seek it not." Abu-al-Darda' said, "I would rather learn one point than spend my night in continual prayer;" and again, "The learned and the learner are partners in righteousness while the rest of

---

[173] Ahl Adhikr, people of remembrance meaning scholars see Quran 21:6-7
[174] Look up footnote num 9
[175] Referring to the fact one should travel as far as China to look for knowledge. Not literally go to China.
[176] The key to these treasure boxes is to ask questions

men are barbarians in whom there is no good." He :also said, "Be learned, or a learner, or an auditor but never anything else lest thou perish." 'Ata' said "[Attendance at] an assembly of learning atones[177] [the evil of attending] seventy places of entertainment." "Umar said, "The death of a thousand worshippers who spend their days in fasting and their nights in continual prayer is a lesser calamity than the passing away of one learned man who is aware of what is lawful before Allah and what is unlawful. "Al-Shafi'i said, "Seeking knowledge is better than supererogatory works." Ibn-'Abd-al-Hakam said, "I was [once] at Malik's place studying at his feet when the hour of noon[178] arrived. Thereupon I closed my books and put them away in order to pray; but he said, `What you have risen to perform is not better than what you were doing provided your intentions are good." Abu-al-Darda' also said, "Whoever should regard that rising early for study is not *jihad* [reveals himself] deficient in reasoning and intellect."

ON THE EXCELLENCE OF TEACHING

the evil of attending] seventy places of entertainment by the following words of Allah: ".... And may warn their people when they come back to them, haply they may take heed to themselves", (9:123) by which is meant teaching and guidance. Allah also said, "Moreover, when Allah entered into a covenant with those to whom the scriptures had been given, and said, `Ye shall surely make it known to mankind and not hide it' ...' (3:184),"meaning thereby that teaching was incumbent upon them. And again He said, "But truly some of them do conceal the truth, though acquainted with it."(2:141) Here Allah has ruled against concealing the truth as he has with regard to concealing evidence when He said, "He who refuseth [to give evidence] is surely wicked at heart." (2:283) The Prophet said, "Allah does not give the learned any knowledge unless He enters with them into the same covenant He has entered into with the prophets - namely, to make it known and not conceal it." Allah also said, "And who speaketh fairer than he who biddeth to Allah and doeth the thing that is right?" (41:33) and again, "Summon thou to the wav of thy Lord with wisdom and kindly warning;" (16:126) and also" And teach them `The Book' and Wisdom."(2:123)

[As to the evidence of the excellence of teaching] in tradition, the Apostle of Allah, on sending Mu`adh to al-Yaman, said to him, "That, through you, Allah may lead one man [unto Himself] is better for you than the world and all that is in it." He also said, "Whoever acquires but one section of knowledge in order to teach men, will be given the reward of seventy of the righteous." Jesus said, "He who has knowledge and shall do and teach, the same shall be called great in the Kingdom of Heaven." The Prophet said, "When on the day of resurrection Allah says unto the worshippers and the warriors, 'Enter ye into Paradise', the learned would say, 'By virtue of our learning have they attained their piety and fought for Thee'. Then Allah would say unto

---

[177] Amends, removes..Etc.
[178] The Prayer (*Salat*) of Dhuhur

them, 'I regard you alike with my angels: intercede and you will have your intercessions accepted.' They then would present their intercessions and enter into Paradise." This cannot result except from knowledge which is made active through teaching not from passive knowledge which is inert. The Prophet said, "Allah does not take away knowledge from men after He has given it to them, rather it vanishes with the passing away of the learned. Thus whenever a learned man passes away, whatever [knowledge] he had perishes with him. When finally there are none left but ignorant leaders they will give uninformed opinions whenever consulted, leading men astray and confusing themselves." The Prophet also said, "Whoever has any knowledge but conceals it, will, on the day of resurrection, be bridled with a bit of fire." He also said, "How excellent' a gift and how admirable a present is a word of wisdom which you hear and inwardly digest and then carry it and teach it to a brother Muslim: verily it is equivalent to a year of worship." And again, "Accursed is the world and all that is in it except the name of the exalted Allah and him who shall follow in His way, be it a teacher or one taught." The Prophet also said, "In truth Allah and His angels as well as the heavens and the earth, even the ant in its hill and the whale in the sea, will bless the man who teaches his fellow men." He also said, "A Muslim gives his brother Muslim no better benefit than a `fair' tradition which had reached him and which he consequently imparts. He also said, "A good word which the believer hears and follows and also teaches is better for him than a year's worship."

One day the Apostle of Allah passed by two assembled groups: the members of the first were calling upon Allah and offering their supplications, while the others were instructing men. Whereupon he said, "These beseech Allah; if He wills He will grant them their request and if He wills He will withhold it; whereas those teach men and verily I was not sent but as a teacher." Then he turned and sat among them. He also said, "The knowledge and guidance which Allah has sent me to declare are like unto heavy rains which fell over a certain locality. One spot absorbed the rain and put forth herbs and much grass; another spot held the waters with which Allah benefited men who drank therefrom, watered the earth therewith, and then planted it; and a third spot was flat, it held no water and put forth no herb." The first part of the parable signifies the one who reaps the benefits of his own knowledge, the second signifies the one whose knowledge is of benefit to others, while the third stands for him who enjoys neither.

Muhammad also said, "When a man dies all except three of his works perish, namely, a permanent endowment for charity, useful knowledge, and righteous progeny that bring honour upon his memory." And again, "He who leads to something good is like him who does it." He further said, "Envy[179] is unlawful except regarding two categories of persons: those to whom Allah has given wealth and power to spend that wealth rightly, and those to whom Allah has given wisdom with which they regulate [their lives] and which they teach." The Prophet also said "Allah's mercy is upon my successors." On being asked, "But who are your successors?" he replied, "My successors are those who keep my laws and teach them to Allah's people."

---

[179] Envy is used here in the sense of Ghibtah. Ghibtah is permissible for the reason that when one sees that a person has been graced by Allah (subhana wa ta'ala) with certain gifts and qualities, he also desires to be blessed with those gifts.

[As to the evidence of the excellence of teaching] in the sayings of the Companions, `Umar said, "Whoever shall relate a tradition and thus induce someone to do according to its precepts, will, with the [actual] doer be equally rewarded. "Ibn-'Abbas said, "All things even the whale in the sea will intercede for him who teaches men good." One of the learned men said, "The learned man occupies the position of an intermediary between Allah and His creatures; let the learned, therefore, be mindful how he occupies this position."

It has been related that Sufyan al-Thawri[180] arrived in 'Asqalan where he tarried[181] but no man questioned him [or sought his knowledge]. Whereupon he said, "Hire for me a beast of burden in order to depart from this city, for it is a place where knowledge does not prosper." He had not said this except in solicitude over the excellence of teaching in which lies the preservation of knowledge. 'Ata' also said, "I came upon Sa'id ibn-al Musayyab while he was weeping, at which I said. 'What causes you to weep?' He answered, 'No one seeks from my any information.' It has also been said that the learned men are the lights of the ages; each is the torch of his own age and through him his contemporaries obtain light." Al-Hasan said, "Had it not been for the learned:, men would have become like animals." For it is through teaching and instruction that men are brought out of the category of beasts to that of human beings. 'Ikrimah said. "Verily a price is set upon this knowledge." When asked that it was, he replied, "It is to be given to him who can keep it well and not lose it." Yahya ibn-Mu'adh said, "The learned have more compassion for the follow

ers of Muhammad than either their fathers or mothers." "How is that?" he was asked; to which he replied, "Their fathers and mothers shield them from the fires of this world while the learned protect them against the fires of the next." It has been said that in the process of learning the first [step] is silence, followed by listening, then retention, then doing, and finally imparting. It has also been said, "Teach what you knows to him who does not know and learn from him who knows what you do not know. If you would do this you would learn what you have not known and would retain what you have already known." Mu'adh ibn-Jabal said, (I have also come across the same saying described as a *marfu*[182] tradition), "Acquire knowledge, for its acquisition is [acquisition to] the fear of Allah, its pursuit is [equivalent to] worship, its study is [equivalent to] praise, searching for it is [equivalent to] jihad, teaching it to him who does not know is [equivalent to] almsgiving, and imparting it to those who are worthy is meritorious. Furthermore, it is the bosom friend of the lonesome, the companion in solitude, the guide [to religion, the comforter in both] happiness and misfortune, the aid to the lonely, the relative among strangers, and the beacon on the road to Paradise. Through it Allah exalts a few and

---

[180] Sufyan ath-Thawri ibn Said (716–778) was a Tābi' al-Tābi'īn (3rd generation after the prophet) Islamic scholar, Hafiz and jurist, founder of the Thawri madhhab or school of taught .He was also a great hadith compiler (muhaddith).
[181] Got delayed or intended to stay for a while.
[182] Elevated. A Hadith which is traced back directly to Rasulullah (Sallallahu Alaihi Wasallam) is called Marfu'

makes them leaders in virtues, chiefs and counsellors worthy of emulation, pioneers in righteousness whose footsteps should be followed and whose deeds should be observed. The angels seek their friendship and with their wings they touch them to gain thereby their favour. The .living and the dead, yea even the whales and the fish of the sea, the lions and beasts of the field, as well as the heaven and its stars intercede for them, because knowledge is the protection of hearts against blindness, the light of the eyes in darkness, and the fortification of the body against decay. Through it man attains the dignity of sainthood and the loftiest ranks. To reflect upon it is [as meritorious] as fasting and its study, as continual prayer. Through it Allah is obeyed, worshipped and glorified; through it he admonishes and forewarns; through it His unity is declared, and through it also [man] abstains from sin. Through knowledge the ties of relationship are made close by kindly deeds, and the lawful and the unlawful are made known. Knowledge is like an *imam* whereas works are his followers. Knowledge is bestowed upon the fortunate and from the unfortunate withheld".

EVIDENCE [FOR THE EXCELLENCE OF KNOWLEDGE] FROM REASON

The purpose of this section is to comprehend the excellence and value of knowledge. Nevertheless, unless excellence is in itself understood arad its meaning determined it will not be possible to acknowledge it as an attribute to knowledge, or to any other trait besides. Similarly, whoever expects to determine whether or not Zayd is wise without having understood the meaning and essence of wisdom, is sure to go astray.

Excellence is derived from the infinitive to excel, which is excrescence. When, therefore, of two objects which are similar, one has an extra characteristic, that object is described as excelling the other, no matter what its excellence may be. Thus saying that the horse is more excellent than the donkey means that the horse shares with the donkey the capacity for carrying burdens, but excels it in charging, wheeling, swiftness, and beauty. However, should a donkey possess a ganglionar growth[183] it would not be described as more excellent, because the ganglion, through an excrescence on the body, is in reality a defect, an imperfection. In addition the animal is sought for its useful qualities, not for its physical features. If you then understand this, it will be clear to you that knowledge excels when compared with the other attributes, just as the horse is distinguished when compared with the other animals. Furthermore, while swiftness is an excellent [feature] in the horse, in itself it has no excellence. Knowledge, however, is in itself an absolute excellence, apart from any attribution. It is the description of Allah's perfection, and through it the angels and prophets were imbued[184] with honour. The fleet horse is better than the slow. Knowledge is, therefore, an excellence in the absolute and apart from any attribution.

---

[183] A nonproportional growth
[184] Inspired

A precious and a desired object may be of any of three categories: what is sought as a means to an end, what is sought for its own [intrinsic value], and what is sought for both. What is sought for its own [intrinsic value] is nobler and more excellent than that which is sought as a means to an end. The dirham and the dinar are objects sought as means to an end to. secure other objects. In themselves they are only two useless metals; and had not Allah made it possible to transact business through them, they would have been the same as pebbles. Happiness in the hereafter and the ecstasy' of viewing the face of Allah are sought for their own [intrinsic value], while physical health is sought both for its own [intrinsic value] and as a means to an end. Man's health, for example, is sought because it is a guarantee against bodily pain, and also because it helps [man] to reach his ends and [secure his] needs. Similarly, if you would consider [the case of] knowledge, you would discover that it is in itself delightful and therefore sought for its own [intrinsic value], and you would also find it a way which leads to the hereafter and its happiness, and the only means whereby we come close to Allah.

The greatest achievement in the opinion of man is eternal happiness and the most excellent thing is the way which leads to it. This happiness will never be attained except through knowledge and works, and works are impossible without the knowledge of how they are done. The basis for happiness in this world and the next is knowledge. Of all works it is, therefore, the most excellent. And why not, since the excellence of anything is revealed by the quality of its fruit? You have already learnt that the fruit of knowledge in the hereafter is drawing near to the Lord of the Universe, attaining the rank of the angels, and joining the company of the heavenly hosts[185]. Its fruits in this world, however, are power, dignity, influence over kings, and reverence from all to an extent that even the ignorant Turks and the rude Arabs are found naturally disposed to honour their teachers because the latter are distinguished by a great deal of knowledge derived from experience. Even the animal does by nature honour man because it senses that he is distinguished by a degree of perfection exceeding its own. These are, then, the excellence of knowledge in the absolute. As shall be seen later, the different branches of knowledge vary, and with their variation their excellences vary.

The excellences of teaching and learning, in view of what we have already said, are therefore manifest. For if knowledge is the most excellent of things, the process of acquiring it would then be a search for the most excellent, and imparting it would be promoting the most excellent. For human interests extend to both the material and the spiritual worlds, and no order exists in the latter without existing in the former because this world is a preparation for the next, and is the instrument which leads to Allah anyone who uses it as such, a home for him who takes it as a dwelling place. The affairs of this world, however, do not become orderly except through human activities. These activities, crafts, and industries are divided into three categories:

The first involves four fundamental (activities) without which chaos would rule the world: agriculture for raising food-stuffs, weaving for manufacturing clothes, architecture for erecting houses, and politics for establishing human relationship and society and for promoting co-operation in the control of the means of living.

---

[185] Another name for angels

The second involves such activities as are auxiliary to any of the above-mentioned fundamental activities. Thus iron craft is auxiliary to agriculture as well as to several other industries, and supplies them with their respective tools and instruments such as the implements for carding and spinning cotton preparatory to its weaving.

The third involves such activities as are supplementary to the previously mentioned principal industries, e.g., the process of milling and bread-making in relation to agriculture and the process of laundering and tailoring to weaving.

The relation of these principal activities to the order of things in this world is as the relation of the members of the body to the whole, because the members of the body are also divided into three categories. These are fundamental like the heart, the liver, and the brain; auxiliary like the stomach, veins, arteries, and sinews: or supplementary and ornamental like nails, fingers and eyebrows.

The highest of these activities are the fundamental, and of these the highest is politics [as employed] in unifying [people] and in reform. For that reason this discipline demands of those who pursue it a degree of perfection greater than that required by any of the other disciplines; and in consequence it is inevitable that the politician should subordinate to himself, and make use of, the other profession.

Politics, bent on reform and on guiding people to the straight path which [insures] salvation in this world and the next, is [in turn] divided into four classes: the first, which is also the highest, is the [religious] polity of the prophets which involves their jurisdiction over the thoughts and actions of the privileged few and the common folk alike. The second is the [civil] polity of the caliphs, the kings, and the sultans, which involves their jurisdiction over the actions, but not the thoughts, of the privileged few and the common folk. The third Is the intellectual polity of the learned man, who know Allah and His will and who are the heirs of the prophets, which involves jurisdiction only over the thoughts of the privileged few since the understanding of the common folk is too low for them to benefit, and their power of discrimination is too weak to observe and emulate their actions, and are, therefore, subject to no compulsion or restraint. The fourth is the ["ecclesiastical'] polity of the preachers which involves jurisdiction only over the thoughts of the common folk.

Next to the [religious] polity of the prophets, the highest is, therefore, the intellectual because of its service in disseminating knowledge, in diverting the souls of men from the destructive and undesirable traits, and in guiding them to those which lead to happiness and are praiseworthy, all of which, in the final analysis, fall within the purpose of teaching. We have only said that the intellectual activities are more excellent than the other professions and activities because the superiority of an activity is known by three things:

1. By examining the native endowments of man through which the activity is realized, as in the case of the superiority of the theoretical sciences over the linguistic. Wisdom is attained through the intellect while language, through the sense of hearing (and intellect is superior to the [mere] sense of hearing).

2. By examining the extent of its usefulness, as in the case of the superiority of agriculture over the goldsmith's craft.

3. By observing die object. of its operations, as in the case of the superiority of the goldsmith's craft over tanning; the object of the one is gold while that of the other is the hide of a corpse.

It is further apparent that the religious sciences, which are the knowledge of the path to the hereafter, are comprehended through the maturity of the intellect: and as we shall see later, clear understanding and clear intellect are the highest attributes of man, because through the intellect the responsibility of Allah's trust[186] is accepted, and through it man can enjoy the closeness to Allah.

Concerning the extent of its usefulness there is not the slightest doubt since it contributes to happiness in the hereafter. And finally, how could the merit of an object of an activity be denied when the objects with which the teacher deals are the hearts and souls of men. The noblest being on earth is the human and the noblest in his essence is his heart with whose perfecting, cleansing, purifying, and leading to Allah the teacher is occupied. Thus on the one hand the work of the teacher is a (form of] praise to Allah and on the other hand a (form of] stewardship. It is in fact the highest form of stewardship because Allah has bestowed upon the heart of the learned man knowledge, which is His most intimate attribute. Hence the learned man is like the keeper of Allah's most valuable treasures and has permission to give from them to all who need. What rank is, therefore, higher than that in which the servant is an intermediary between his Lord and his fellowmen, to draw them closer unto Allah and to lead them to Paradise to which the pious repair. May we, through the Grace of Allah, become one of them, and may He bless every chosen servant.

[End of Section I]
Section II: is on On praiseworthy and objectionable branches of knowledge

---

[186] *"Indeed, we offered the Trust to the heavens and the earth and the mountains, and they declined to bear it and feared it; but man [undertook to] bear it. Indeed, he was unjust and ignorant."* Al Ahzab 33:72

Advice from long-term Tayba students

We asked some of our most accomplished and long-term students, who themselves were incarcerated or are still incarcerated, to offer some advice on studying Islam. Here are the responses they sent to us:

Q: What mindset and attitude should a student have?

A student should have the mindset and attitude that pushes him to acquire as much knowledge of the Deen as possible in order not only to live according to what has been prescribed for us but also to make a contribution to society upon his release. A teacher once related what one scholar said about mindset and attitude: If a person has a place to pray (develop the spirit), a place to exercise (develop the body), and a place to study (develop the mind), then what the person has is a training ground" (Khalil).

"Positive and clear mindset with no distractions (tv, radio, celly, friends etc.)" (Isa).

"A believer should have a positive mindset or attitude in whatever he/she is involved in. One of the ways of accomplishing this is by first clarifying one's intentions and removing any impurities from them. Then he/she must constantly check them for the possible return of these old impurities or any new ones. In my earlier years of studying, my intentions were filled with so many impure reasons and purposes. They varied from receiving an Ijaza (degree), to being known as a great teacher, to pleasing other people, etc. A degree shouldn't be the reason or purpose for studying or acquiring knowledge. It should be for the sole purpose of developing a relationship with the Owner of all Knowledge. This relationship surpasses any degree or Ijaza. The acquisition of knowledge shouldn't be to obtain the contentment of one's relatives, friends or teachers. Relationships change, people come and go; everything is impermanent except Allah (SWT). Never allow them to be the motives for your striving to learn your Deen, for it can be a hindrance. There is nothing wrong with your loved ones being happy with your achievements, but your goal should always be the pleasure of Allah (SWT). When I first arrived to prison I decided to go back to school and complete my education. I felt that an education would hopefully prove to my parents and family that I was making a change for the better. But when I lost my parents to death, I also lost my desire for studying. I learned from that experience that Allah's contentment should always be the goal and everything else secondary. The acquisition of knowledge shouldn't be with the concept that you are doing it to teach other people, because you can't explore yourself when it is done with some other ambition. Lastly, one must understand the loftiness of this knowledge. I was listening to a lecture a day ago, "Advice to the Seeker of Knowledge," by Shaykh Al-Habib Kazim al-Saqqaf. He said some extraordinary things, in my lowly opinion. He said, "The first courtesy that a student of knowledge should show, is to acknowledge the loftiness of this knowledge. These sciences that we learn, be they fiqh, tasawwuf, tajweed, should be implemented in our lives. By one implementing them it is like one learning how to work a rocket, then getting inside and embarking on a journey to a place where you might be able to have direct perception into the knowledges that the Prophets (AS) came with. So, one should give it its due. By sacrificing his/her time for it, by being constant in the acquisition of knowledge and couple his/her learning with the practice. Because there is no benefit in learning something you don't practice it. By coupling one's knowledge with action, Allah (SWT) discloses to that person the realities of this knowledge. These knowledges may seem simple, but they are really profound. The profundity of them can only be known if one implements them. So, by knowing the immensity of these sciences, one will actually try to live them, because even though they seem small, the benefits are actually immense. If one was to study a small book on tajweed, which may take a week, the immensity is far greater than that. Because in knowing how to recite the Qur'an, one knows how to address his/her Creator. By knowing how to address your Creator, one also knows that these are articulations of the words of Allah (SWT), which is the eternal speech of Allah (SWT). Then, one can hear it as a Divine Address coming to him/her." He continues in another place, "These knowledges that one learns are like little keys and their treasures are repositories of Divine Knowledge which are disclosed to one later. By knowing its worth, sacrificing one's time for it and by giving it its due, one will have an opening by which he knows its worth, by the permission of Allah (SWT)" (Muhammad Amin).

"As a student my mindset should be to always respect, pay close attention and never interrupt the murshid while he or she is teaching. My attitude should always be spiritually sound, pious and highly appreciative of sacred learning at the feet of our Shaykh's" (Taahir).

"We should be focused on becoming beacons of light to our families and communities. This should be done while simultaneously seeking Allah's, Subhaanahu wa Ta`Aalaa, Face and embodying the Noble Character of the Rasooluallah (saw)" (Abdul Muhaymin).

"Forget about the time that you have to serve and focus on the time that you have to learn" (Aqil).

"One of complete gratitude that Allah has given them the time and resources to study w/ competent teachers! we all know the fitna that spreads when people have to guess as to the intention of Allah and His blessed msngr concerning a Quranic verse or noble hadith! be grateful! buckle down and take advantage of the favor of Allah to you!!!" (Tabari).

"Their mindset should be one of appreciation and thanks for the opportunity to study with a scholar who learned excellent knowledge via traditional Islamic scholarship and methodology. An attitude of thankfulness goes a very long way, because it leaves the student with no room to take knowledge for granted. This knowledge is for attaining closeness to Allah Ta'ala by observing His limitations, specifically those that are obligated for us; so, with the mindset of understand what is obligated should enhance our attitude of learning this at whatever cost, as soon as humanly possible" (Ahmad).

"A student should be open minded and willing to learn, when it comes to building one's own knowledge in terms of new ideas and concepts. Moreover, a student should be of a positive attitude and not get frustrated and willing to give up when it comes to one's studies, always maintaining a need to grow in terms of one's intellect. Having a clear and positive mind will help anyone learn in a more productive and efficient manner" (Sergio).

"They should first be thankful for the opportunity to study traditional Islamic knowledge. They should recognize this as a tremendous blessing from Allah. They must remember that as their knowledge grows so do their responsibilities while their excuses begin to vanish" (Juan).

"A student should be very determined , hungry, and excited and waste no time. He should realize that there is a difference between Sacred knowledge and "information." The student should be desperate and chase knowledge like it is leaving and whoever has it will be a millionaire. The student must realize there is no time to waste, just because we are in prison and have plenty of it is not an excuse to waste it, rather we should be thankful and use each of its precious moments" (Sulaymaan).

"If we look at the great 'ulāmā or scholars of Islām we will see they were characterized by five main qualities that lead to their success, they are: High Himma (spiritual ambition), Sabr (Patience), and tawadu' (humility). If we are to succeed ourselves as students of knowledge we must strive our utmost to inculcate these qualities into ourselves. I will expound upon each of these qualities individually now:
A. High Himma. The student of 'Ilm or sacred knowledge should have an extremely high desire/ambition to learn sacred knowledge and practice it in their life, this desire/ambition is called "himma" in Arabic. The only way one will be able to attain this high level of himma which the Prophet (salla Llāhu 'alayhi wa sallam), Sahaba (Radi Allā 'anhum), and 'ulāmā had is by realizing the greatness of 'Ilm or sacred knowledge in the sight of Allāh (subhāna wa ta 'alā). When we truly appreciate the merit of sacred knowledge, and the great status of those who learn and teach it, then we will find the himma to become people of sacred knowledge ourselves.

Every Tayba Foundation course starts with a section by Shaykh Rami (may Allah preserve him) called "Advice on studying", this section shows the merit and importance of sacred knowledge in Islam. I will not repeat what Shaykh Rami mentioned there and the serious student should reference that one. One of the greatest inspirations in my own journey was the section on sacred knowledge found at the beginning of the book "The Reliance of the Traveler" translated by Shaykh Nuh Keller, which list many of the Ahadith on this subject and discusses its merit, I would also suggest reading that.

I would now like to mention a few points of benefit on the subject of sacred knowledge: Allah and His Messenger (salla Llāhu 'alayhi wa sallam) have emphasized learning sacred knowledge ('ilm) in many Qur'anic verses and Ahadith (Plural of Hadith). Allah says in his Book, "He gives hikmah (wisdom) to whom He wills, and whoever is given hikmah has indeed received tremendous good. Only the people of intelligence take heed" (Qur'an 2:269). The Mufassirun (scholars of Tafsir or Qur'anic commentary) say the word "Hikmah" (translated as wisdom) means "knowledge of the Deen and beneficial knowledge one practices" (see "Quraan Made Easy" by Mufti Elias). The Prophet (salla Llāhu 'alayhi wa sallam) said, "whomever Allah wishes well for He gives a deep understanding of the Deen (fiqh)." He also said, "Accursed is this world and all that it contains, except for the Dhikr (Remembrance) of Allah, someone learning sacred knowledge or someone teaching it." The last hadith I would like to mention is the words of the Prophet (salla Llāhu 'alayhi wa sallam), "A single 'Alim (scholar) is harder on the Devil than a thousand worshippers."

The last hadith has much depth of meaning and I will mention a few points related to it. The whole of Islam is based on learning sacred knowledge and then practicing it. The first thing a believer must learn is the attributes of Allah that He necessarily possesses and what attributes that don't befit Him, knowing and believing this is what makes one a Muslim. If one doesn't learn the proper knowledge of 'Aqida or Islamic creed one's whole Islām could be rejected. So the first obligation of a Muslim is to learn the science of 'Aqida and then to believe in it. Likewise, Allah has commanded us to worship him in the way that he sees fit, according to the rules and regulation he has lard down, we can only do this by studying the science of Fiqh or Islamic Law. If we neglect learning the knowledge of Fiqh we could be worshipping Allah for years but have it rejected from Him due to mistakes made due to our ignorance. So a worshipper who has no knowledge can have his worship rejected, or he can be easily mislead by the Devil, whereas the 'Alim or learned Muslim will be safe from these pitfalls, and that's why the Prophet (salla Llāhu 'alayhi wa sallam) said what he did.

We cannot "obey Allah and His Messenger" as Allah's commanded us over and over again in the Qur'ān if we do not know what we have been commanded to do or prohibited from doing, the only way to fulfill this command is by learning. And this is why the Prophet (salla Llāhu 'alayhi wa sallam) said, "Learning is an obligation upon every Muslim." For this reason, Islam has been a religion steeped in learning and teaching, which places special emphasis on scholarship, and which highly honors scholars.

Now one of the things we should realize is almost all the problems we see in the Ummah (Muslim community) today is due to ignorance of the Deen, and the only cure is to learn Sacred knowledge and then teach it to others. The prison environment is no different than the situation the Ummah on the outside is facing, indeed the level of ignorance on the basics even of Islamic belief and practice is more dire amongst prisoners, who have almost no access to scholars and materials on traditional Sunni Islam. Many of the issues we have between each other, administration, and other inmates in prison is due to ignorance of what the deen really teaches on many issues and how to properly conduct ourselves. We owe it to Allah, the Prophet (salla Llāhu 'alayhi wa sallam), and the Ummah as a whole to rectify this situation by becoming people of sacred knowledge, this is mere gratitude to Allah for the blessing of Islam.

We should realize not only is it a Fard 'Ayn or personal obligation to learn the deen for personal application our lives, but it's a Fard kiffayah or communal obligation to have scholars to teach the Deen to the community, we are in an age where this Fard kiffayah is being neglected and we do not have even 1/10th of the scholars we need. As the Prophet (salla Llāhu 'alayhi wa sallam) said, "Allah will not take away knowledge all at once. Rather, He will take it away by taking away the scholars (in death). Then the people will take the ignorant ones as their leaders and they will give answers without knowledge so they will be misguided and they will misguide." And as Shaykh Rami commentated "So, if we do not want to make ourselves another sign of the time, we must be a part of reviving the sciences of the Deen."

In the prison environment our situation is even worse, we have had almost no access to scholars until Tayba Foundation started their Distance Learning Program, and it's virtually non-existent to find inmates who have Ijāzā (certification) to teach others. We have been presented with an immense opportunity through Tayba Foundation to not only learn our Fard 'Ayn but also to fulfill a Fard kiffayah by training in the Islamic sciences in order to gain Ijāzā to teach others, thus helping to rectify the situation our Ummah finds itself in. Realizing all of the above and the pressing necessity our community is in should give us the Himma needed to embark on this journey of gaining 'ilm. One of the greatest lectures I've heard on this subject and which inspired me in this area is "Ignorance: The Disease of our Time" by Shaykh Muhammad al-Yaqoubi, I encourage anyone who can obtain that lecture to do so (IslamicBookstore.com sells it).

B. Ikhlās (sincerity): Allah says, "And they were not commanded but to worship Allah, to be sincere in their worship of Him and to following the pure religion" (Qur'ān 98:5). The 'ulāmā say the greatest act of worship after the Fard 'Ayn is learning sacred knowledge, it being superior to even nafl fasting and prayers. Sincere learning is an act of worship; we have been commanded to make Allah our sole intention in doing so. The Prophet (salla Llāhu 'alayhi wa sallam) said, "Deeds are judged according to their intentions, and every man shall receive what he intended..." Our only intention in learning sacred knowledge should be to gain this knowledge in order to draw nearer to Allah and gain His good pleasure. Learning sacred knowledge is one of the greatest means to raise our rank with Allah, it is also one of the greatest means to spiritually transform ourselves. The scholars of Tasawwuf (Purification of the Heart) say their whole method of purifying the soul is based on: 'Ilm, 'Amal, and Hāl. 'Ilm is learning sacred knowledge,

'Amal is putting that knowledge into practice, and Hāl is the resultant spiritual state that comes about from putting that knowledge into practice. So the student of knowledge should make the niyyah or intention learn this knowledge in order to gain Allah's pleasure and draw nearer to Him and to spiritually transform themselves. There is huge Barakah (Divine Blessings) that descend upon the people of sacred knowledge. One should renew their intention each tome they study. One's intention for studying should never be to gain prestige, fame, gloat over people, etc... One of the things I like to think about is even if I was in solitary confinement for the rest of my life, never seeing another human being again, would I still find the himma to memorize the text and learn? Thinking of this is a good barometer of my level of Ikhlas & a reminder that I should only intend Allah by my studying.

C. Shukr (gratitude): In the verse of Qur'ān I quoted earlier Allah told us that whoever is given Hikmah (wisdom or knowledge of the Deen) has been given a tremendous blessing. One thing to realize is that if we are not grateful for a blessing then Allah may very well strip it from us, and the way to keep a blessing and have increase in it is to be grateful for it, as Allah informs us in the Qur'ān. The 'ulamā say true gratitude or shukr is manifested in the heart, tongue, and limbs. By thinking of and appreciating a blessing that's the shukr of the heart, by praising and mentioning a blessing often that's the shukr of the tongue, and by using the blessings of Allah for what they were created for (i.e. to obey him) that's the shukr of the limbs. So the student of sacred knowledge must be extremely grateful they're been blessed with the opportunity to study under scholars, they must teach this knowledge to others, and they must implement this knowledge in their lives.

One of the things I would like to remind the Tayba students is what a great blessing and opportunity you have been presented with through the Tayba Distance Learning Program. Those of us who spent years in prison without access to scholars and materials know what a great blessing this is. Shaykh Rami has dedicated his life to teaching and training prisoners, as have other Tayba staff, there is no one else out there doing that. Shaykh Rami is not just some average joe but a top notch scholar who studied overseas many years and was authorized (given Ijāzā) to teach others, with an isnād (chain of transmission) extending back to the Prophet (salla Llāhu 'alayhi wa sallam). Our community on the outside is in dire need of scholars with ijāzā to teach them and they are in high demand, so the fact a scholar with Ijāzā has finally decided to dedicate all of his time to teaching inmates is a huge blessing. Usually scholars with ijaza are only available to study under in bigger cities like L.A., San Francisco, New York, etc... and even Muslims on the outside have to travel or move to study under scholars with Ijāzā, or they have to take an online course at the cost of a couple hundred dollars each.

What I'm getting at is we have been blessed with an opportunity most of our brothers and sisters on the outside don't even have. Likewise, we should realize each course we take with Tayba cost $225 and all of that is being paid by the donation of brothers and sisters out there who care about you. When Allah has blessed is with so much – people dedicating all this time and money to you – we should show our gratitude to Allah by applying ourselves fully 100% to our studies. Not turning in all of our work assignments, missing deadlines, and dropping out of the program are great acts of ingratitude. We must fully apply ourselves.

D. Sabr (Patience): Allah (Subhana wa wa ta 'alā) says in the Qur'ān "Seek assistance with sabr and salaah" (Qur'ān 2:45). The 'ulāmā say patience is composed of four parts: Patience in maintaining ones acts of worship, Patience in avoiding the prohibitions, Patience with the Decree of Allah, and Patience with the servants of Allah. The student of knowledge must have patience with all these things. We as prisoners are in an environment that often requires extreme patience ~ often we are surrounded by negative influences a people, loud noises and distractions, etc... I had a letter from Shaykh Nuh Ha Mim Keller to his Murids or students in prison that started out by saying "As-Salāmu 'alaykum to all currently in the school of the Prophet Yusuf", & this letter really made me reflect on the Prophet Yusuf ('alayhi salam) and how our situation resembles his – he was forgotten by his people on the outs yet he spent his time in the worship of his Lord and maintained extreme patience. "The school of the Prophet Yusuf" is the school of learning patience.

We as students of knowledge in prison must have much sabr. All students of knowledge must have the patience to maintain our program we've set up for ourselves to study and memorize. As Shaykh Rami has pointed out, knowledge is a precious thing and Allah will only let you have it if you struggle. Gaining knowledge is a full time job and you will have to sacrifice your time, sleep, habits, etc... in order to succeed in it. Likewise, as we gain knowledge and implement it in our lives we will face those who are not aiding us in that, sometimes being a person of Taqwa can be a lonely path in here and we must also have patience with that. Sometimes due to the immense volume of letters and calls Tayba receives we may have to wait a couple months for responses, we must also have patience with that. But of we don't give up and we maintain patience on this Path of gaining sacred knowledge we will see in the end how all we did was worth it. Allah says in the Qur'ān He is with the Patient and will guide to his Path those who struggle for his sake.

E. Tawdu' (Humility): If one has ever meet 'ulāmā or sat with them one will be struck with how humble they are; they are people of extreme rahma or Mercy. With the more knowledge we gain the more humble we should become. We should realize all knowledge we have is a gift from Allāh, and the only reason we know what we do and have the ability to obey Allah is because He has given us the Tawfīq or Divinely given success to do so. Nothing puts a distaste in peoples mouths more than those who act arrogantly or lord their knowledge over others. In the Muwatta of Imām Mālik it's related, "Malik related to me (Yahya bin Yahya), that he heard that 'Isa bin Maryam, peace be upon him, used to say, 'Do not speak much without the mention of Allah for you will harden your hearts. A hard heart is far from Allah, but you do not know. Do not look at the wrong actions of people as if you were lords, but rather look at your own wrong actions as if you were slaves. Some people are afflicted by wrong actions and others are protected from them. Have mercy on those who are afflicted and show gratitude for His protection." (Abdus Salam)

Q: How can a student increase their motivation to learn?

"By keeping in mind that his learning is an investment in him/herself. Whatever the person learns will benefit him/her in this world and the next, insha Allah" (Khalil).

"My motivation was wanting to be able to do my worship properly to Allah and the fact that I was surrounded by ignorance (muslim/non-muslim). Every prison seemed like the blind was leading the blind, I just got fed up and starting studying" (Isa).

"I would constantly reflect on my state and goals and remind myself of where I wanted to be and question if I was making any progress and adjust my habits and attitudes accordingly" (Abdul Muhaymin)

"Realize that learning is your greatest means to drawing closer to ALLAH and remaining ignorant is a worse crime than the one committed in the first place" (Aqil).

"By starting a study group. constantly show others /share w/ others what is available and encourage them to participate" (Tabari).

"Knowing the rewards and benefits of studying is a key motivation. Implementing what one learns will allow them to taste the sweetness of the experience of studying sacred knowledge and it will motivate them to want to learn more. Seek out those individuals who love studying sacred knowledge. Pass on the knowledge that you have understood through a qualified teacher and implement it. By this you will become a source for others. You will be like a running stream through which others can quench their thirst. Like a stream that continues to run due to its connection to a source (body of water), you must maintain your connection to the studying of sacred knowledge" (Muhammad Amin).

"Always make your day's lesson your dhikr – your morning, afternoon, and evening wird. I often read, in various books, the biographies of great ulema (scholars) and it motivates me greatly to know what they did, and the hardship they went through to attain it; it increases my himma (zeal) and strengthens my iman (faith)"

"To increase one's motivation it is a good idea to focus your energy on what you do want rather than what you don't want. A student should be more open minded when it comes to taking the advice of others, in terms of working on one's attitude and desire to work on the weaknesses of one's ability to learn" (Sergio).

"By remembering what it was like when they lived in a state of ignorance. They should look around them and see how those who have not come to Islam live their lives. They should also look at those Muslims who spend no time studying conduct themselves. Also they should read the stories of the scholars who have attained true success" (Juan).

"A student's motivation is increased through stories. Especially by the companions in books such as "Beauty of the Righteous" and the "Ranks of the Elite" by Abu Nu'aym Al-Asfahani (Hilyatul Awliya wa Tabaqatul Asfiya), because once students see the heavenly glory and honor knowledge brings, that will be enough, especially former convicts who sought glory in haram ways, now it's the time to seek the glory of the Ridhaa Allah. Nothing motivates me more than to read about Sa'a ibn Abi Wayqar in the battle of Qadsiyyah praying the 80 ra'kah salatul fath in a dusty turban in the palace of Kirsa, belittling the dunya, Allahu akbar!" (Sulaymaan).

"The greatest piece of advice I can give on how to motivate oneself to learn is to keep the company of those dedicated to sacred knowledge, keep the company of brothers or sister who are into studying. If you cannot find this company in the people around you then turn to the books like the ones before you by Imam Zarnuji and Imam Ghazzali included in this course. Every time I read Shaykh Rami's "Advice on studying" it increases me in himma. Likewise reading the biographies of various 'ulāmā such as in the back of "The Reliance of the Traveler" and elsewhere always motivates me.

We must also realize the things that will cause us to lose himma and avoid them. Keeping the company of negative people and the worldly will definitely have a bad spiritual effect on you and should be avoided. Even keeping the company of Muslims whose main focus is the latest TV show, card games, or the latest gossip on the yard should be avoided. The 'ulāmā say if you increase in the physical you'll increase in the spiritual. Some of the greatest thieves of our time is the Television and the radio, and in my own journey I found the minute I totally gave them up my himma increased, my memory improved, and my spiritual state with Allah deepened.

As for daily things we can do, we should turn to Allah and ask Him to make this task easy for us – the best time is to wake up in the last third of the night to pray 2 rakas Tahajjud, even if only 30 minutes before Subh, and ask Allah to increase you in your himma and ability to retain what you learn. Tahajjud is a time when Allah answers du'a and all the 'ulāmā I know pray it. When the Prophet (salla Llāhu 'alayhi wa sallam) woke up he would say, "La ilāha illā Ant, subhānaka – llāhumma wa bi hamdik, ataghfiruka li dhanbī wa as'aluka rahmatak, Allāhumma Zidnī 'ilman wa lā tazigh qalbi ba'da idh hadaytanī, wa hab li min ladunka rahma, innaka Antal Wahhāb." (Translation: "There is no god but You. Glory be to You. O Allah, to you belongs all praise. I ask Your forgiveness for my sins and I ask You for Your Mercy. O Allah, increase me in knowledge, and do not lead my heart astray after You have guided me. Bestow on my Your Mercy, for You are the Ever-Bestowing One.") Likewise, after Subh the Messenger of Allah (salla Llāhu 'alayhi wa sallam) would say, "Allāhumma innī as'aluka 'ilman nāfi 'ā, wa 'amalan mutaqabbalan, wa rizqan tayyibā." (Translation: "O Allah, I ask You for beneficial knowledge, acceptable deeds and goodly sustenance.") So we can also use these du'ā to ask Allāh to increase us in our knowledge" (Abdus Salam).

Q: How can a student best manage their time to study?

"It requires a lot of self-discipline, which means a student has to sacrifice doing some things that he/she likes to do. But if the student prioritizes correctly, the student will be able to exert sufficient effort in his/her studies while being able to enjoy the things he/she likes" (Khalil).

"What things should he or she consider when managing time to study in an efficient manner? Best time to study was in the morning before and after fajr. Everyone was asleep and it was quiet. Late afternoon before dinner reviewed morning lesson" (Isa).

"What things should he or she consider when managing time to study in an efficient manner? When I am functioning in a sound mental and spiritual manner I try to take around thirty minutes or so before Subh and review what I learned the day before and what I will be learning for that day. I will then take my memorization lessons and break it down into manageable parts, usually 5 to 6 sessions throughout the day of 25-30-33 times in each session and I end the day with at least 50 recitations in the last session. In between each recitation session throughout the day as time permits I am constantly reading and reviewing what I am memorizing and I talk about it with a brother to help me to remember the info. and to share the info. as I am learning. I try to take my extra funds and buy as many of the the reference books that I can along with other supplemental materials such as Mishkatul Masaabih and other books of Hadith and Fiqh etc" (Abdul Muhaymin).

"How can a student best manage their time to study? What things should he or she consider when managing time to study in an efficient manner? Try to schedule study session at the same time when going to study and be consistent as to days and time" (Taahir).

"The best thing to have as a student of knowledge is a daily schedule one never deviates from, I have found it most beneficial to write my schedule down and then tape it to my wall. Now when picking the times for your daily studying try to figure out the times when you will have the most quiet and can chant the Arabic out loud without disturbing others ~ if you can go to the yard in the morning I've found that to be a good quiet place to memorize, or if you have a celly who works or goes to the yard at a certain time of day then utilize that time to stay in the cell to memorize. You have to put first things first as a student of knowledge, and sleeping in in the morning or going to yard when the pod is quiet is not the best choice when you could be using that time for study. I've also found it helpful to find a celly who is willing to keep their TV or radio plugged into their headphones and who doesn't talk a lot. I've found the best time of day for memorization to be early in the day when it's quiet, and the best time of day for writing the projects for each course to be latter at night once I lock down. Just try to analyze your situation and pick a schedule that fits and don't deviate from it no matter what.

As stated previously one should study where they won't be disturbed or will not disturb others. Studying in the Middle of the pod at midday where there's a bunch of hollering is not a good choice, for example. I've also found the prison library and chapel to be good places I can study in quiet.

One should not put on the nāfs more than it can bear or it may very well kick back and over-turn one's program. A little daily effort is better than a lot that dwindles to nothing, so make your daily schedule something that's realistic and maintainable, increase with increments over time. One can make a vow with Allah each day to stick to one's schedule and if one doesn't then do some disciplinary measure to train the nāfs, like giving away one's dessert or one's dinner tray for example. One can also reward the nāfs, if it sticks to its schedule of study for the week treat it to something you like on canteen (otherwise don't)" (Abdus Salam)

"What things should he or she consider when managing time to study in an efficient manner? If one has a large sentence of 10 years plus, then he should try to commit at least 3-5 years of that time to serious study if the can without working. Take on learning as a full time job with no distractions. Give yourself 3-4 day a week of exercise in the morning or afternoon and always leave the evenings to yourself and your studies. If you dont fall asleep with an open book in your hand at least twice a week, you are shortchanging yourself" (Aqil).

"What things should he or she consider when managing time to study in an efficient manner? to spend at least one hr per day per subject at a minimum...you have the time,use it wisely" (Tabari).

"The first thing one needs to do is root out their wants from their needs. Then, prioritize your studies in light of these needs. Focus on no more than two subjects at a time, but one is always preferable. This way, one allows his mind to be fully focused on the subject matter at hand. By studying one subject or text at a time, more time is given to the process of reviewing and memorization, if one desires memorization. Leisure time is a foreign concept to Islamic tradition, it is something new. If one needs a break or some downtime, then make sure it benefits the mind, spirit and body. The believer is always aware of his/her time. Al Hajj Malik Shabazz (Malcolm X) said, "I don't trust one who doesn't wear a watch." This was because he thought that the person who didn't keep track of time, wasn't concerned with how he/she used it. Don't be too easy on the nafs, nor too hard. These are two extremes and the line between them is very thin. So, walk it very carefully. Remember the nafs loves the two extremes" (Muhammad Amin).

"What things should he or she consider when managing time to study in an efficient manner? Know your own schedule. When do you normally wake up, go to bed, when is chow called, when is it quietest, what is your cellmate's schedule, what agitates them, and so on. None of these sorts of things can be taken lightly, because if they are they can be a part of the reason you fall off of your studies. When you set a time, you must stick to it as it will get away from you" (Ahmad).

"A student can best manage their time to study be developing a time log, as to manage their times to study. This time log should reflect the time one studies and they should not divulge from this study time" (Sergio).

"They can do so by planning their week ahead of time. Try to foresee when they will have at least 45-60 minute blocks of time where they will not be disturbed. Allow some flexibility in this by allotting more study time than they believe they will need in case they get an unexpected doctor's appointment or a visit" (Juan).

"Stop watching TV. Wake up after fajr because it's quiet and the best thinking is done then, utilize the qaylullah nap, and put your books near you so you're motivated to learn and they are easy to reach, go on over your lessons last thing before bed. Eat showt quick meals, walk fast, don't vain talk too much, only work out 1 hr - 1 ½ hr a day, and jog" (Sulaymaan).

Q: Where should a person study? Where should they avoid studying?

"A person should study wherever they will be less likely to be distracted. In a situation where it is practically impossible to avoid distractions, drowning out those distractions is possible ... and the student will know best how to do that for him/herself. Just as an example, I used to spread my study material on the bunk in a way that forced me to turn my back on everyone. Then, I would insert my earbuds without any music playing. It didn't drown out the noise completely, but it put the noise in the background enough to allow me to study peacefully. Or the person can go to the library. The library is usually a quiet place" (Khalil).

"Keep good company pick quiet places to study where you won't be distracted, and decrease in the things that distract one from Allah like Television and radio" (Abdus Salam).

"Best place was in the cell if your cell-mate was not there. Dayroom was good in morning time due to people working but when sports are on avoid dayroom, yard was a good place to walk and memorize" (Isa).

"In a prison environment I found that the assigned room is often the best place to study. If you are staying in an open-dorm then earbuds will probably need to be collected and used . You can also us the Chapel, Library, or the far end of the Rec Yard. Stay away from Common Areas and the TV rooms and other closed-in crowd gathering areas" (Abdul Muhaymin).

"Study where there are minimum to no distractions. As mentioned the evenings are the best when the climate is settled and no movement. A place where there is little to no traffic, like in ones room. This is best for all of your resources are there for cross reference. If there are a group of brothers then focus on small things to cover and memorize while together and remind each other of the importance of taking advantage of the time together. LEAVE OFF ANYTHING THAT STEALS TIME AND IS OF NO BENEFIT. Like focusing on the alleged deviance of this guy or that guy and the like. Avoid places that has much traffic as it will create many distractions and just steal your time" (Aqil).

"In the quiet spaces...chapel,room, alone on the rec.yard...take your ear plugs to isolate yourself from surrounding distractions" (Tabari).

"If it is disliked or forbidden to pray there, then it's best not to study there either. Relieve yourself of all distractions that you can, and then study. It may be your cell, the library, or in the wing/tier with other students. Every individual knows that place and the best time to study at that place" (Ahmad).

"A person should always study in a quiet place free from all distractions. Unfortunately for us here in prison it's very hard to find a quiet place free from all distractions. The best place to study is your cell. If you have a cellie that likes to talk allot or likes to watch/hear his T.V out loud, it would be a good idea to explain to him that you are going to study at certain times of the day and you require of him to respect that time by not having his T.V out loud. In contrast the worst place to study is the dayroom. I have witnessed many inmates who are taking college classes trying to study in the dayroom. It is a very bad place to study because every minute someone is constantly approaching you to find out what you are doing. Avoiding such a noisy environment is essential for one's concentration and retention" (Sergio).

"The places of studying should be left to the discretion of the student. But the place designated should be absent of distraction and impurities. Anytime after fajr and before dhuhr are identified as the best time. Also, one shouldn't load up on food and drink before studying. Overeating extinguishes the light of intelligence. When you overeat, you like to sleep" (Muhammad Amin).

"They should study wherever they feel most comfortable, preferably a place that has a large surface that allows you to spread out your study materials. For me this is hard to do in my cell because I have such a small desk. I also do not like to be around mine or my cellmate's TV/radio. Avoiding studying at tables where people usually play table games. They will sit by you regardless of seeing you study" (Juan).

"The mosque and library. Never study in the gym, only study in the yard if it is peaceful, it varies by institution. Make a nice little "study niche" in your cell, be creative, personally I don't sleep on my mattress so I rolled it up and use it as a table. If your cellmate does not give you space, then you'll have to learn to study on the unity, but you should maintain a serious demeanour so people will give you space and know not to bother you when studying" (Sulaymaan).

Q: How can they incorporate breaks and rewards into their routine of studying?

"There are several studies that suggest a student's retention decreases after more than 1-2 hours of straight study. Therefore, a student should set his mind to study for no more than 1-2 hours and, as a reward to him/herself, do something from which the person derives joy" (Khalil).

"I studied in intervals and if I got tired or lazy on one subject I went to another" (Isa).

"I wouldn't encourage breaks, but a change in subject matter. The incarcerated are already on a break. Prison life is a break from life and the everyday responsibilities of bills, family, real challenges, etc. Use any breaks you decide to take to do dhikr/fikr or trade ideas with other students of knowledge. The reward should actually be provided by outside sources, like a teacher. It should reflect the parent rewarding the child for good works. But we have to be very careful with this reward system, especially with the initial seeker of sacred knowledge. The desired reward for them should be that they see their relationship with Allah growing. They should also understand that the completion of the text is the actual reward from Allah" (Muhammad Amin).

"I incorporated breaks and rewards into my routine as a student studying by practicing my Arabic and learning a surah on my down time from studying" (Taahir).

"I would typically take an hour or two each day to not deal with anything. I would take a nap, go out to talk with my Sahaba, or look at a movie if there was something that I wanted to look at. After I complete each lesson I would normally take time to fix myself a something that is outside of my normal routine and take 4-6 hours to kick back outside of my normal routine like an extra movie or something else" (Abdul Muhaymin).

"How can they incorporate breaks and rewards into their routine of studying? Use the day to break up and take your intervals. Exercise, leisure and the like. As the daytime in most cases is when one can get access to other parts of the facility. So never try to compete. Allow that to accomplish these needs" (Aqil).

"Look at all the material, divide it according to the time you have to complete it,and set a minimum amount of daily work u must accomplish to finish the course on time,but try to do more than the minimum amount 'cause things come up which set you back" (Tabari).

"Each person seems to approach this differently; however, 5 days on and 2 days off is a good method for me, depending on if I'm trying to memorize the text or not. Otherwise, the two off days are still used for review" (Ahmad).

"Every so often students should take a break from studying to relax their mind and not get "burned out" in terms of studying. Take regular breaks. Your brain functions best when fueled with oxygen, water, and glucose. Every 20-60 minutes, get up and stretch. Drink water. If hungry, snack on fruit, which contains glucose. Stretch and walk around for a few minutes. When you resume studying, not only will your muscles be more relaxed, but you brain will have more oxygen as well. Finally, avoid getting distracted while taking a break" (Sergio).

"Always be sure to schedule a break every 50 minutes if you plan to go for two or more hours at a time. I like to have a hot cup of coffee or cold drink of water. Be sure to get up and move around to get the blood flowing" (Juan).

"Breaks have to be earned. Only when you've crammed so much into your brain and heart do you take a break. Studying burns calories, you're gonna need chocolate and coffee (or tea). The only reward is the pleasure of Allah at death. The only worldly rewards is receiving the knowledge and 'ijaza to teach, and pass on the knowledge and start a sadaqa jariya for the qabr. There should be no rewards until after the semester. The reward is making Shaykh proud" (Sulaymaan).

Q: What kind of exercise, health and diet concerns should a student have?

"Avoid trying to study on a full stomach and do not eat and study at the same time. Coffee got my blood flowing but was not good for my diet due to the packs of sugar I use to use" (Isa).

"A student should have physical and spiritual exercises as a student, working out and doing daily dhikers. Health and diet concerns should consist of voluntary fasting and consuming if possible only Halal food" (Taahir).

"What kind of exercise, health and diet concerns should a student have? A person should be sure to eat breakfast every morning or at least on those days they plan to study. They should also stay well hydrated. A sugary snack in the middle of a long study session is OK as brain glucose levels may go down and need to be replenished quickly" (Juan).

"A student should make sure everything they eat is obtained from a halāl source and by a halāl means. What this means is any meat we eat should be slaughtered by Muslims or Jews (so get on a Halal, kosher, or vegetarian diet in your prison) as that's the only Halāl meat available in this country. Meat from the Super-Market or regular prison chow line is not halāl according to any

Islamic scholars from the 4 Sunni Madhhabs, there's many fatwas available on this. What we eat has a huge effect on our character and the acceptability of our deeds to Allah, there being many hadith which show the du'ā and salāt of someone nourished on the unlawful is rejected by Allah. All of our energy to study and memorize comes from what we eat, so one of the student of knowledge's first concerns should be eating the halāl. Also avoid eating food stolen from the prison kitchen, from gambling, or obtained from an inmate or prison "store" (where people borrow things and pay back an increase – this is riba and 100% haram). Also realize one's health is an Ammana or Divine Trust from Allah, so stay healthy by working out and not overeating. The Prophet (salla Llāhu 'alayhi wa sallam) said "The strong believer is better than the weak believer, though there's good in both." Someone who maintains their physical health can worship Allah better and longer" (Abdus Salam).

"It is good to take at least 30-45 minutes at least 3-5 days a week to do some type of exercise. We should also do the best that we can to avoid eating from the dining hall things that can raise doubt in our hearts if we are capable of doing so. Everyone's situation is different and some of us are struggling more than others so we have to be honest about what we can do and what we are willing to sacrifice. Also, do not try and be tough. If you are not feeling well go to medical, and if you are taking medication(s) take them as prescribed and as needed" (Abdul Muhaymin).

"Each individual is different. But at least get to the yard a few times a week and relieve the pressure. Exercise, jog, play sports or the like. Its healthy to do so and keep the balance. Also it keeps you from becoming lazy sitting around all day" (Aqil).

"Never underestimate the significance of eating halal only food. Avoid processed foods as much as possible, and keep to physical activity and du'a for a long healthy life to spread the knowledge we are learning" (Ahmad).

"The body should be given its right with regards to proper rest and a pure halal well-balanced diet. As for exercise, we must keep it in the right perspective. Working the body out to the point of exhaustion, which hinders acts of worship, is blameworthy. Aiming to obtain a "bedroom body" and not to strengthen the body for worship is blameworthy. Our Nabi (SAW) has been reported to have said, "work is worship." So, if one is going out to a job everyday and, in the process of working, they are moving their limbs, then they have met the requirements given their body's movement. There is an exercise that the inmates do that are called burpees. They resemble the movement of the prayer. Therefore I'll suggest that the believers increase their rakats, especially at night, and you may just produce the same results. At the minimum you will definitely build up your spiritual bank account. But, if the doctor orders more, then I would hope you listen to him/her" (Muhammad Amin).

"Good, nutritious food in prison is hard to come by, so everything in moderation especially when you are studying. too much sugar make u sleepy,a little sugar helps to stay focused. too much exercise make you sleepy at the time of study,light exercise at the time of study keeps you alert" (Tabari).

"A student should always have a healthy lifestyle free from ail sort of vices that might affect their study habits, always remembering to get plenty of rest, sleep, and have a proper diet" (Sergio).

"A student's health and dieting concerns should be legitimate. The food really influences the membrane, and laziness in the enemy. Learn tai-chi breathing techniques so you don't eat too much, a lot of water, tea and protein. Only eat halal and do cardiovascular exercises either at night or first thing in the morning, peanuts and fish are necessary. Eat pastries instead of candy bars because of the starch we need, don't eat pasta at night, don't eat after 8:00 pm and fast so you don't have to worry about food and just study" (Sulaymaan).

Q: How can a student maintain focus and concentration on studies while in the environment they are in?

"The student will be able to focus and concentrate much more if he/she participates in study groups with other Muslims in ta'leem, etc" (Khalil).

"A student has to separate himself from others, find tables or benches that are empty. A student must try to avoid the prison politics as much as possible and not to be distracted by the non-muslims and their activity. A muslim should always mind his own business!" (Isa).

"By studying in the morning before or after salat while others are still sleeping or late at night when everything is quite" (Taahir).

"Constantly recite Qur'aan when you can, make Dhikr, recite Salawaat on the Prophet(saw), and keep making Tahmid, Tahlil, and Tasbih of Allah,Ta`Aalaa. Remember that the Prophet (saw) said to make your tongue move with the Dhikr of Allah until the people think that you are mad" (Abdul Muhaymin).

"Focus on the time you have to learn and not the time you have to serve. The time you have to serve is fixed and done, (unless one is working on an appeal). So why focus on it. It has to be done, so just do it! But within that time is where you make benefit of the time you have to learn. Don't lose it or waste it! Once one realizes that he is there as a student and not as a prisoner, then he should be fine, Insha ALLAH" (Aqil).

"A study group. questions always present themselves, be ready! seek knowledge! ask questions!" (Tabari).

"Distractions constantly tug at our minds, and, like an unruly child, the unfocused mind dashes from one distraction to another. Everyone has experienced losing focus for a minute, an hour, even a day. Some people are most alert in the morning, whereas others learn best at night. Still others think best in the middle of the day. I personally find that the best time to study is early in the morning before and after Fajr, since at that time the noise is at its lowest. In addition, to maintain focus, they should try to associate with those inmates who are going to be a positive influence in terms of their daily life and studies, others who will motivate them in terms of their studies" (Sergio).

"They should remember that rarely will they have a perfectly quiet place to study and that part of the struggle in attaining knowledge are the distraction of the dunya. Go into study with the mindset that you won't allow yourself to become distracted by being distracted" (Juan).

"In the words of Shaykh Ibn Ata Allah, "Seek out those people whose state elevates your state and their speech calls you to the dhikr of Allah." The lives of people who do this are less complicated, and you will always find them in areas that are in harmony with the shari'ah. Try to avoid unnecessary people, places and things. If they are fardh or sunnah then engage them. Avoid haraam, makruh and mubah to the best of your abilities" (Muhammad Amin).

"The only truly safe people in prison are muslims. The student of knowledge must realize that his studies protect him from himself and others. Generally, in prison one has to be mildly reclusive and well-mannered when forced to interact if necessary, otherwise the student should spend most of their time in a neat, fragrant organized cell and be in and out when going to the chow hall and gym, and if they are having a good study flow at that time they should just skip that meal or trip to the gym. Also a student might have to sacrifice some programs, school and jobs which are the most distracting" (Sulaymaan).

Q: What advice on communication with the teacher, other students, chaplains, staff, etc would you have for a student?

"Just be patient, people respond on their schedule, not yours. Be clear in what you are asking using as few words as possible. Prioritize your questions" (Juan).

"There are etiquettes that must be observed that guide the student-teacher relationship. But in general, Muslims should use eloquent speech no matter who is being addressed" (Khalil).

"A student should seek another student to study. Students should get to know and develop a relationship with chaplains and police staff who are Islam friendly due to being able to get copies or getting your books etc" (Isa).

"Know the etiquettes of student and teacher relationships, always be on time for study sessions, come prepare with study materials, text, books, paper, pen, etc. Save questions for teacher after session in order not to interrupt the flow of studying. Give respect at all times to teachers, chaplains, staff, etc. Be serious when coming to learn scared knowledge and ready to put into practice as a servant to thy LORD swt what you are blessed to learn. Don't ask teachers, chaplains or staff questions you can get answers for from fellow students or research answers thy self. Never think cause you study more, have more knowledge then other students, teachers, chaplains that you are better than them. Always be mindful of the (diseases of the heart)!!!!" (Taahir).

"Never hesitate to ask questions of your teachers if you need to. Try to always engage in conversations with other students, chaplains, and staff that allows for the information you are learning to embed itself in you and give you a chance to explore alternative outlooks and questions that you can share with your teacher" (Abdul Muhaymin).

"Whenever the student of Tayba Foundation encounters anyone regardless of his/her status in life, it should be with a character reflective of our beloved Nabi (SAW). We will encounter people in this environment, and in life in general, who display unpleasant behavior towards us. This behavior may incite in us a response that is unpleasant. But, if we can separate the action of others from the idea of their true spiritual ability, then our response stands a better chance of being one of compassion, rather than hostility and anger. Allah has Divinely placed in every human being the ability of being beautiful, compassionate, loving and caring. This potential is established in every one of us, but many are unaware of this. Allah (SWT) has given mankind guidance, which we can use to assist one another in awakening to this spiritual potential. This guidance will remove the veil of ignorance that lies between the human soul and their Lord (SWT), which is the cause of our suffering from the pains of hostility, anger, rudeness, greed, violence, envy, vanity, and more. Non-Muslims, as well as many Muslims, are trapped in this circle of spiritual death. Therefore, by you and I knowing this, we are able to restrain our nafs from responding in a way that is displeasing to Allah and is a misrepresentation of the character of Nabi Muhammad (SAW). We don't get angry, hate or act unpleasant towards the person, but towards the act. In fact, one's heart should fill-up with overwhelming love and compassion due to our sadness over their ignorance. We extinguish unpleasant character of others with the love of Nabi Muhammad (SAW). So, when we encounter officers, inmates, family members or others who display behavior unbecoming of a human being, then know that they are totally unaware of this inherent spiritual potential that they possess. Allah (SWT) tells us to repel evil with good, because this is the natural response of a soul that is awakened. My beloved brothers and sisters in this faith, being spiritually alive and healthy allows you to overcome any display of bad character by others. If they happen to be hostile, angry, abusive, pimps, drug dealers, murderers, even homosexual, love of the Nabi (SAW) will move you to approach them with the spirit of compassion. I am not excusing the behavior, or advocating keeping the company, but you will be amazed at how Allah (SWT) can affect someone with a small act of kindness that will bring them to spiritual awakening. Think about it!" (Muhammad Amin).

"Always maintain sabr (patience) with Tayba and don't allow delays in response to discourage you. Shaykh Rami is very busy and his load is heavy, know if it takes awhile to get a response its not because he doesn't care, Tayba gets a ton of mail. Try not to overburden Tayba with long letters but keep the letters brief and to the point. If you send a couple questions in at a time you'll get a quicker response than if you send in 50. Try not to make more than one or two request at once. It's okay to send a reminder if the delays been long (over 3 months), but don't lose patience, and maintain proper Adab.
As for other students we should honor them as Muslims and fellow seekers of sacred knowledge, this is a high rank with Allah. Realize people learn at different paces and have patience. As a general rule do all you can to serve your brothers and sisters.
As for prison administration realize you are a representative of Islām and the best Dawah is in action, have patience and do not allow your anger to get the best of you. If you run into people who are antagonistic towards you or Islām realize its a test from Allah, if you can rectify the matter by going to their superior or through a grievance process then do so, if you can't then just maintain patience and make du'ā to Allah. Losing one's temper will never make matter better by only worse, realize it's all the Qadr of Allah. As stated, we are in the school of the Prophet Yusuf (i.e. the school of patience), view it as an opportunity to gain the love of Allah by demonstrating patience" (Abdus Salam).

"If one has access to a teacher then, they need to try and maximize that time throughout the week with them. Again in the daytime if possible. And have your lessons, questions and ideas ready when you contact the teacher, This way, you don't waste his time or yours" (Aqil).

"Have patience! the teacher is doing everything he can to facilitate ur learning. same w/ the fellow students, everyone is not at the same level of learning(or have the same capacity for absorbing information) and Allah loves those whose facilitate ease for others" (Tabari).

"In Akhdari we are taught to maintain dignified speech. IT seems that this is more for retaining our dignity regardless of what sort of speech is directed at us. This is how our beloved Prophet, Allah bless him and give him peace, lived and acted in light of harshness guided his way in many forms. … As Muslims this is how we should be. With regard to adab (etiquette) towards our teacher and other students, this is our duty as Muslim to ensure their rights are upheld at all cost.

Teachers should be respected and spoken to as we speak to our parents and deal with them" (Ahmad).

"Always ask questions when it comes to doubts or confusion in terms of your studies. If you don't understand the material you are studying make side notes and write whatever questions comes to your mind. Always respect the teacher and what they are teaching you" (Sergio).

"Raise your hand, don't talk back, be gentle, lower your eyes, be patient, make your questions simple, realize your teacher is human too and only Allah has all the answers. Remember "mas' ta 'ta'at" and at some point you're going to have to do your own research and consult your heart, don't use the shaykh as a crutch, but only when necessary" (Sulaymaan).

Q: What goals should a student have?

"That must be determined by each individual student. However, what I could say is that a student should identified goals for him/herself and then vehemently set out to accomplish them. The student should know that it is okay to modify goals after periodic assessments, so long as he/she continues to strive towards his/her goals" (Khalil).

"The main goal a student should have is to learn 'ilm in order to apply it in their life and become spiritually transformed through that, all for the sake of Allah. For those who have the ability they should seek to memorize the text in Arabic with its meanings in English in order to gain ijāzā. The main way our deen has always been transmitted is through the ijāzā system, and we need to become part of the solution to the problems our 'ummah is facing through helping to revive the ijāzā system by gaining ijāzā ourselves and teaching people. An 'alim or scholar is essentially someone with ijāzā in multiple Islamic sciences/Text, and the Tayba Foundation offers a way for us to become 'ulāmā ourselves" (Abdus Salam).

"Goal should be to get closer to Allah. A student before studying or setting a goal should ask himself why am I studying? In prison I found that people studied to be the most knowledgeable, studied to debate others, studied to please others. A student has to ask himself why am I studying?" (Isa).

"To study for the sake of learning the deen to be a better servant, father, son, husband and giver to the community. To be willing to teach others what they have been blessed to learn" (Taahir).

"To seek Allah's, Subhaanahu wa Ta`Aalaa, Face and improve your character and understanding and practice of the Deen" (Abdul Muhaymin).

"His goal as is the goal of every believer is PARADISE! It's no different, but his should be his focus on his studies. Anything else is like "Double Jeopardy" You are already serving time from your life that you can never get back, then on top of that you are losing any benefit in that time? It really can't get worse than that!" (Aqil).

"To remove ignorance from himself and to help the ummah w/ his knowledge" (Tabari).

"At the least, to learn the personally obligatory rulings that pertain to him. Outside of that, in light of the disservice that Islam is receiving in prison by way of the inundation of Salafi / Wahhabi teachings and materials, we should feel obliged to pass this message on and help restore Islam to its truest and traditional form, and possibly add to the perspective of our conditions as prisoners, ex-gang members, drug addicts and users, etc" (Ahmad).

"The main goals for a student to have are to build upon one's prior knowledge and always be willing to learn new concepts and ideas" (Sergio).

"They should be mostly realistic with the educational level you bring to the course. If you read at a 6th grade level do not be embarrassed if you do not perform as well as someone who reads at a post-high school level. (Here is a not to Tayba instructors: Most prisons have inmates take reading and math tests which measure their levels in those subjects. Before taking on a new student it may be a good idea to request a copy of these performance evaluations" (Juan).

"The student should seek to be a scholar and friend of Allah, even if he'll never attain this, but still must realize he is only a student and only knows a little bit and can never surpass the salaf in virtue and knowledge. He should start high because even if he lands low, it might still be higher than what he initially expected. Also he must realize he needs knowledge for a sadaqa jariya like raising a righteous child, writing a book or making a masjid, these are the only things that might really matter one day" (Sulaymaan).

"One should set goals that are reasonable to achieve. I remember telling Shaykh Rami (May Allah preserve him), that I should be further in my studies than where I was at the time. Then I said to him, "I guess this is where Allah wants me to be." Shaykh Rami responded by saying, "Amin, that's actually a high maqam (station)." Later in my reflection of our conversation, I realized something so true, as well as false. What the Shaykh said was true but, concerning me, it was false. Sometimes we may confuse a) striving and exhausting ourselves to accomplish a task, but falling short or not getting the end results we expected, with b) desiring to complete a task, but being unable to due to laziness and procrastination. An example of a) is when we strive to complete a book in six months, but it takes seven to eight months instead. We did everything that could be done, but Allah decreed for you to complete it in that time. One can say MashaAllah, this is what Allah wanted. An example of b) is when you intend to complete a book within six months, but instead it takes one or two years. Then, we cannot truly say this is not where Allah wanted you to be--this is what you desired for Allah to decree for you. There is a big difference. People use this as an excuse for not accomplishing what needs to be accomplished or at least making a sincere effort. They will say, "I guess this is where Allah wants me to be," or "Allah hasn't written for me to learn Arabic or fiqh." The focus should be, "What effort have you made?" Back to the question of goals. Make the Door of Allah your goal, it will put everything else in your life in the right place" (Muhammad Amin).

Q: How can a student use study partners or a study group?

"Identify other Muslims who are just as curious and eager to learn as oneself. Then, take advantage of the "chapel" times, as well as getting together on the yard (where violence is less of a concern)" (Khalil).

"Study partner worked well for me because we had the ability to go back and forth. I was never fond of study groups, they always ended in debates" (Isa).

"If one can find fellow brothers or sisters to study with that's a huge blessing and will help everyone to motivate each other. Getting together to chant the Arabic poetry of a couple lines of a text a day for 30-60 minutes can really cement it in one's memory, and this is a method used traditionally in much of the Muslim world to memorize. Likewise reading a couple lines of poetry or a section of the Matn (concise text) and its commentary in group and then repeating review on ones own before the next study session, then testing each other, will help one learn. Once one gains ijāzā in a text and holds classes or individual study sessions it will help one to retain what they've learned and help their increasing of skill at expounding on the text" (Abdus Salam).

"A student could use a study partner to go over words they might be learning in Arabic, to read Qur'an in Arabic plus learn surahs. In study groups students could go over material of a text they are learning from a teacher, also ask questions they might have written down in which they didn't fully understand" (Taahir).

"If there are Brothers who are trying to learn but have not yet taken the initiative to sign-up take the time to seek them out and have individual conversations or suggest that they set-up a time that you all can get together to talk about what you are learning. Try to do this in a way that does not lead them to believe that you think that you are better than them or give them a reason to run from you whenever they see you coming. Be easy with the Ilm and the people. If there are Brothers at your facility who are a part of the Tayba program you can find time to sit down and allow each brother to review each lesson that they have completed that will allow everyone to ask questions and engage in some positive discussions about the subject matter. You can each take time to help with pronunciation and encouragement" (Abdul Muhaymin).

"If there are other serious brothers to study with, then this is great. Meet regularly to remind and encourage each. Memorize together small amounts that can be accomplished between meetings" (Aqil).

"Either be the leader or be the attentive student or a supporter of the circle of knowledge" (Tabari).

"By reaching out to other students, reading and discussing the material, leaving questions or things they don't fully understand" (Ahmad).

"A student can have others critique their work and give advice as how one can improve their communication, writing ability, and general study habits" (Sergio).

"Sometimes it helps to orally verbalize what you believe you've learned from the courses so using another student or Muslim as a sounding board tests your ability to impart what you've learned. Also it is good to hear out-loud what you think you know" (Juan).

"Never argue with your study partners. Talk about besides Islam sometimes (as long as it is halal), befriend your partner and don't always enforce Shariah on them, realize you're just as flawed. Sit down everyday together with coffee and snacks and pace yourselves, assign homework to each other, and elect one person as the leader of the group to facilitate and keep the peace" (Sulaymaan).

Q: How should one read through the material and review it?

"One should read through materials with a questioning mindset. Much of the traditional Islamic literature is technical and one can misinterpret text if questions aren't frequently asked" (Khalil).

"Student should do an initial read without understanding then the second time start jotting notes or making marks in his book" (Isa).

"I believe it's good to read at least 10 mins of the material in the early morning as a new student, after a week increase reading to 20 mins, on the third week reading should increase to 30 mins and stay there. Reading must be often and consistent. As for reviewing material, my advice is to go over what was read earlier that morning with a fellow student later that day" (Taahir).

"I found it easier for me to read the material then go back over it line by line. Afterwards, I listen to the lecture on each lesson and take line by line notes and then I locate the relevant Aayaat and Ahadith that are in the lecture and some that are in accordance with what the teacher has shared. Then I constantly review each lesson before moving on to the next one as I follow the memorization schedule I previously shared" (Abdul Muhaymin).

"If one has a teacher, then that's great and they can go over their study materials and then review it with the teacher for corrections or clarifications. If one does not have a teacher then, they should learn what they have from their materials and just try to build upon it. BUT NEVER SHOULD THEY IMPOSE THAT UPON ANYONE ELSE AND THINK THAT THEY HAVE SOME RANK! THIS IS DELUSION AND A TRICK FROM SATAN! KNOWLEDGE SHOULD HUMBLE YOU! IF NOT, THEN IT JUST BECOMES INFORMATION, AND THE DEVIL HAS INFORMATION, EVEN MORE THAN ANY OF US, BUT IT DOESN'T BENEFIT AND HUMBLE HIM. SO DON'T BE LIKE SATAN" (Aqil).

"Read through the entire material 1x, to understand layout,nuances,objective of the author and teacher. then commit to the next level of mastery, then the next etc" (Tabari).

"A number of times and very carefully. Take note of the what stands out as new or odd. Always find a time of the day for review to retain where you had left off or learned last" (Ahmad).

"One should read through the material carefully and if doubts exist, reread the material and ask questions as to clarify material one is reading" (Sergio).

"They should keep a pencil or highlighter in their hand to make note of passages that they feel are relevant. Do a quick scan of the entire book so that you may get an idea of what topics might repeat themselves" (Juan).

"By reading, writing, and reciting it. Also he should write down all the vocabulary, take short footnotes, don't be scared to use the English dictionary if some words are not understood, follow the mahdam method even if you don't want to memorize the text. Apply what you've learned and share it with someone as it helps you understand it" (Sulaymaan).

"Everyone has their own methods that work but the method I've found most helpful is to read through the whole text one time in English without trying to memorize anything, while doing so I highlight or take notes on points that really stood out to me. Then I read through the text again slowly, taking a small portion each day and trying to memorize it (in English), I also write any questions out I have for the instructor as I do so. As for memorizing the text in Arabic I do this while working on the above. The 1st thing I do is a word for word translation of the complete text, I will do a line of Arabic (half a line of poetry) on lined paper, then 2 lines below I'll write each words meaning in English under it and the page its root can be found in the Hans-Wehr Dictionary, then 2 lines below that I'll write the other half of the line of poetry in Arabic, then 2 lines below that I'll write the English meanings and their reference in the Hans-Wehr, then 2 lines below that I'll write Tayba Foundations translation of that verse/line. I number each verse of Arabic on this paper. Usually this translation process of the whole text takes one to two months if I spend 2-3 hours a day on it. Once done I commit to memorizing a couple lines at a time, I also make flash cards for the Arabic words of each individual word as spelled in the text, putting Arabic on one side of the card (made out of lined paper) and English on the other. So on top of going over my memorization of each line in Arabic a couple times each day (as outlined in Shaykh Rami's "Advice on how to study") I will also spend at least 30 minutes reviewing my flash cards each day. I do not go onto a new line until I fully have mastered the lines I was working on; this usually takes a couple days. One must also spend 15-20 minutes a day chanting the whole portion of the text ones already memorized other wise one will start to lose it, even once the text is fully memorized chant it one time at least a day" (Abdus Salam)

"One of the methods that I use in reviewing my notes is lecturing to the unseen world. I make wudhu and sit on my bed like the shuyukh do. Then, I act as if I am teaching to the world of the angels and jinn. It helps in knowing the material and memorization. One year, I taught most of Imam Akhdawi to a group of brothers from memorization. The class was discontinued around the section of prayer, but I have no doubt I would have completed that class in that method had it continued. In order to do this you have to be in an area where you don't disturb others. So, if you have a cellmate, wait until he or she leaves for the recreation yard or for some other activity of the day. Then sit and teach!" (Muhammad Amin).

Q: What advice would you have on improving memory?

"Only thing I could think of is repetition. Repeating over and over what one wants to memorize" (Khalil)

"What advice would you have on improving memory? dhikr beeds and repetition" (Isa).

"To improve memory I think it's good to read line of material, close your eyes and repeat it to self three times. The same goes for memory of Qur'an or Arabic words" (Taahir).

"I found obedience to be the key for me. Whenever I'm disobedient to Allah, I struggle with my studies and memorization. So, maintain strict obedience to Allah and His Messenger (SAW) and you will notice the difference. After all, it is Allah (SWT) who bestows upon us both knowledge and ability" (Muhammad Amin).

"Remove yourself from people, places and activities that would cause you to be divided in your attention. Only allow your mind and heart to be attached to what is absolutely necessary" (Abdul Muhaymin).

"The brain is a muscle like any other, and if you work it out by memorizing each day one will see one's strength and skill improve over time. It's absolutely imperative to stick to one's daily schedule of memorization and reviews. I also find it helpful even outside my study sessions to test myself on what I've reviewed for the day, such as after meals and after each salat. Keep striving and your memory will improve. Personally I may spend all day trying to memorize something and when I wake up the next day I can't remember, but when I wake up and re-memorize the text that's when it finally sticks, the second day. Always start each study session by asking Allah to make it easy for you and to give you Tawfīq; and use the du'ās each morning we outlined earlier" (Abdus Salam).

"Try to keep your sight and hearing away from the Haram. The more garbage you put in, the less room there is for goodness. Purify your intention and desire to seek the pleasure of ALLAH. Then, ALLAH will facilitate the rest, Insha ALLAH" (Aqil).

"Repetition and active study groups! constantly talk about the material! ask questions! seek answers! dig into the information" (Tabari).

"Start small, finish big. Memory is like a muscle and has to be developed. If one wants to begin memorizing, then they have to repeat numerous times and give oneself time to gauge how much and how often it takes one to achieve their goal" (Ahmad).

"Get plenty of sleep, rest, and have a proper diet for this will improve one's health and memory. Learning is enhanced by frequent practice sessions of sufficient length over time. Organizing and rehearsing your material will definitely improve your memory. Reviewing one's material silently and with great concentration is essential. Looking for key concepts, main idea, and supporting details of what one's is studying is also helpful. I personally find reciting the study material very helpful. As I read aloud, I add any related information that comes to mind. Sometimes I pretend that I am explaining the information to someone who is not taking the class but is interested in the information. Then I look back at the study material and compare the information there with what I have been saying. Another technique I use is, I visualize what I am studying and I tried to create a picture in mind of the material. For example, when I was studying the section of wudu from the Mukhtasar of Imam Al-akhdarii I was able to memorize the section very easy by visualizing myself performing every act wudu. Finally, rewriting the material without looking is very effective. This physical activity of writing engages your brain in a new way. Thus, the process helps to strengthen the neural networks related to the information" (Sergio).

"Get a good night's sleep. Sleep is when your brain hardwires what you've learned during the day. Try not study when you are too tired. A good indicator that you are too tired is that you read a page and cannot recall what you just read" (Juan).

"Relax. Just keep repeating the information with a song-like rhythm and do it 4 lines at a time. First do wudhu, face the qiblah, and go hard after salah, later sit down and relax with the coffee on your chair or bed and go slow. Practice after fajr first thing after salah, as you just woke up and last thing before sleep so you dream about it. Say this dua: [Arabic] and send blessings on the prophet before and after with basmalah and whatever part of the Quran you're trying to remember" (Sulaymaan).

Q: What advice do you have on note taking?

"Most texts have sections. Notes should be taking in chronological order corresponding with the sections of the texts. This makes it easier to go back and review notes. Within the notes, key concepts and ideas should be highlighted" (Khalil).

"I still till this day mark my books using different color pens or post-its" (Isa).

"Make your handwriting legible enough that you can read it later on. Also always note what page or point in the recording your note came from, it will save time later on" (Juan).

"Before the audio transcripts were available and we had to take notes on all the audio lectures I would almost record everything and all relevant points. Al-hamdulillāh the audio transcripts have saved me a lot of time with this and I mainly take notes or underline parts of the text that stick out to me now. I also number the whole Arabic text and then number the audio lecture for easy reference to the Arabic line that is being commentated on. I use different colors for underling different things – for example: Red for Qur'an or Hadith quotes, Green for a principle being taught, Black a particular point that I like, Purple for an explanation of an Arabic word, etc... In the back of each book I'll write a short index of the main points page numbers for easy reference, for example on "Prohibitions of the Tongue" I would put "Example of Murabit al-Hajj on misinterpreting word Najm in Qur'an pg. #30", "Difference of opinion within one Madhhab and reasons for that pg. #132", "Mukhtasar of khalil is the most advanced book in Maliki Fiqh pg. #138", etc... So one must devise methods to make each text more easily navigable" (Abdus Salam).

"I believe it's good to put a sticker next to line or paragraph and write note on it. Do not ever write in a text of sacred knowledge, take notes on paper, we must always preserve the text" (Taahir).

"Be meticulous when taking notes. If you remember a Ayah or Hadith that compliments the teacher's lecture make sure to add it to your notes to enhance what you are being taught. Do not mix your notes up with other information that you may have compiled, make sure that each lesson, section, and book that you are studying are kept together and that they are kept neat and secure" (Abdul Muhaymin).

"Notes are very important and also aid the memory. So never think that you don't need taking notes. Especially in the beginning of one's journey of seeking knowledge" (Aqil).

"I found obedience to be the key for me. Whenever I'm disobedient to Allah, I struggle with my studies and memorization. So, maintain strict obedience to Allah and His Messenger (SAW) and you will notice the difference. After all, it is Allah (SWT) who bestows upon us both knowledge and ability" (Muhammad Amin).

"Start w/ major points that need to be remembered. then upon revisiting the material,refine ur notes and the info u want to remember.then more refining etc" (Tabari).

"When I read a text, I take note of things that are new to me or worded differently than I've heard or read them before. If it is a large section, than I make it my business to write out the entire section to help me retain the information. If it is audio, then I use the same process, but I stop the recording and listen as much as it takes to write out the information" (Ahmad).

"Always take notes in an outline form, be sure to highlight important ideas, and don't be afraid to write notes for yourself in the margins of your textbook. Go over notes of previous sessions and prepared a list of questions. While listening to the audio lessons, listen actively for key concepts, main ideas, and supporting details. If there are concepts you don't understand, write it down and put a questions mark in the paragraph related to the material of your textbook. Furthermore, make sure your notes are accurate, complete and understandable. Finish partial sentences, define key words, fill in space with missing information, and correct misspelling. Afterwards, if you still have gaps or confusion in your notes, review that particular section in your book or ask the Sheikh for more clarity" (Sergio).

"Keep your notes organized, but exclusive to you. Write everything, relax and make it like a journal, it's note not a resume, make your writing messy, use key terms, be brief and take notice of key points and summarize each section of the text" (Sulaymaan).

Q: What advice do you have on writing an essay?

"Writing isn't easy. However, a good essay can be written if one has a solid introduction; the rest of the essay should follow" (Khalil).

"Write the easy based on some way the text has fixed a situation around you or influenced a change in your life, write it from the heart" (Abdus Salam).

"Keep it simple, a beginning, middle and ending on the subject you are writing about" (Taahir).

"Essays are very good for your studies as they allow you to express your understandings from your studies. Essays per subject is a great tool to refine your understanding and reinforce precision in the materials learned" (Aqil).

"Write a draft of your essay as you you begin to near the completion of the text. Write it as if you are talking with someone opposed to talking to someone. Although there may be times when it is necessary to change your presentation always remember that you are writing to display your understanding of the material and , Inshaa'Allah, your ability to teach/relay the information to others so that they can learn from you and also understand it as you do so" (Abdul Muhaymin).

"Think about what u want to say,and then find the words that best express what u r feeling. dont be discouraged, this is something which takes time and effort" (Tabari).

"Like speaking, always talk about what you know in a way you enjoy it" (Ahmad).

"Always follow the proper format for writing an essay, and especially, have others read your essay as to make improvements and corrections to it. If you get to choose the topic, select one that truly interests you. For you will enjoy writing about something meaningful to you, and your grade will probably improve as well. Even if the Shaikh assigns the topic, look for an approach to the topic that appeals to you. Once you know what you are going to write about, start immediately. Write something, anything about the topic, even a few brief notes. This effort engages your unconscious mind, which will continue mulling over the topic even while you're involved in other activities. Later when you are writing, these unconscious ideas will bubble into awareness and help you write with more depth" (Sergio).

"Be prepared to re—write it at least three times. Write more than you think you'll need. You never know what will be important and anyway plan on cutting a lot out in revision. Never use a word you just looked up in the dictionary because you think it will make you look smarter. If it does not fit your style of speech it can make the flow of the piece disjointed. Always use simpler words that you are comfortable using unless you really need to in order to convey a more precise meaning and a simpler word won't do" (Juan).

"Come from the heart, don't lag, use similes and metaphors, quote history and other information, speak to the reader by "Hey reader!" imagine you're giving a college lecture or that you're 'Ali at the Battle of thaybar, take 'Ali's advice on speaking as he was the best "toastmaster."'" (Sulaymaan).

Q: How did you overcome the challenges of the prison environment to remain steadfast in your deen and your studies? What personal strategies should be used if you/they ever feel/felt tempted to give up due to the challenges of their circumstances?

"Masha Allah. I think one helpful strategy is to talk with other brothers/sisters about what one is experiencing. The Imam (chaplain) should also make him/herself available to provide counsel to those who seek it. And, it is okay to sometimes take a break from studying, but don't take too long of a break because you could fall out of the habit. Studying is a habit" (Khalil).

"A student must surround himself with other muslims and also choose as a sahaba someone who is like minded. Physically I was in prison but mentally I was at home, my studies ended up being my escape from prison. I use to see brothers give up on Islam due it being so many rules and struggling to pray. Quitting or giving up was not an option, my circumstances actually made me hunger knowledge more" (Isa).

"By keeping ALLAH swt first above all else in my life, being connected to those on the path as righteous servants, being steadfast in congregational salat daily. The personal strategies one should always use if ever feeling tempted to give up is share these thoughts with a friend or chaplain. Remember that one is where they are by an act of their own hands. Be very mindful that only the strong survive so it's a must that he or she continue to Strive, Struggle and Be Strong" (Taahir).

"I constantly asked Allah, Subhaanahu wa Ta`Aalaa, to help me, guide me, fill me with Ilm&Hikmah, Bless me with `Aafiyah, etc. and whatever else I felt that I was lacking at that time. Prayer and Fasting was also very helpful along with Salawaat Alaan Nabi (saw)" (Abdul Muhaymin).

"All of the answers above are an answer to this question. First your focus is that you are not here as a prisoner, but as a student, trying to maximize the time spent there. Balance your days with exercise and sports or the like. And never feel sorry for yourself! ALLAH is giving you a gift through this experience. Don't fail by getting sidetracked by what is going on around you. Wake up everyday seeing that its another day to learn more, not another day incarcerated" (Aqil).

"These are the best circumstances for someone to take time out to study. reflect on what Allah has done. no matter what led to the actual detention, Allah has given you another chance to get it right, show your gratitude w/ actions and dedication, not just lip service!" (Tabari)

"Never take on too much at one time. It will cause you not to do anything as a reaction to not getting it all done properly. It is waswasa. Shaykh Nuh says: it is Shaytan "upping the ante." … Prison, for me, was an environment that created steadfastness in me. It made me see what distractions really are. To remain steadfast, you have to see what is or can potentially hold you back and push them to the side. … Likewise, surround yourself with like-minded folk. Bad company drains your himma and clouds any progress you may have made" (Ahmad).

"This is a heavy question and I'll try to be concise. The greatest means I actually had to remain steadfast in my deen was/is my studies, they occupy me with using my time beneficially and keeping me focused on positive. The greatest hurdle in prison is negative people, you must learn to surround yourself with positive people focused on learning the deen, if you can't find them then turn to books to help inspire one, "Hayatus Sahaba: The Lives of the Sahaba" is one of the best books to read a daily section from. I try to think about what the Sahaba, 'ulāmā, and Awliya attained through this deen and it inspires me to want to spend my all to attain what they did. Avoid harām war stories about crime, drugs, women, etc..., do not listen to them or share them. Television and Music glorify the haram and keep the desire for it alive in our hearts, get rid of them 100%. One must re-learn halāl activities that are fun, one can't study all the time or you'll burn out, try to learn a hobby like bead work, wood work, drawing, crochet, etc... work out every day, go to the library, etc... If one learns to recite Arabic and has a portion of Qur'an, they recite everyday it will be better than Music and will fill the heart with serenity. Arabic Nasheeds and Qasidas (classic Islamic poetry that is sung) are also a good nafs release. Never lose hope and make du'ā to Allah, if you fully apply yourself He will aid you. People who make exceptions to the laws laid down by Allah suffer the most, the deeper our level of submission the more peace one will find. We must inwardly find the serenity and peace Islām offers, Islām must be more than a set of rules otherwise it will become too heavy for you. The way to attain this inner peace which is a sanctuary in our environment is by detaching from negative people, studying and implementing Islamic knowledge, increasing in one's Qur'anic recitation and Dhikr, reading inspirational Islamic books, and finding Halal activities like working out or a hobby. Change does not happen overnight but by incremental changes, add a little each week or month and over the years you'll see huge change. Know Allah loves you and never lose sight of that, that's why He lead us to Islām and to scholar through Tayba Foundation, to show us how to draw nearer to Him. Know the shaytān hates this and his goal is to make you give up, he will send waswasa or Satanic Doubts your way. Reject them and pay no thought to them. If you can't or are struggling seek advice from Tayba Staff and other trustworthy knowledgeable Muslims, no one will judge you but we will only try to help you.

You have been blessed with an immense opportunity to study this deen, show Allah you're grateful by fully applying yourself. You only get out of something what you put into it. Know the journey to Allah as a student of knowledge is a long process and takes much patience, start will a little change and increase over time and you'll see huge changes in your life and level of knowledge. Pray to Allah for success" (Abdus Salam)

"Always maintain a positive attitude in terms of my studies and have a desire to learn new ideas and concepts. It is very important to associate with those inmates who will be a positive influence in terms of your studies. Never give up in terms of your studies for this will only bring regret in terms of your later goals in life. Be certain that in learning your deen and applying what you have learned properly, Allah will bless you immensely. Over the course of my time in prison I have faced many obstacles especially with my Islamic studies. A few years ago during a mass search I literally lost all my Islamic material (this happen in another prison not the one I am presently housed). It took me along time to save some money from my paid check of $12.00 dollars a month to build a personal Islamic library. During that search I lost every single book I had. When I returned to my cell, my cell looked as if a tornado had passed by. More than upset I was really hurt. At first it was very discouraging; I thought for a brief moment that perhaps it was not worth studying anymore, but then realized that I was not going to let this event obstruct my desire for learning. Now that I am studying with Tayba I am happy with their teaching methods and concerns for the student. We should never give up in our journey to seek knowledge. No one is exempt from facing challenges, especially in this modern times. If we courageously confront with wisdom and justice whatever challenges come our way, Allah will open the way for us. We should remain steadfast, humble and trust that Allah will deliver us and give us victory" (Sergio).

"I do not allow myself to focus too much on my present, everything is perishing except for the countenance of Allah. So these hard times will pass but in order to build a better future and akhira we need to make sacrifices right now. Early on what helped me stay steadfast in the din is remembering that doing things my way got me in prison and that I need to give this new way of life time to manifest changes in my life for the better" (Juan).

"Realize that knowledge is a soother. It will save us, it will benefit us, use knowledge to help your fellow prisoners. It's amazing how much respect muslims in prisons have without being violent. Mu'aah bin Jabl said "Knowledge is the companion of the lonely," realize Rasolallah went through the worst, with hardship comes ease, try to see Allah's hikma in what is seemingly evil, be thankful, never complain, realize that friends and family are dying and only Allah is our friend and we can only worry about ourselves and be resurrected lonely, naked, and empty handed. When I got the verdict at trial, a Muslim brother was a court officer, wearing his beard proudly, he told me a story of a scholar who spent 20 years in prison for something he didn't do but forgave his enemies because of his chance to become a scholar, which never would have happened if he didn't go to prison. Realize that prison is "Madrasah Yusufiyya." The word "cell" comes from monasteries, prison is a rahma, we're protected from the dunya" (Sulaymaan).

Q: What general advice would you like to share with a student in prison who is just starting to study?

"Set small goals to meet, do not overextend yourself, and be willing to learn from the advice of others, always building upon the prior knowledge you have had. Respect your teacher and the material you're learning from. Do not watch T.V and study at the same time. Have good adab with your Sheikh and pray for him. Finally, do not focus so much on the goal, rather concentrate on the means and trust that after you have put all your efforts and dedication in your studies, Allah will bless you by giving you understanding of the Deen" (Sergio).

"I heard one of my teachers say that some people are amazed at the way scholars retain and deliver knowledge (I'm one of those people); it's absolutely incredible. But he also said that what isn't seen is the years and years of studying--the time and the energy--that the scholar has put into learning. It isn't easy and it's a long process, but at the end of the day, learning is going to benefit the student the most" (Khalil).

"A new student must Avoid or gradually decrease his desires in music, t.v, friends etc.... Anything that could be a distraction" (Isa).

"That knowledge is power so take advantage of it. Be as passionate about your learning the deen of Islam as one might be for sports, exercise, trying to gain your freedom, etc" (Taahir).

"Take it easy on yourself. Do not start off doing so much that you can not maintain what you started. Build yourself up to a level that you can maintain and take breaks throughout the day. For every hour that you study take about a 10-15 minute break make Dhikr and be patient with yourself" (Abdul Muhaymin).

"Don't look or focus on the end of your time, but rather look and focus on the beginning of your studies!!!" (Aqil).

Be persistent! stay seeking and Allah will guide you! have noble goals knowing Allah will help u to reach them" (Tabari).

"Know why you are studying, and get to it. Many, many others have not been provided this chance, and Allah Ta'ala has given you this blessing of knowledge to obey Him and worship Him. "Whoever Allah wishes will for He grants him understanding of His deen," said our beloved Prophet, Allah bless and grant him peace" (Ahmad).

"What general advice would you like to share with a student in prison who is just starting to study? If you begin to feel really frustrated take a few days off from your studies. Ask someone who has been studying for a while for advice and support" (Juan).

"Don't overwhelm yourself. Be like 'Ibn Hajr Asqalan, and know your brain is not harder than a rock. Trust in the qadr. Whatever you are meant to learn won't miss you and whatever was meant to miss you will never come, Allah is the teacher and guide. But work hard, don't be lazy and don't eat so much that you go to sleep after. Study fiqh" (Sulaymaan).

Q: What general advice would you like to share with a student in prison who has been studying previously?

"Don't give up studying; we can never acquire too much information" (Khalil).

"Islam is special and do not try and study Islam like your in school (high school, college) Islam is life long and your degree is with Allah. Studying Islam should be looked at as long term success and not short term pleasure" (Isa).

"May Allah Ta'ala increase you in knowledge, forgive you your sins, and allow what knowledge you have learned to be a proof for you and never against you" (Ahmad).

"Keep striving for Allah and don't become complacent. Do the things outlined in this paper that will help you raise your himma. One of my greatest fears I have is what if Tayba Foundation seized to exist, I remember those days when it didn't, this always inspire me to strive harder as I don't know how long this blessing or opportunity will exist. I ask Allah to preserve and give Tawfiq to Tayba Foundation, its staff and volunteers, and all of its student. As a final note I'd like to thank Tayba foundation for the opportunity to share the above advice, it has been a great reminder to myself who is always most in need of any advice I give, I ask Allah to give me and all the Tayba Foundations students benefit through it and the Tawfiq to implement it. Allahumma Amin!" (Abdus Salam).

"Never stop reading. Do not always try to read a book straight through like a novel. Read a few pages and take the time to investigate what is being discussed and take notes and do your follow-up research. Constant Dhikr and Salawaat along with manageable amounts of Prayer and Fasting. May Allah, Subhaanahu wa Ta`Aalaa, Bless you all to walk among and reside with His Awliyaa and Fuqahaa until you gain their Station and go on to be raised with them on the Day of Yawmul Qaiyaamah and be granted entrance to His Jannah" (Abdul Muhaymin).

"If what you have been doing is working, then continue and and work harder to get better. If it is not working then take a step back and reexamine your schedule and find out what's not working so to fix it. But please don't continue on wasting time! Your are oppressing yourselves. And this Deen is for liberation, not for oppression. May ALLAH be with you always" (Aqil).

"Get back to studying, the ummah needs you !!!" (Tabari).

"It is never too late to restart your studies, for it is obviously never too late to learn in life" (Sergio).

"Be careful of thinking you know it all. I recently made a mistake in studies because I did not carefully read the instructions. Re-read all instructions and remain humble and patient" (Juan).

"Continue to study, make sure you are studying for the right reasons and most important that you are studying the right material and following the path of Prophet Muhammad (pbuh)" (Taahir).

"Whoever has been studying recently should get off his high-horse, rebuke himself for his arrogance and realize he is not a scholar and can't give fatwa from one hadith book or because he knows tajweed. Islaam is broad. There are many scholars, never stick to one scholar or book and try to destroy whoever is in your path, the difference of opinion are a mercy. Don't just study fiqh, to some tazkyyah and tasawwuf. Don't claim to be a "super-shariah muslim" then go to buddhist service or do yoga, but criticize sufism, stick to the Sunnah and do some sufi meditation (from the sunnah), remember you are mud" (Sulaymaan).

A Useful Study Guide

The following Study Guide was developed for an online academy now known as SeekersHub (previously SeekersGuidance). Although the guide was designed for online students, we chose to include it in this course material for your review because you are a student studying by distance and correspondence, the advice in the guide would naturally apply you. There are a lot of similarities between studying online and studying in a course by correspondence like the ones you are doing with Tayba. Wherever it says "online" just substitute the word "correspondence" to make it relevant to your studying situation with Tayba.

A Guide for Students By SeekersGuidance "We did not attain unto this knowledge except by way of exaltation (i.e. of the knowledge and deeming it something great)"

Imam al-Halwani "The most beloved actions to Allah are those performed consistently, even if they are few." Prophet Muhammad ﷺ

Dear Student, By taking a Seekersguidance course, forming a SeekersCircle or joining us for classes at SeekersHub, you have set your foot on the path of learning the religion and striving to perfect your faith and practice. Staying on this path requires commitment, consistency, and an understanding of the etiquette of seeking religious knowledge. What follows is an overview of the etiquette of learning, as well as a number of learning strategies to aid you in mastering the material you are learning.

The Proper Etiquette (Adab) of the Seeker by Ustadh Tabraze Azam – –

Our tradition is deeply rooted in proper manners (adab); or the right way of doing things. For this reason, the scholars have always stressed its importance in training new generations of students in order that they may be fit to receive the Prophetic light.

Imam Zarnuji (Allah be pleased with him), the author of the excellent work Instruction of the Student and the Method of Learning (Ta`lim al-Muta`allim fi Tariq al-Ta`allum), writes that it is of the utmost importance that one has deep respect for the knowledge one is studying and its people.

Imam Ghazali (Allah be pleased with him) mentioned that, "We didn't attain unto this knowledge except by way of humility". Similarly, Imam al-Halwani (Allah be pleased with him), a great Hanafi, is reported to have said, "We didn't attain unto this knowledge except by way of exaltation (i.e. of the knowledge and deeming it something great); for I have not touched a single piece of paper except in a state of ritual ablution (wudu)".

Furthermore, Ibn Jama`ah (Allah be pleased with him) noted in his work, Memoir of the Listener and the Speaker in the Training of Teacher and Student (Tadhkirat al-Sami` wa'l Mutakallim fi Adab al-`Alim wa'l Muta`allim), that one should appear before one's teacher in a state of purity, of clothing and body. One should be focused in one's state, not tired, hungry, or otherwise. This is in order that one can fully benefit from the teacher and his instruction. When one realizes the greatness of that which is being sought, those it is being sought from and that one is seeking to attain a portion of the Prophetic inheritance, one humbles oneself, is in awe of knowledge and its people and gives one's all. The etiquettes (adab) to follow are many. The more one adheres to them, the greater the benefit one attains. "Act upon that which one knows, and Allah will grant one knowledge of that which one knows not."

The Five Inward Manners of Seeking Knowledge

1. Intention • Have a high intention of why you are seeking knowledge. Is it to seek the pleasure of Allah (may He be exalted), or are you seeking knowledge to show off?

2. Clear & Defined Goals • Have a clear sense of what you are seeking, and define what your goals are for seeking knowledge. What are you trying to achieve? How are you going to go about seeking knowledge? Do you want to be able to teach others?

3. Veneration • Have a deep respect for scholars, writings of scholars, books , and for knowledge itself. Scholars are inheritors of the Prophet (may Allah bless him and grant him peace). • Maintain a state of ablution (wudu) when studying.

4. Adab (Manners) • Have proper adab (manners) - you can only have adab if you learn about it

5. Consistency • Learn something every day and review every day. Our lives are busy, but at the same time we should set aside some time every day to learn. Establish a routine for study. • Seeking knowledge should become intrinsic for the true seeker

The Five Outward Manners of Seeking Knowledge

1. Repeat and Review

- Commenting on this advice, Shaykh Faraz Rabbani tells us that by repetition, even donkeys learn so there is no reason why we humans cannot learn through repetition.
- Review:
    - Key Concepts, conditions, and integrals because if you understand these clearly, you understand what you are studying.
        - Definitions (e.g. What is ghusl? What is wudu? What is wiping?)
        - Shaykh Adib Kallas (rahimahullah) said that matters are known by their definitions.
        - So, it is of utmost importance that one learns the definitions of what is being studying.
        - Definitions bring out the meanings of things

2. Take Notes
- Take notes while listening, but also make your own notes on readings that are prescribed or supplemental material described in the lecture
- Have pen and paper to jot down the most important things described or items to be researched at a later time
- Diagram what you are studying because diagramming helps to visual concepts
- Diagramming helps you actively engage in what you are learning.
- A seeker of knowledge is called a seeker because they are an active participant in learning. The term "seeker" means that you are the one who is searching and acquiring knowledge. You are not being sought for knowledge.
- Example: Seekers ask "What else can and should we be reading?" when studying a topic with a teacher.

3. Ask
- The Prophet ﷺ said, "The cure for confusion is but to ask".
- We shouldn't be scared to ask questions from our teachers because if we don't ask, it may lead to confusion and misunderstanding. Questions should, however, be asked with the proper etiquette and manners.
    - Asking is half of knowledge
    - Part of why it is half of knowledge is to know how to ask a question, and the right way of asking questions
    - Ask also to confirm what you do understand because Ilm is decisive knowledge so it is imperative to make sure your understanding is correct.

4. Extra Readings

- You must do extra readings in a guided way, not randomly.
- The strong student of knowledge is one who learns the core of their knowledge through teachers but at the same time they continue reading to gain breadth of knowledge.
- You can potentially read many things, but you would be foolish to read books above your current level of understanding. So, ask what is appropriate
- Anytime you are studying one book, try to read a similar book on the same level • This will deepen your understanding of any topic

• Read actively

5. Prepare for class

   • The best way to prepare for a class is to prepare so much that you know the subject better than the teacher
   • It is important to prepare for class, just as you prepare to go to school or work.
   • It is best to read and understand the text of the section being discussed, however, if nothing else, read over the text of the section.
   • When reading, you may encounter questions which you can then ask when given the opportunity
   • Many teachers say that one should prepare for five hours for each one hour of class, however, others have recommended less time for preparation.

Five Strategies for Successful Online Learning

1. Plan

   • Set aside regular work time during the week. Online classes are not easier than face-toface classes; they require just as much actual studying time.
   • Plan ahead so you can attend the live sessions.
   • If possible, make sure you have a private space where you can study.
   • Have at least one back-up in place should your computer or Internet connection fail. If a friend or family member's computer isn't available, use your local library.

2. Motivate Yourself

   • Online classes take a tremendous amount of self-motivation. Remember why you are taking this course -- to seek the pleasure of Allah. Be as strict with your time as you would were you signed up for a face-to-face class.

3. Participate

   • Take part in the online forums. Attend the live sessions with questions prepared.
   • Speak out if you run into any questions. In the online class, the body-language and other non-verbal cues instructors and classmates might pick up on when you are struggling are absent. If you have a question, ask.

4. Maintain adab

- It can be easy to let our adab slip when we aren't actually sitting in front of our teacher.
- Be thoughtful when preparing your written questions and responses.
- Be aware of how the written word can be misread or misinterpreted. Always re-read what you post before others see it. Being overly "concise" can be misread as abruptness. Writing in all caps is typically interpreted as shouting. For more, see the Netiquette Home Page in Recommended Readings, below.
- Always be your best self in your online classes.

5. Take your online learning seriously.

- When life gets busy, it's easy to let an online class slip down your priority list. Take the online class just as seriously as any face-to-face class you might take.
- Again, remember why you are seeking sacred knowledge. Make your initial intention a high one, renew your intention throughout, and stay committed. Final Advice • Students should listen to the lessons at least once, while taking notes. These notes may then be studied as often as necessary.
- Students may listen to the audio repeatedly, while commuting or while doing other rote work, and with repetition the student will gain mastery of the material covered.
- Students are encouraged to ask questions as they arise, while listening to the audio • Assignments and review questions which are given should be honestly attempted and completed within reasonable time
- Students should pace themselves so that they are listening to a regular amount of course material daily or weekly (according to their own preference). It is to the students' advantage to follow any recommended lesson completion dates.

Some Recommended Readings & videos

[1] Instruction of the Student: The Method of Learning
[2] Memoir of the Listener and the Speaker in the Training of Teacher and Student
[3] Imam Ghazali's Book of Knowledge
[4] The Book of Knowledge from The Gardens of the Righteous (Riyad al-Salihin)
[5] The Path of Muhammad: A Book on Islamic Morals and Ethics
[6] Ten Adab of Seekers of Knowledge - Notes by Ayaz Siddiqui
[7] How to Take Notes like Thomas Edison
[8] How to Take Lecture Notes
[9] Geek to Live: Take study-worthy lecture notes
[10] Netiquette Home Page Videos & audio

[1] Habib Umar's advice to Students of Knowledge
[2] The Etiquette of Seeking Knowledge
[3] The Virtues of Seeking Knowledge
[4] The Way of Seekers SeekersGuidance free Answers service

Study Tips for Distance Learners

We here at Tayba have looked at many different sites, articles and blogs to see what advice has been given for distance learners. We have gathered many of these lists of the and then categorized them according to the manner below. Please read through this entire study guide, giving yourself time to digest and fully comprehend each section.

1. Time Management and Scheduling
2. Study Environment and Space
3. Mindset, Motivation and Attitude
4. Exercise, Health, Breaks & Rewards
5. Focus, Concentration & Distractions
6. Reading
7. Communication
8. Goals
9. Study Groups
10. Organization
11. Review the Material and Notes
12. Memory
13. Choosing What to Read and Choosing Resources
14. Habits For Learning
15. Review your Habits, see what works best for you

1-Time Management and Scheduling

Sura Al Asr

The Prophet ﷺ said: *"Take advantage of five matters before five other matters: your youth before you become old; your health, before you fall sick; your wealth, before you become poor; your free time before you become preoccupied, and your life, before your death."* (Narrated by Ibn Abbas in the Mustadrak of Hakim & Musnad Imam Ahmad. Sahih).

Ibn Abbas narrated that Prophet Muhammad ﷺ said: "*There are two blessings which many people lose: (They are) health and free time for doing good.*" (Bukhari 8/421).

The Prophet ﷺ used to make the following du'a,
"O Allah! Make life a means for every dimension of goodness."

One very moving hadith is related by Ibn-Abbas; the Prophet ﷺ said, "Grab five things before five others: your youth before your decrepitude, your health before your illness, your wealth before your poverty, your leisure before your work, and your life before your death." [al-Hakim in al-Mustadrak]

Rasul Allah ﷺ said, "The two feet of the son of Adam will not move from near his Lord on the Day of Judgement until he is asked about five (matters) concerning his life - how he spent it; about his youth - how he took care of it; about his wealth - how he earned it; and where he spent it; and about that which he acted upon from the knowledge he acquired." [Tirmidhi]

Over the years in teaching and advising students, the one thing I hear constantly from people who are not able to be full time students is "I don't have any time." The reality is that we do have time, we just don't manage it properly. As with all blessings, we should manage them well and cherish and protect them. For a student, it is especially important to manage time well. Here are some tips:

- Beginning on the path of knowledge can seem like a huge task. Begin by taking small regular steps that are consistent. A Chinese wisdom says, "The journey of a 1000 miles begins with a single step."
- Don't fall into procrastination and say, "I will study once I have some time." Rather, take the initiative to carve out some time in your day as it is now. Be sure to consider all the necessary aspects of your day.
- When planning out your study routine, be as realistic as possible and don't place a burden too heavy to carry. If Allah does not place a burden on us more than we can bear (Quran 2:286), then we shouldn't place on our ourselves that we can't bear.
- Once you have a routine for studying, follow it religiously. Treat it like your prayer times in that you always have to make time for them and if you miss them, you have to make it up. But try not to miss it and stay consistent as "The most beloved actions to Allah are the ones which are consistent, even if small" as the Hadith states.
- You don't have to study every day. The traditional Mahdara system of study has a five day study week and a mandatory weekend. You may choose less than five days. What is important is that is regular.
- You should not wait for time to appear for you to study in; you have to be proactive in creating spaces within your day's time to study. Make sure to factor in all aspects of your daily routine. Once you create a routine, stick to it.
- Use a journal, notebook, planner or calendar to write down your routine and plan. You do not need to memorize your plan, rather keep your memory space for other things.
- Having a schedule can prevent frustration in the student. You will find yourself making gains towards your goals as well as not overburdening yourself. You will also find that you don't have to cram in study sessions in irregular intervals. It is better to spend one hour a day over a five day period than to have one day a week with five hours straight. But if you can't spread your studies over a week, then once a week is better than nothing at all.
- In a later section we will discuss the importance of studying with another person or a group. When others make their schedule to accommodate you, respect their time and sticking to the routine becomes even more important.
- Make sure to factor in break times in your study routine. This will be discussed further in another section. Most people cannot study for 4 or 5 hours straight. So break studies into smaller sections taking a short (timed) break in between or give yourself a reward. Breaks and rewards will be discussed further in another section.
- If you find yourself having difficulty in creating or following a study schedule, then you might have an issue with motivation or attitude towards studying. This will be discussed in a later section. If you change your attitude, you may find it easier to create and follow a study plan.

Tips on creating and checking a study plan:

- Decide the times and place that you will study. Make sure it is both a time and place where you will not be distracted and your mind will not wander.
- Give yourself some time to find the right routine. To achieve this, you will have to review your study habits every week. After each review, you can make adjustments to your schedule.
  - As an example, some people find they study better at the end of the night and will go to bed early. Others find waking up difficult so will study late into the night and then sleep until fajr time. Work with your nature and don't try to crush your self (nafs).
  - You might find that you get more out of a certain time. Some people find 30 minutes after fajr is better than 2 hours after dhuhr.

Term/Weekly Calendars and Daily Schedules

- The Term Calendar provides you with the big picture, the weekly calendar a smaller picture and the daily schedule the smallest picture of your planning.
- Term Calendars: At the beginning of a term, make a calendar for the whole term with all the important dates and deadlines on it. Be sure to include other responsibilities and deadlines that you have that need to be balanced with your studies.
- Weekly Calendars: At the beginning of each week (whichever day it is that you choose to start your week), sit down and plan out your week. Make changes as needed throughout the week. Don't be afraid to shuffle things around if the need arises.
- Daily Schedule: This may seem like too much planning, but you will find that it does not take that much time to sit down each evening and roughly plan out what you need to complete the next day.
  - Note items that you need to cover the next day.
  - Note items from previous days that need to be caught up.
  - Note anything that may take a good amount of time from you.

- **<u>Have a List of Priorities for your Studies and Assignments.</u>** The further you advance in your studies, you will find that your workload will increase. One thing many students find when they are studying is that there are never enough hours in the day to get everything done. Usually by the end of the day, you will be tired and so you should get through the most difficult items first and leave the more easy items until the end.

- **<u>You should have protected times and spaces for you to study.</u>** A later section will discuss study spaces. For study times, try to have blocks that are at least 40-50 minutes. The optimum would be blocks of three hours as studies have shown that three hours is the most productive block time. The other thing to note about the 3-hour block is that it takes 15 minutes to "get into the mode" of whatever you are doing. So plan 15 minutes to settle into the 3 hour block. Then note that every time you break that block of study, it will take 15 minutes to get back into the mode. So avoid distractions as best as possible. That is why the block of time should be "protected."

- **Schedule in your other activities.** Every student will have time they need to dedicate to family, work, projects, community, friends, hobbies, personal interests, exercise, etc. Don't get into the habit of making your studies last and saying you will get the studies done after you get everything else out of the way. Give your first time in the day to studying and then take care of things that you need to attend to.

- **Expect the Unexpected.** There are always things that will come up. Don't get frustrated when they do, but try your best to deal with them in a way where you don't sacrifice your studies. If something comes up and can be delayed do that but if it needs to be attended to right away, then by all means deal with it. Treat the missed study time like a missed prayer in that you will have to make it up at some point.

- **Don't cram your study sessions.** If you feel like you have to cram all your studies for one week into a few hours, then you need to review your schedule. Your studies should be evenly distributed throughout the week. Think of the example of rain; if it all comes down in a single downpour, the ground cannot soak it up but if it comes down in a slow steady trickle, then the ground has time to soak it up.

- **Be regular in your studies.** The famous Hadith states that "The actions most beloved to Allah are the most consistent, even if little." A regular routine of studies is more likely to be a cause of you succeeding in your studies than using random times to study.

- **Studying at the same time of day.** We are creatures of habit, and that can work for or against us, depending on the type of habit that we acquire. It can be used to your advantage to create a habit of studying at the same times every day. It will become part of your daily routine and you will be mentally expecting and planning for it each day. If something comes up, don't worry about that. Just get your schedule back to normal as soon as you can.

- --

- **Each study time should have a specific goal.** Simply studying without direction is not effective. You need to know exactly what you need to accomplish during each study session. Before you start studying, set a study session goal that supports your overall academic goal (i.e. memorize 30 vocabulary words in order to ace the vocabulary section on an upcoming Spanish test.)

- **Never procrastinate your planned study session.** It's very easy, and common, to put off your study session because of lack of interest in the subject, because you have other things you need to get done, or just because the assignment is hard. Successful students DO NOT procrastinate studying. If you procrastinate your study session, your studying will become much less effective and you may not get everything accomplished that you need to. Procrastination also leads to rushing, and rushing is the number one cause of errors.

- **Start with the most difficult subject first.** As your most difficult assignment or subject will require the most effort and mental energy, you should start with it first. Once you've completed the most difficult work, it will be much easier to complete the rest of your work. Believe it or not, starting with the most difficult subject will greatly improve the effectiveness of your study sessions, and your academic performance.

    - Because many distance learning courses are self-paced with no set schedule, time management is an important part of distance learning. Students may want to keep a calendar with assignment due dates, scheduled webinar lectures and exam dates marked. They can then manage the workload by scheduling the work that needs to be accomplished each week. Students are also recommended to schedule class time, study time and discussion time.

    - If the prof doesn't lay one out for you, make a weekly schedule that details what you need to complete each week (eg. Week 1, chapter 1, 2; Week 2, chapter 3, 4, 5 etc.). Be certain to consider deadlines for assignments, quizzes etc. to make sure you will have covered the material in time.

    - Make a second calendar with all the course due dates/deadlines on it. From here work backwards to determine when you need to start the assignment, essay etc., to be sure you can meet the deadline.

    - Set out a weekly scheduled 3 hour block (either altogether, or broken up) that will be devoted solely to that course. Think of this as equivalent to the time you would spend in class, so it should be at the same time every week and don't skip it!

    - Differentiate between "classwork," and "homework." Class work is the lecture component that you would normally be doing with a prof, but are now doing on your own during a set time (see 3 above), while homework is work done in excess of this which is just like homework you do for any other course. Do each one in the specific allotted time you have given yourself and don't skip any of it – it will catch up with you later!

- **Organize a Study Timetable.** Because Correspondence Courses require a self-motivated person, it is essential that you have a study regime that you can stick to. Most of the time you will have a Timetable or Class Schedule, and if you are studying by Correspondence, then classes will be set aside for you, these are *not* Free Periods, but scheduled time for your Correspondence Class.

- **Never Procrastinate.** You must proactively work on assignments. Instructors can usually tell when an assignment was thrown together at the last minute! Start future assignments early and build them day by day. For example if you have to write a paper that is due one week from today, you should research the topic for the first two days, create a mindmap or outline on the third day, and write the paper on the fourth and fifth days. Use the sixth day to revise and to send the work through any required online grammar or plagiarism checkers. Once you get your reviewed paper back, make any cosmetic changes, and turn it in!

- **Make sure to spend enough time on a course.** The books you will be studying are not designed to be quickly read through. You must spend a lot of time with them until you know them inside and out. Some of you will work towards memorizing the Arabic or maybe just the English. But even if you don't memorize, study the book until you "own it." Don't schedule the bare minimum amount of time to just go through the material. Schedule enough time for you to master the material.

- Final Advice about time management: Pace yourself. This is not a sprint, it is a marathon. Remember the Hadith that Imam Zarnuji mentioned about the riding beast that is driven into the ground.

2-Study Environment & Space

- **Find a dedicated study space.** Some students will spend the first 20 minutes of their study time just looking for somewhere to study. A key to ongoing time management is to find a dedicated study space free from distractions where you can concentrate. If you want to change up your study space, that's fine, just make sure to find a study space that works and stick with it.

- **Eliminate lifestyle distractions.** Technology offers unprecedented ways to access new information. However, it also creates distractions that prevent you from concentrating on your research. Stick to academic websites, silence your phone, and turn off your wireless connection as soon as you have enough information to write.

- **Where you study is important.** A lot of people make the mistake of studying in a place that really isn't conducive to concentrating. A place with a lot of distractions makes for a poor study area. If you try and study in your dorm room, for instance, you may find the computer, TV, or a roommate more interesting than the reading material you're trying to digest.

  The library, a nook in a student lounge or study hall, or a quiet coffee house are good places to check out. Make sure to choose the quiet areas in these places, not the loud, central gathering areas. Investigate multiple places on-campus and off-campus, don't just pick the first one your find as "good enough" for your needs and habits. Finding an ideal study place is important, because it's one you can reliably count on for the next few years.

Finding a Good Place to Study

- One of the keys to effective studying is finding a good location. It's difficult to study in a room full of distractions. However, the ideal location for you may not be the ideal study location for someone else. You may not like studying somewhere private, or even very quiet, but you do want to make sure that you study at a location that is conducive to your method of learning, allows you to concentrate, and is free of distractions.

- The reason why it is not always recommended to study in a quiet area is because some people learn better in a room with background noise. While studying in a library with people constantly coming and going, librarians restocking books and people talking is distracting to some, it's the perfect study environment for others. Some students prefer studying in a small cubical where they will not be disturbed by noise or any other visual stimuli, while others like studying right in the middle of bustle and commotion.

The following are general guidelines for selecting a study location. Since everyone has individual study preferences, there is no one best study location for everyone.

Create a routine

- Develop a routine by studying in the same place and same time on days you plan to study. Everyone has a personal preference as where they study, whether it's in a library or dorm room. Regardless of your preference, we recommend studying in the same place. Just make sure to study in a location without distractions. For example, if you like to watch television, it is probably not a good idea to study in a room with a television.

- Although it may seem monotonous, it's beneficial to establish a studying routine. This will get you into the habit of studying, and before you know it, it will take little effort to get motivated to study.

Find a location that's comfortable

- It is counterproductive to study for extended hours at a time in an uncomfortable environment. For this reason, you should find a place to study that is comfortable. You want to make sure you do not suffer any back, wrist, or other physical discomfort while you study. Even small discomforts can eventually result in more serious physical problems. It's also a good idea to make sure you have all the materials you need to study, such as pens and books, nearby your study area.

- It's also good idea to study in a well lit area since it can be difficult to study with poor lighting even if the environment is perfect. Studying in the basement of library may seem the perfect location, but if there isn't any natural light, it will have a negative effect.

Evaluate your study preferences

- Each individual has unique learning styles, methods and study preferences. Consequently, you should first determine how you learn best before deciding on a study location. You should also know what it is that is most distracting to you. As mentioned, some people can study in noisy environments while others can't. After selecting a study environment best suited your individual preferences, conduct frequent evaluations to determine whether your study sessions are productive. If not, reassess your study location.

Create study rules and follow them

- If your study sessions are unproductive, or you're struggling with motivation, establish some personal study rules. After you have established some rules, be sure to tell your parents or other trusted family members and friends to follow up with you. A common rule many people set for themselves is scheduling specific timeframes for studying with periodic breaks. If don't have anyone to follow up with you, it's still a good idea to establish study rules.

Make sure you're not distracted whiles you're studying.

- Everyone gets distracted by something. Maybe it's the TV. Or your family. Or maybe it's too quiet. Some people actually study better with a little background noise. When you're distracted while you're studying you (1) loose your train of thought and (2) you're unable to focus -- both of which will lead to very ineffective studying. Before you start studying find a place where you won't be disturbed or distracted. Some people this is a quiet cubicle in the recesses of the library.

Find a Study Space that is best suited for your subject.

- If you are studying Agriculture, then try using the Library or Agricultural Plot or Shed. If you are studying Computers, go to a computer room where you have access to a Computer, Printer and Internet. Your study space should be quiet and clean, it is best to do your work in a classroom rather than the playground *It may be tempting to study at your Lunch Seats, but this can be quite distracting*

Study Corner at Home You are at school about 6 to 8 hours a day, 5 days a week, you sleep approximately 9 hours a day, and you will probably have out-of-school activities such as sports and work.

- This only leaves you with a few hours a day to study at home. Therefore it is important that you have a quiet study space with almost everything at your fingertips. Ensure that you have a tidy and neat desk, with drawers and folders dedicated to each subject. Have a pencil tin and pencil case, with highlighters and markers, assorted colours of pens, pencils, ruler, Eraser, and anything you may need. *Lighting* is important, so if your bedroom or study light isn't appropriate or bright enough, buy a lamp or light that shines over your head and in front of you. The worst thing is straining your eyes and the second is being too cold or too hot. To prevent this, make sure you have a heater or air-conditioner and if your unable to have one in your room, try having a fan or a wheat bag. You can also use water bottles, Warm Cups of Hot Chocolate or Tea, (Coffee doesn't help) and layers of clothing.
- Keep a clean and tidy study corner at home. This way you will always have a suitable work area.
- Make sure all study areas are *ergonomically correct*. Feet on ground, back straight, keyboard and desk at same level of your hands, and the screen of computers a safe distance away from your face.

3-Mindset, Motivation and Attitude

Motivation has a strong influence on how well you do your job. Students often develop a "Slave Mentality." That is, they see themselves performing tasks which are required by their teachers but which are utterly meaningless to them.

In contrast, the students who see how their schoolwork fits into their plans for themselves become willing workers. It is quite true that "you can do anything you want to do" because wanting makes the necessary work easy.

Determination to work does not mean the same as motivation. "Will Power" will not work over a lengthy period of time. You can force yourself on occasion, but there are definite limits to the success of such an approach.

How to Gain Motivation

Step 1: Decide what you're trying to do in college. (You may need a counselor or other advisor to help with this, but that's why they're there.) Find out exactly how you go about achieving what you want. (What classes are required. Equally important, what classes aren't required. How long will it take you? How much will it cost?) With this information you can see the end of the tunnel. You can see yourself progressing, and you can avoid a lot of "wheel spinning."

Step 2: Make college your job. Don't let the incidental business of earning a living and leading a social life interfere with your central task of getting through school. If something **must** be neglected (and good planning can usually avoid this), then neglect something other than school. Your job is probably a short-term, dead-end proposition anyway. Don't get bumped out of school just to work 48 hours a week for the minimum wage.

a. Real students own their own books, have a suitable place to work, and keep their materials conveniently available.

b. Most distractions come from within you. If you have trouble concentrating, try to see what's bothering you and take steps to eliminate it. Most problems yield to direct action, but you must do the acting.

Step 3: Set short-range goals

a. Analyze your study task. What do you want to achieve? How can it best be done?

b. Set a definite time limit. You can get as much done in one hour as six if you know you must. Work expands to fit the time available.

c. Evaluate your success or failure. You can learn best from making mistakes, provided you recognize that they **are** mistakes.

d. The student must focus his or her attention on whatever needs to be remembered. If you intend to remember something, you probably will.

e. The student must be "sold" on the course. Why is this subject worth knowing? Correlative reading may enhance the student's interest. For example, historical novels are a marvelous way to learn history. The greater the knowledge, the greater the interest.

Don't forget to learn!

Studying isn't just about passing an exam, as most students look at it as. Studying is an effort to actually learn things, some of which you might actually care about. So while you'll have to take your share of classes that have little or nothing to do with your interests, you should still look for interesting things to take away from every experience.

By the time you'll realize what a great opportunity school is, you'll be well into the middle of your life with a lot of responsibilities – children, mortgages, career pressures, etc. Then most people have neither the time nor energy to go back to school. So take the time to learn some stuff now, because you'll appreciate the opportunity later on.

1. How you approach studying matters

Too many people look at studying as a necessary task, not an enjoyment or opportunity to learn. That's fine, but researchers have found that how you approach something matters almost as much as what you do. Being in the right mindset is important in order to study smarter.

Sometimes you can't "force" yourself to be in the right mindset, and it is during such times you should simply avoid studying. If you're distracted by a relationship issue, an upcoming game, or finishing an important project, then studying is just going to be an exercise in frustration. Come back to it when you're not focused (or obsessed!) by something else going on in your life.

Way to help improve your study mindset:

- *Aim to think positively when you study*, and remind yourself of your skills and abilities.
- *Avoid catastrophic thinking.* Instead of thinking, "I'm a mess, I'll never have enough time to study for this exam," look at it like, "I may be a little late to study as much as I'd like, but since I'm doing it now, I'll get most of it done."
- *Avoid absolute thinking.* Instead of thinking "I always mess things up," the more objective view is, "I didn't do so well that time, what can I do to improve?"

- *Avoid comparing yourself with others*, because you usually just end up feeling bad about yourself.

Have the Proper Mindset

Realize that studying can't be crammed in while feeding your kids lunch or during your coffee break at work. Learning takes time and consistent effort to be successful. Be prepared to spend a significant amount of time working on your courses. It's been said that success is 99 percent perspiration and 1 percent inspiration. This is as true for the world of studying as it is for the world of working.

Be aware that not all parts of your studies are going to be interesting. Some parts could be dry and boring so you need to keep a positive attitude to remain interested. If you don't, your mind will wander and you'll find yourself focusing on the other tasks you need to complete in your life instead of getting your money's worth out of the courses you bought.

Keep Yourself Motivated

As an adult, you may feel that it's silly to give yourself little rewards for doing well in school. After all, you may think, the final ultimate reward will be holding that degree in your hand. But it could be years before you get that degree or diploma so give yourself a break and thank yourself for your dedication to your studies. It'll help keep you motivated and the reward doesn't need to be anything spectacular. Treat yourself to resting in front of your favorite television show, a night out visiting friends or even that chocolate bar you've been craving for a while. Just be careful not to allow these rewards to become an excuse not to study or a way to interrupt your studies.

Resilience

The key to successful preparation, participation, time management and organization is persistence and determination. Even with the best intentions, it is easy to fall behind or miss a lecture. But, by maintaining dedication and commitment to one's educational goals, distance learning students can take advantage of a unique learning opportunity and possibly build toward a new career.

Preparation Students should prepare for their courses by reviewing the syllabus and course objectives, taking note of any scheduled presentations, lectures, assignment due dates and exam dates. Distance learning students should also familiarize themselves with the course delivery method, assignment submission process and means of contacting the instructor and classmates.

Relax. Your professors want to help you. Don't be afraid to ask for help when it's necessary.

Be Proactive. Because at school you have heavy study loads anyway, as well as family commitments, relationships and social lives, it is essential to be proactive. If a section of work is due on Friday, and it's only Monday, get stuck into it, once it's out of the way, you will not have to worry about it. If you have a *BIG* assignment due in a month, try to get most of it done in the first few weeks, and then plan to have it finished a week prior to the Due Date. This way you won't be cramming and working till the early hours of the morning trying to finish it.

Be Happy With Your Study Efforts Don't be too hard on yourself. Doing a Correspondence Course can be hard, and it takes guts, determination and confidence in yourself that you can do it. At times your marks may fall, other times you may get 100%. Whether you achieve the best, or strive to be the best that *you* can be, that's all you can ask for. Don't be too hard on yourself if you don't do as well as you had hoped, or that you find you didn't answer a questions right. You have already proven that you are dedicated to the subject, so just make sure you stick to it and keep trying. Study is only beneficial if you put in the effort.

As a distance learning student, you will find that being pro-active and engaged in your personal learning experience will pay off in good grades and depth of learning.

Be motivated

As a distance student you'll need to be a self-directed learner. To ensure that you can do this, you need to be highly motivated. The best way to stay sharp is to have a clear goal in mind for what you want to achieve through your education. If you are working toward a degree, your goal may be to finish your degree and change careers.

Be confident

Before you take your first distance course, look through the book. You should also be confident of other skills that are involved in university learning, such as reading university-level textbooks and writing papers.

4-Exercise, Health, Breaks & Rewards

- **Get exercise. Eat right. Get plenty of sleep.** Yeah, you've heard this before, but let us say it again. Get exercise, eat right and get plenty of sleep. If you're not at your peak, you won't be able to focus or concentrate, nor will you have the energy or stamina to get your studies completed efficiently. Going to bed an hour early, can make all the difference the next day in your ability to make the best use of your time.

- **Don't replace protein with caffeine.** Protein and complex carbohydrates are an energy source that won't leave you jittery.

- **Walk Before An Exam.** It's been proven that exercise can boost your memory and brain power. Research conducted by Dr. Chuck Hillman of the University of Illinois provides evidence that about 20 minutes exercise before an exam can improve performance.

- **Exercise to release stress.** Instead of succumbing to anxiety or pressure until studying seems impossible, find a productive outlet to express your frustration. Physical activity releases endorphins that reduce stress and depression, and it's completely free.

- **Take care of yourself first - Eat well.** Nutrition plays a huge role in your ability to learn. Instead of depending on sugar and caffeine -- and weathering the crashes that follow -- drink plenty of water and make sure you get enough fruits and vegetables. A well-rested, well-nourished, hydrated body is capable of staying awake and alert without help from chemicals.

- **Take care of yourself first - Get plenty of rest!** Your brain needs to recharge regularly in order to process and absorb new information. Sometimes all-nighters are inevitable, but don't let it become a habit, because sleep-deprivation can prevent you from learning or thinking critically. Give yourself permission to make up for lost sleep, too.

- **Keep healthy and balanced.** It's hard to live a balanced life while in school, I know. But the more balance you seek out in your life, the easier every component in your life becomes. If you spend all of your time focusing on a relationship or a game, you can see how easy it is to be out of balance. When you're out of balance, the things you're not focusing on – such as studying – become that much harder. Don't spend all of your time studying – have friends, keep in touch with your family, and find interests outside of school that you can pursue and enjoy.

Finding balance isn't really something that can be taught, it's something that comes with experience and simply living. But you can work to try and keep your health and body balanced, by doing what you already know – exercise regularly and eat right. There are no shortcuts to health. Vitamins and herbs might help you in the short-term, but they're not substitute for real, regular meals and a dose of exercise every now and again (walking to class is a start, but only if you're spending an hour or two a day doing it).

Look at vitamins and herbs as they are intended – as supplements to your regular, healthy diet. Common herbs – such as ginkgo, ginseng, and gotu kola – may help you enhance mental abilities, including concentration, aptitude, behavior, alertness and even intelligence. But they may not, either, and you shouldn't rely on them instead of studying regularly.

- **Be active in your study Don't get *stuck in a rut*, if you are getting tired during study, go for a walk and stretch, have a glass of water or juice and do some heart-pumping activities.** If it's late at night, and your tired, go to bed, many students try to over-lead their brains with study and assignments. Sleep is when your brain reinforces the efforts made during study and helps make your *short term* memories into *long term*.

- Energy Deprivation can become a problem after continual use of computers and studying.

- If your work station is not *ergonomically correct* then you will have soon find you will be having back problems, sore joints and muscles, as well as poor circulation.

- **Stretch and be active during study.** Make sure you stretch and walk around every 15 minutes, to keep blood circulating and keep your brain awake.

- **Study, Study, Study...**Relax. There will be times that you have to put the hard yards in, during exams, or over the holidays. Be sure that you make as much of an effort to keep up with your work, and when your holidays and breaks do come around, make sure you take full advantage of them. If you go to a camp, sit back and relax, and don't worry about school.

- **Get exercise. Eat right. Get plenty of sleep.** Yeah, you've heard this before, but let us say it again. Get exercise, eat right and get plenty of sleep. If you're not at your peak, you won't be able to focus or concentrate, nor will you have the energy or stamina to get your studies completed efficiently. Going to bed an hour early, can make all the difference the next day in your ability to make the best use of your time.

5-Focus, Concentration & Distractions

- **Prevent Getting Side Tracked.** A Correspondence Course is self-motivated, it is very easy to get sidetracked and lose concentration, this can happen by seeing a friend and talking to them, getting distracted by music, or coming across a website and not doing your work. A good way to prevent getting distracted and keeping on track, is to eliminate the distractions. Remove all music devices, (at school other people may have them, try not to become distracted), when using the Internet or computer, don't stray off your scheduled task, if a friend comes over to you, tell them you will only be a few minutes and ask if you can talk later and explain that you are busy. (Most friends will understand). If you do become distracted, save your work, and pick up doing the scheduled task at a later time, when you are not tempted by distractions.

6-READING

- **Be an active reader.** Be a text detective: ask your text good questions and it will yield good answers.

- **Avoiding Study Traps like (traps in bold and solutions in plain text):**

  1. **"I Don't Know Where To Begin"** Take Control. Make a list of all the things you have to do. Break your workload down into manageable chunks. Prioritize! Schedule your time realistically. Don't skip classes near an exam -- you may miss a review session. Use that hour in between classes to review notes. Interrupt study time with planned study breaks. Begin studying early, with an hour or two per day, and slowly build as the exam approaches.
  2. **"I've Got So Much To Study . . . And So Little Time"** Preview. Survey your syllabus, reading material, and notes. Identify the most important topics emphasized, and areas still not understood. Previewing saves time, especially with non-fiction reading, by helping you organize and focus in on

the main topics. Adapt this method to your own style and study material, but remember, previewing is not an effective substitute for reading.

3. **"This Stuff Is So Dry, I Can't Even Stay Awake Reading It"** Just attack! Get actively involved with the text as you read. Ask yourself, "What is important to remember about this section?" Take notes or underline key concepts. Discuss the material with others in your class. Study together. Stay on the offensive, especially with material that you don't find interesting, rather than reading passively and missing important points.

4. **"I Read It. I Understand It. But I Just Can't Get It To Sink In"** Elaborate. We remember best the things that are most meaningful to us. As you are reading, try to elaborate upon new information with your own examples. Try to integrate what you're studying with what you already know. You will be able to remember new material better if you can link it to something that's already meaningful to you. Some techniques include:
   - **Chunking**: An effective way to simplify and make information more meaningful. For example, suppose you wanted to remember the colors in the visible spectrum (Red, Orange, Yellow, Green, Blue, Indigo, Violet); you would have to memorize seven "chunks" of information in order. But if you take the first letter of each color, you can spell the name "Roy G. Biv", and reduce the information the three "chunks".
   - **Mnemonics**: Any memory-assisting technique that helps us to associate new information with something familiar. For example, to remember a formula or equation, we may use letters of the alphabet to represent certain numbers. Then we can change an abstract formula into a more meaningful word or phrase, so we'll be able to remember it better. Sound-alike associations can be very effective, too, especially while trying to learn a new language. The key is to create your own links, then you won't forget them.

5. **"I Guess I Understand It"** Test yourself. Make up questions about key sections in notes or reading. Keep in mind what the professor has stressed in the course. Examine the relationships between concepts and sections. Often, simply by changing section headings you can generate many effective questions. For example, a section entitled "Bystander Apathy" might be changed into questions such as: "What is bystander apathy?", "What are the causes of bystander apathy?", and "What are some examples of bystander apathy?"

6. **"There's Too Much To Remember"** Organize. Information is recalled better if it is represented in an organized framework that will make retrieval more systematic. There are many techniques that can help you organize new information, including:
   - **Write chapter outlines or summaries**; emphasize relationships between sections.
   - **Group information** into categories or hierarchies, where possible.
   - **Information Mapping.** Draw up a matrix to organize and interrelate material. For example, if you were trying to understand

the causes of World War I, you could make a chart listing all the major countries involved across the top, and then list the important issues and events down the side. Next, in the boxes in between, you could describe the impact each issue had on each country to help you understand these complex historical developments.

7. **"I Knew It A Minute Ago"** Review. After reading a section, try to recall the information contained in it. Try answering the questions you made up for that section. If you cannot recall enough, re-read portions you had trouble remembering. The more time you spend studying, the more you tend to recall. Even after the point where information can be perfectly recalled, further study makes the material less likely to be forgotten entirely. In other words, you can't overstudy. However, how you organize and integrate new information is still more important than how much time you spend studying.

8. **"But I Like To Study In Bed"** Context. Recall is better when study context (physical location, as well as mental, emotional, and physical state) are similar to the test context. The greater the similarity between the study setting and the test setting, the greater the likelihood that material studied will be recalled during the test.

9. **"Cramming Before A Test Helps Keep It Fresh In My Mind"** Spacing: Start studying now. Keep studying as you go along. Begin with an hour or two a day about one week before the exam, and then increase study time as the exam approaches. Recall increases as study time gets spread out over time.

10. **"I'm Gonna Stay Up All Night 'til I Get This"** Avoid Mental Exhaustion. Take short breaks often when studying. Before a test, have a rested mind. When you take a study break, and just before you go to sleep at night, don't think about academics. Relax and unwind, mentally and physically. Otherwise, your break won't refresh you and you'll find yourself lying awake at night. It's more important than ever to take care of yourself before an exam! Eat well, sleep, and get enough exercise.

Know and actively use reading skills.

Strategies for Reading Textbooks

Reading textbooks may not be fun, but being able to is important. Throughout middle school, high school and college, textbooks will be a big part of your reading. Understanding how to read and use them effectively is key to academic success.

Before You Read

Textbooks can be boring, tedious, and full of detail. Jumping right into a textbook without having a general idea of the central themes and topics can make texbook reading that much more challenging. We learn best when we move from general to specific.

Previewing and developing a big picture of a text before reading will enable you to better identify what's important as you read and make it possible for you to retain the detail.

Preview. The steps below will help you preview a text and enhance your comprehension and retention.

- Review all chapter headings and subheadings.
- Glance over any pictures, charts or graphs in the section you'll be reading.
- Read any bold or italicized words and make sure you understand them.
- Read the chapter summary.
- Review any end of chapter questions.

Question. Developing a set of questions you want to answer before you start reading a text provides direction and focus as you read the text. Once you've previewed the text, make a list of questions you want to find answers to as you read. How do you do this? Easy. While you're previewing the text, turn each heading and subheading into a question. For example, if the heading is "Root causes of the American civil war," then your question may be "What were the root causes that lead to the American civil war?"

While You Read
The following strategies will help you maximize your comprehension and retain information while reading textbooks.

Reflect. From reviewing chapter headings, subheadings, bold or italicized words, ask yourself what you've already learned. Now as you read:

- Answer the questions you developed while previewing the text.
- Try and predict the answers to the questions and find out if your predictions are correct.
- Read aloud. Reading aloud improves comprehension and retention of information.
- Develop a picture in your mind of the concepts presented. Visualizing information, concepts or material presented make it much easier to remember.
-

Highlight. As you read through your text, highlight important passages that support central themes and concepts. Be selective. If you're highlighting more than 20% of a passage you're not being selective enough.

- As you read, try and identify important concepts and facts that could be likely test questions. Underline and identify these concepts with a "Q" in the margin.
- Circle with a pencil key terms and vocabulary. Write a short definition for each in your notes or in the margin of the textbook.

- Take well organized notes on the backside of your corresponding class lecture notes. This way your lecture notes and textbook notes for the same topic will be easy to access and review in preparation for the test.
- Make visual aids, including, picture, graphs, diagrams, or tables, to help visualize what you're reading. Visualization is a great way to take information that is complex or difficult and make it easy to understand and remember.
- Write a brief summary of the central themes and ideas in your notes. Being able to develop a summary of what you learned will help you master the material and retain the information.
-

After You Read
What you do after you read a text, can be almost as beneficial to learning and retention, as reading the text itself.

Recount. Once you've finished reading a text or passage, sit down with someone else and tell them what you read and what you learned from the text. Explaining aloud what you've learned from reading is arguably the most effective way to promote mastery of material and improve retention. Joining a study group is a great way to have the opportunity to share with others what you've learned from your reading.

Review. Review. And then review again! Within a day of your initial reading, spend 20 to 30 minutes–depending on the amount of material covered–reviewing your notes and the information you learned, reciting the main points and topics. This will move the information from short-term to long-term memory. Each week spend about 10 minutes reviewing your notes and the highlighted parts of your text. Reviewing will make sure you're prepared when test time arrives.

When Textbook Reading is Challenging
Texbook reading is typically more difficult than other forms of reading, but sometimes it's downright challenging. If you're faced with reading a challenging textbook, we recommend the following:

- **Read aloud.** Reading aloud improves reading comprehension and retention of information. Reading aloud allows you to hear what you're reading which enables the brain to process the information more effectively and remember what it heard.

- **Change positions.** Reading passages from textbooks gets tedious and boring really fast. Being stuck in the same position the entire time you read only adds to the monotony. Try reading standing up for a while, or change positions every once in the while.

- **Read the text again.** Each time you read a text again you'll pick up something new, retain more information and find it easier to understand. It's not uncommon to read the same passage from a textbook several times before you're able to fully understand and retain the information.

- **Search for key words.** Read sentences removing the adjectives and adverbs. This will cut to the meat of the sentence and help you identify what's being said and what's really important for you to know.

- **Jump around in the text.** Sometimes it's beneficial to skip around and read different parts of a chapter or section in a textbook. For example, jumping to the end of the chapter and reading the chapter summary, before reading the chapter, can greatly enhance focus, direction and understanding as you go back and read the actual chapter.

- **Mark it.** If you come across a passage or section of the text that you just don't understand, underline it and put a mark next it in the margin of your book. When you're done reading your text, you'll have several marks throughout the chapter. Once you get back to class, you'll know what questions to ask your teacher or professor.

- **Take a break.** If you're just not making headway with the text you're reading, take a break, regroup and come back to tackle it later with a fresh pair of eyes.

- **Turn to the web.** When all else fails, "Google" it. The web is a plethora of information. And these days there are websites that address, and lend understanding, to just about every topic or subject.

Things to Consider...
Here are a few more things to consider when reading textbooks.

What to Read

Every teacher and professor is different. Some weight their tests and quizzes heavily on what's found in the textbook, while others rely almost entirely on their lectures. At the beginning of the semester try and find out if exams will be based primarily on information obtained through in-class lectures or from reading the text book. This will help you know where to focus your time.

Where to Study

Finding a peaceful, comfortable location, away from distractions, where you can focus, is essential to reading textbooks effectively. Learn more about finding a good study location.

When to Read

When you read is just as important, if not more important, than where you read. Reading textbooks can be tedious and boring. The last thing you want to do is read when you're fatigued, tired or it's late at night. Reading textbooks requires that you're alert and attentive. We recommend reading for about 30 to 45 minutes at a time then taking a short break to reinvigorate your mind and body.

How to Retain It

The best way to retain information from textbooks is to (1) read aloud and (2) discuss what you've read with other people. Reciting text information moves it from your short-term to long-term memory and ensures subject mastery.

7- Communication

- **Meet and get to know faculty.**

- **Don't be afraid to ask for help**

Don't be afraid to reach out to tutors, professors, and classmates if you think you're falling behind. Whether you have trouble understanding a new concept or just need help managing your time, college is full of people who know exactly what you're going through.

- Know what the expectations are for the class

Different professors and teachers have different expectations from their students. While taking good notes and listening in class (and attending as many of the classes as you can) are good starts, you can do one better by spending some time with the instructor or professor's assistant. Talking to the instructor early on – especially if you foresee a difficult course ahead – will help you understand the course requirements and the professor's expectations. Maybe most students in the class are expected to get a "C" because the material is so difficult; knowing that ahead of time helps set your expectations, too.

Pay attention in class. If the instructor writes something on the whiteboard or displays it on the screen, it's important. But if they say something, that's important too. Copy these things down as they're presented, but don't zone out completely from what the instructor is also saying. Some students focus on the written materials without regard for what the instructor is saying. If you write down only one aspect of the professor's instructions (e.g., just what they write down), you're probably missing about half the class.

If you get a particularly bad grade on a paper or exam, talk to the instructor. Try and understand where things went wrong, and what you can do in the future to help reduce it from happening again.

- **Participation & Communication**

Online learning programs include participation, just like traditional on-campus programs. In distance learning, students participate by attending lectures, taking part in discussions, using email and mail to stay in communication and keeping up with required reading and assignment deadlines.

Studying alone without classmates or an instructor can lead some students to feel isolated or frustrated. Students can help alleviate these feelings by logging in to the course daily, participating in group discussions, reaching out when frustrated or confused and sending emails to share ideas and ask questions.

- **Expect fairness.**

Avoid asking for favors that would be unfair to other students. If you have a legitimate need, your professor will be more willing to work with you than if you just want to whine about a grade.

- **Don't go over his head.**

In extreme cases, online students may find it necessary to complain about a course to the school administration. But, it's almost always best to solve problems directly with the professor. If you have a non-urgent complaint about the course, work with the instructor or save it for the evaluations.

- **If web communications break down, ask for a phone meeting.**

Sometimes emails and internet chats just don't cut it. If you have a concern that isn't getting solved online, ask your professor to set up a phone meeting. If you live near the school's brick-and-mortar campus you may even want to meet in person.

- **Ask politely.**

Even an online professor is in the wrong, it's always smart to keep your communications polite. Remember that emails, message board posts, and chat discussions are often saved.

- **Introduce yourself.**

As soon as you begin an online class, take a minute to introduce yourself to the professor. Say hello in a class chat or drop him a quick email. You'll be more comfortable dealing with someone you know if a problem arises.

- **Use our communication tools**

It's also a good idea to contact other students taking the course. You may be able to email each and go to chat rooms to talk. The more you communicate with others, the more you'll feel connected. Using tools such as Moodle email, and the student practice site for group work in Collaborative which provides real time interaction, you will be able to share documents and work on projects together and it is available 24/7

Explain to your parents, friends, neighbors, community members your situation. Most people are positive towards school, some...are not so positive. Make sure you explain to those around you what you're doing, more often than not, you will be able to have a quiet study time, but make sure that they understand that a Correspondence Course means that you don't have a Teacher to help you if you have questions, and in many situations, you may not have the resources right at your fingertips. This is when those around you need to be active in helping you to learn, by driving you to a library on the weekend, or making sure you have folders and cardboard for assignments.

Utilize Face-To-Face Meetings Many Correspondence Teacher's will provide face-to-face teaching every term or a few times a year. This is a great opportunity to meet your teacher, and other students studying the same subject as you.

- If you get stuck on a question, ring or email your Correspondence Teacher, all teachers have a responsibility to their students to help them... Correspondence teachers have a greater responsibility as they are teaching students over a large area, and not just at the one school.

- Distance learning students must take a far more active role in learning and accessing information than traditional students in face-to-face classrooms. Written messages or posts from the professor and classmates replace other means of direct communication, and course materials are posted online. Rather than simply sitting through a class and jotting notes, you must take the initiative to download and read lectures and course materials.

Read the Syllabus and Use it as a Roadmap

The syllabus is your course guide. It contains not only information about the professor, grading requirements, and class and assignment schedules, but also instructions on how to access online forums and e-texts. You should download and save the syllabus as soon as you have access to it.

A good syllabus provides a kind of "roadmap" to success. Read it thoroughly and ask questions if any points are unclear. You may need to ask question via email, a forum post, or even through a phone call to the instructor. Don't discount all the means of communication that are available to you.

Never discard the syllabus as an irrelevant document. Print it, and know it top to bottom. This will help you schedule your time for completing assignments, as well as facilitate planning your personal life around your academic life.

8-Goals

Set goals. If you don't know what you want to achieve as a student, you won't know how to get there or if you've accomplished things.

Set individual academic and personal goals.

Setting and Achieving Goals

A goal is something that you want to accomplish or achieve at some define point in the future. There are generally two types of goals, short-term goals and long-term goals. Short-term goals are goals you want to achieve in the near future (i.e. in a week or two) and long-term goals are goals you want to achieve down the road (i.e. by the end of the term.) Setting realistic goals and accomplishing those goals is the key to achieving and maintaining academic success.

However, not all goals are appropriate goals. In order for your goals to be appropriate they need to be in line with what you desire to accomplish academically. You goals must also be clear. If your goals are not clear they effort you put towards achieving these goals will lack direction and focus.

In preparing your goals follow "The Three W's of Goals".

- First **WRITE** down each of your goals.
- Second, each goal should state **WHAT** you want to accomplish.
- Finally, you need to identify **WHEN** you'll accomplish each goal.

For example, an appropriate goal might be the following:

I will brainstorm a list of potential science projects (what you will do) for the science fair by December 3 (when you will accomplish the goal). Characteristics of good goals include the following:

- **Achievable.** Setting goals that are so lofty that there is only a slight chance you'll be able to achieve them is not part of effective goal setting. Make sure the goals you set push you to excel but are well within your skillset and ability to accomplish.
- **Realistic.** Setting a goal to get straight A's when you're approaching the end of the semester and failing most of your class may not be realistic. A realistic goal may be to pass all your classes and get a few A's and B's.
- **Flexible.** Don't set such rigid goals that you can't modify your goal if circumstances change. Also, set goals that allow you to achieve some success even if you don't achieve your entire goal.

Ultimately, you want to set goals that will provide you direction and motivation to succeed academically.

Set Long-Term Goals

Your educational experience should help you achieve your goals. As a distance learning student, you understand how the flexibility of learning can be integrated into your lifestyle and career path. Setting both short- and long-term goals gives you the impetus to create the life that you want and the career that you will enjoy.

Setting Goals

- Goal #1: "I will succeed in this course."
- At the beginning of a new course, look through the materials. Break the lessons/assignments into manageable chunks. You might not have time to do a full lesson in one night, so plan for how much you can do, then stick to it until you're done.

A good way to stay on top of your work is to set goals. The more you do now, the easier it will be at the end. Break large tasks down into smaller parts. For example, if you have a paper due at the end of the course, break it down so you do part of it each week. Ensure that you accomplish the goals you set for yourself by the end of each week. When it comes time to pass in the paper, you'll be glad you did this.

9-Study Groups

Use helpful resources. The old adage, if at first you don't succeed, try, try, try again, while useful for many of life's situations, isn't always the best philosophy when you're strapped for time and can't figure out your chemistry homework. As you progress through middle school, high school and then into college, it's wise to rely on the help, expertise and knowledge of others to assist you with the learning process. Smart friends, tutors, study groups, and even the Internet, are useful resources for tackling complex subjects and making the most effective use of your time.

Join a study group. Study groups offers several advantageous to students, least of which is the ability to cover more material faster. Working in a study group makes it possible to research and learn about various topics quickly. Each member is assigned a topic and then provides a summary to the group.

Participate in study groups will help in sharing the load of reading and studying with other students – you will learn better by teaching them, and you will be exposed to ideas you didn't come up with on your own.

Study groups usually meet before big tests, but many students have realized how helpful it is to help one another throughout the school year. You can exchange notes, quiz each other, and most importantly, hold each other responsible for showing up to each session.

Practice by yourself or with friends

The old age adage, practice makes perfect, is true. You can practice by yourself by testing yourself with either practice exams, past quizzes, or flash cards (depending what kind of course it is and what's available). If a practice exam isn't available, you can make one up for yourself and your classmates (or find someone who will). If a practice or old exam from a course is available, use it as a guide – do not study to the practice or old exam! (Too many students treat such exams as the real exams, only to be disappointed when the real exam has none of the same questions). Such exams help you understand the breadth of content and types of questions to expect, not the actual material to study for.

Some people enjoy reviewing their materials with a group of friends or classmates. Such groups work best when they're kept small (4 or 5 others), with people of similar academic aptitude, and with people taking the same class. Different formats work for different groups. Some groups like to work through chapters together, quizzing one another as they go through it. Others like to compare class notes, and review materials that way, ensuring they haven't missed any critical points. Such study groups can be helpful for many students, but not all.

Use study groups effectively.

Ever heard the phrase "two heads are better than one"? Well this can be especially true when it comes to studying. Working in groups enables you to (1) get help from others when you're struggling to understand a concept, (2) complete assignments more quickly, and (3) teach others whereby helping both the other students and yourself to internalize the subject matter. However, study groups can become very ineffective if they're not structured and if groups members come unprepared. Effective students use study groups effectively.

Support and Encourage Fellow Classmates

If you cultivate a positive atmosphere with your fellow students, you will build a constructive relationship that will help you as well as others—which is try in any class, but even more important in a virtual class.
You will get accustomed to asynchronous learning and will figure out how to best be supportive and encouraging through just the text on the screen. Make sure that your posts are constructively positive even if you are pointing out that a statement is incorrect or an idea is tenuous. Create an online learning space that reinforces respect and values others' ideas. Remember, everyone needs encouragement to achieve his or her goals.

Contribute to Discussions

One of the secrets to distance learning is engagement. Students who are engaged in discussions show that they are seeking knowledge and understanding.
Take an active role in your education by stepping into a discussion with informed comments. Instructors know who is contributing and who is not. They have access to every forum and post. Often, they can even see how many discussion threads each student has opened and read, even if the student has not written a response.
In an asynchronous environment, discussions can be very lively and active, and become great learning venues—make sure you make yourself a part of it.

Talk About It

- Tell people what you're doing. You're more likely to stick to a course if your co-worker knows you're doing it. If you are studying high-tech or internet development, the person might just know a programmer he can hook you up with for tutoring.
- Ask a friend to check up on you.
- Ask someone to proof your work before you submit it.

Join a Study Group-This Doesn't Have to be Stuffy!

- Join a club. Aspiring financial planners could join a local investing club.
- If you're studying a language like Spanish or Japanese, ask the owners of a local restaurant if they know anyone who might like to do language exchange with you.
- Get a mentor. If you're taking a course related to health or medicine, ask a nurse or pharmacist if you can take them for coffee once a month.
- Search the Internet for bulletin boards or chat rooms related to your topic.

10-Organization

Organize your study materials. If you organize your materials as you proceed through a course, you will retrieve information with greater ease later.

Choose courses carefully, especially during your first year.

Tayba will help you in the beginning by choosing the courses that you are in need of most, such as this one on "How to Study."

Organize your class materials

Instead of keeping one bulky binder or a backpack of loose paper, organize your notes and handouts into separate folders. This makes it easier to find what you need for each exam, keep your homework together, and prevent overwhelming clutter. Color-coding can also help you keep different topics separate.

Bring everything you need, nothing you don't

Unfortunately, when you find an ideal place to study, sometimes people bring things they don't need. For instance, while it may seem ideal to type notes into a computer to refer back to later, computers are a powerful distraction for many people because they can do so many different things. Playing games, going online, IM'ing, surfing the Web, and answering emails are all wonderful distractions that have nothing to do with studying. So ask yourself whether you really need a computer to take notes, or whether you can make do with the old-fashioned paper and pen or pencil.

Don't forget the things you need to study for the class, exam or paper you're focusing on for the study session. Nothing is more time-consuming and wasteful than having to run back and forth regularly because you forget an important book, paper, or some other resource you need to be successful. If you study best with your favorite music playing, make sure your iPod is with you.

Start with the most difficult subject first.

As your most difficult assignment or subject will require the most effort and mental energy, you should start with it first. Once you've completed the most difficult work, it will be much easier to complete the rest of your work. Believe it or not, starting with the most difficult subject will greatly improve the effectiveness of your study sessions, and your academic performance.

Organization

Organization of coursework, due dates and study habits is also required for distance learning. Students are encouraged to set interim goals and deadlines and organize them into a study schedule. Also, it can be helpful to have a regular, quiet study space.

Turn in All Assignments Complete and on Time

The instructor cannot grade your papers if you don't turn them in! Most professors impose a late penalty for overdue assignments, such as 10 percent or points off per day up to three days; after three days, the work is not accepted.
With online courses, students have fewer excuses. You can never say, "I slipped it under your door by the deadline. What do you mean you never received it?" because assignments turned in through the course page will have a digital timestamp that indicates when it was posted. This timestamp is the instructor's ironclad proof the assignment was turned in on time.
Make sure you can see your posted paper or attachment before you log out of the course site.

Follow Online Resources Carefully Week by Week

Most online courses use an online learning system, such as Blackboard, Moodle, or some other customized in-house course management software suite. Your instructor may post additional learning resources to the system along with graded assignments and grades.
The college may also post important enrollment or school information here.
Instructor reserves the right to update course requirements and often those changes are communicated via the online system. Course texts and downloadable assignments are likely to be posted here, too. Take a tour of the system and familiarize yourself with all its features as soon as you have access to it.

Stay Organized

Organization is key to distance learning success! I recommend keeping a physical binder with sections such as syllabus, assignments, and texts and research; or divide the binder into Week 1, Week 2, and so forth. Having a physical binder supports students with flexible schedules (a strong reason many students opt for distance learning in the first place), as it allows them to pick up and go at any moment, despite whether they are in front of a computer or at a wi-fi hotspot.

11-Review the material and your notes

Draft papers. Never turn in the first draft of a paper – always leave time to re-work it before your professor sees it.

Take notes. Use the Cornell, outline, mapping or charting method to condense and synthesize reading, lectures and discussions.

Develop strong listening and note-taking skills.

Develop and improve your writing and speaking skills.

Study Cards

In printing study cards, the student is using kinetic energy (energy in motion), thus making the impression stronger on the brain, and the student will be able to use the cards for overlearning. Another reason for having students make study cards is that they are convenient to carry and flip through for mastery. Reading the cards silently, however, is too passive. Go over the cards orally. A student will not master the cards by passively reading them. Learning requires the expenditure of energy. The student must be actively engaged in producing the sounds, using muscles and burning energy to make the sound.

Take & review thorough notes while in class

Whether you're sitting through a lecture or doing an assigned reading, always take notes. You'll absorb key terms and ideas more quickly by writing them down immediately. Don't be afraid to ask classmates for a refresher if you miss a lecture

Outline and rewrite your notes

Most people find that keeping to a standard outline format helps them boil information down to its most basic components. People find that connecting similar concepts together makes it easier to remember when the exam comes around. The important thing to remember in writing outlines is that an outline only words as a learning tool when it is in your own words and structure. Every person is unique in how they put similar information together (called "chunking" by cognitive psychologists). So while you're welcomed to copy other people's notes or outlines, make sure you translate those notes and outlines into your own words and concepts. Failing to do this is what often causes many students to stumble in remembering important items.

It may also be helpful to use as many senses as possible when studying, because information is retained more readily in people when other senses are involved. That's why writing notes works in the first place – it puts information into words and terms you understand. Mouthing the words out loud while you copy the notes before an important exam can be one method for involving yet another sense.

EARLY REVIEW is most efficient, most productive.

A. Before you attempt to learn new material in class or through reading:

- Glance over previous chapters or notes.
- Run through your mind what you know already.
- Since memorization of new material is most effective when it is associated with the material already known, this process brings all available mental "hooks" to the surface.

B. Immediately after learning:
- Rework your notes, adding material that comes to mind. (Don't recopy; this is wasteful.)
- Order and organize what was learned. (Star, use arrows, additional comments, etc.)
- Integrate new material with what you already know.
- Forgetting is most rapid right after learning. Review helps combat this. Relearning is easier if it is done quickly. Don't wait until it's all gone.

Space initial early reviews to support original learning. Several brief periods spread over 5 or 10 days is usually enough to ensure good recall for intermediate review.

Intermediate review is important when work is spread out over several months or longer. For example, when the final is 4 months away, follow this schedule:

- original learning
- immediate review of limited material same day (5-10 minutes)
- intermediate review of material covered so far, after 2 months
- final review, before exam

Intermediate and final reviews should stress understanding and organization of material.

Final review is a REVIEW, not "cramming" of unlearned material. No new learning takes place except to draw together the final main currents of thought.

- Be brief. Review entire semester's work in 2-4 hours. (Set a limit and stick to it.)
- Outline and organize from memory. Don't bother copying.
- Recite (in writing or out loud to a friend or self)

USE SPACED REVIEW rather than **MASSED PRACTICE**. 60 minutes used in 3 groups of 20 minutes each is more effective than 60 minutes used all at the same time.
- break up learning period for any one subject
- avoid fatigue
- review and strengthen previous learning
- increased motivation, better concentration

12-Memory

Try your best to classify and associate. Many authorities feel that you will master information faster if you learn in groups of seven or fewer at a time.

Try to overlearn through repetition.

Association is a key to memory:

a. You remember approximately 10 percent of what you read.

b. You remember approximately 20 percent of what you hear.

c. You remember approximately 30 percent of what you see.

d. You remember approximately 50 percent of what you hear and see together.

e. You remember approximately 70 percent of what you say (if you think as you are saying it).

f. You remember approximately 90 percent of what you do.

Use memory games (mnemonic devices)

Memory games, or mnemonic devices, are methods for remembering pieces of information using a simple association of common words. Most often people string together words to form a nonsense sentence that is easy to remember. The first letter of each word can then be used to stand for something else – the piece of information you're trying to remember. The most common mnemonic device example is "Every Good Boy Deserves Fun." Putting the first letters of every word together – EGBDF – gives a music student the five notes for treble clef.

The key to such memory devices is the new phrase or sentence you come up with has to be more memorable and easier to remember than the terms or information you're trying to learn. These don't work for everyone, so if they don't work for you, don't use them.

Mnemonic devices are helpful because you use more of your brain to remember visual and active images than you do to remember just a list of items. Using more of your brain means better memory.

13-Choosing what to read/resources

Know and use resources.

Utilize Resources If you have access to a library, make sure that you use it to research and study in. If you have access to a computer and Internet, use them to research and type up assignments. It's no use having resources at your disposal if you are not going to use them.
- Use all resources that are available for your use.

14- Habits for learning

Slow down on tests. Anxiety makes you skip over parts of questions. Read every word carefully.

Learn actively.

Take every extra opportunity to study

If a professor or TA offers an after-class study session or extra credit opportunity, try to fit it into your schedule. This doesn't just give you a stronger safety net in case you make a mistake in the future; it also shows your initiative as a student.

Review your notes, schoolwork and other class materials over the weekend.

Successful students review what they've learned during the week over the weekend. This way they're well prepared to continue learning new concepts that build upon previous coursework and knowledge acquired the previous week.

Always review your notes before starting an assignment.

Obviously, before you can review your notes you must first have notes to review. Always make sure to take good notes in class. Before you start each study session, and before you start a particular assignment, review your notes thoroughly to make sure you know how to complete the assignment correctly. Reviewing your notes before each study session will help you remember important subject matter learned during the day, and make sure studying targeted and effective.

Seek answers from designated areas first.

Professors are eager to help with legitimate problems. But, they don't want to waste time when the answers can be found elsewhere. If you have a basic class question, first seek solutions from the class syllabus, website, and general discussion boards.

Re-read your mail or email.

Written correspondence can often be misunderstood. Whenever sending a correspondence to your professor, re-read to make sure that your message is clear and your tone is intentional.

Listen.

When you receive a response, make sure you pay attention to what the professor is saying. Re-reading his emails will help you avoid missing the details.

Approach before the student rush.

After a challenging assignment or an important test, your professor is going to be inundated with emails. Anticipate any problems and try to approach him beforehand, when he'll have more time to give your concern attention.

Search for One New Idea in Every Class Session, Assignment, and Reading

You are ultimately responsible for what you learn in the course. Every time you post a forum discussion response, read a text, work on an assignment, or interact with other students, you should come away with some new idea or thought about the subject. If you are simply rushing through without thinking, you will not retain the information. However, if you are actively seeking knowledge, you will find it. I suggest writing down what you discover in a notebook and referring back to it each time you start a new learning session. Use what you learn today as a building block for what you learn tomorrow.

Consider How Your Experience Fits Into the Discussion

Education should be relevant and make a difference in your life. Discovering ways that your experience fits into the discussion makes the topic significant and applicable to your job or future education. Some courses naturally build on experience, such as business, sociology, or psychology.

Instructor want to see more than book learning. They want to see that you have synthesized the information and can use it effectively. You will find that because distance learning uses forum posts for discussion, you can take time to formulate a knowledgeable response before you reply. Online discussion questions are great avenues for creating relevance, and discovering the significance of a subject will help you internalize the information.

Ask Questions

If you don't understand something, ASK. It's been said a zillion times: the only dumb question is the one you don't ask.

It's not about memorizing -

It's about learning material that will help you in your hobbies, career, and life. Memorization isn't a bad thing, but make sure you're memorizing because you are really interested in the information, and figure out a way to use the memorized information several times within a few days of learning it. It'll stick if it has real-world meaning.

Review your courses

One great advantage of distance courses is that you are able to view and replay them all or in part as many times as you wish which will allow you to customize your notes and review more challenging information as often as you like.

15-Review Your habits and see what works best for you

Know your learning style. Develop techniques and strategies for compensating for possible differences between your learning style and your instructor's teaching style.

Know Your Learning Style and Use It

- Look for real-world situations and examples of what you're learning about. If you're studying about civil engineering, pay attention to bridges.
- You'll be much more interested if you're involved, not just reading about a topic.
- Put things into practice as early as possible.

- If you're studying accounting, practice by balancing your checkbook.

Celebrate Successes (and mistakes)

- Reward yourself with whatever works for you, along the way. Remember, you chose to do this. Be proud of your accomplishments!

20 Study Hacks to Improve Your Memory

Posted on January 24, 2014 by Andrea Leyden

We've scoured our brains and the internet for the best study hacks to help your brain remember information quicker and easier and ultimately help you do better in your exams.

1. Walk Before An Exam

It's been proven that exercise can boost your memory and brain power. Research conducted by Dr. Chuck Hillman of the University of Illinois provides evidence that about 20 minutes exercise before an exam can improve performance.

Composite of 20 student brains taking the same test

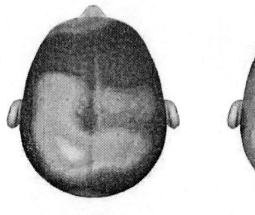
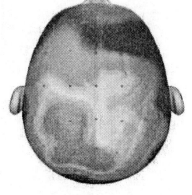

After sitting quietly   After 20 minute walk

Research/Scan compliments of Dr. Chuck Hillman University of Illinois

2. Speak Out Loud Instead of Simply Reading

Although this may make you look a little crazy, give it a go! You will be surprised how much more you can remember when you've said it out loud. **Warning**: Don't try this in a crowded library!

> You're 50% more likely to remember something if you speak it out loud instead of simply reading it over and over.

3. Reward Yourself With A Treat

There are many ways to integrate a reward system into your study habits. Here's a simple way to motivate yourself to study with Gummy Bears:

4. Teach What You Have Learned

The best way to test if you really understand something is to try to teach it to someone else. If you can't get anyone to listen to you explain the Pythagorean Theorem, why not teach a class of stuffed animals!

5. Create Mental Associations

The ability to make connections is not only an easier way to remember information, but it's the fuel of creativity and intelligence. Steve Jobs famously said *"Creativity is just connecting things. When you ask creative people how they did something, they feel a little guilty because they didn't really do it, they just saw something"*.

Mind Maps are an easy way to connect ideas by creating a visual overview of different connections. Read more about the benefits of using Mind Maps to learn here.

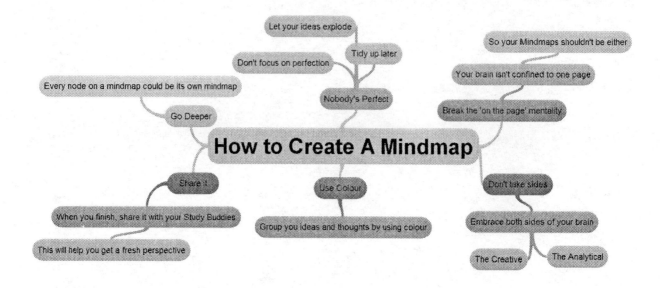

6. Draw Diagrams

Drawing diagrams will help you to visualise information which would be hard to describe. This creates a visual memory in your mind which can be recalled in an exam. You may even be asked to draw or label diagrams such as the human heart in your exam so get practicing!

7. Times New Roman is the Fastest Font to Read

Simply put – there's a reason why Times New Roman is the default font on most applications!

This is easy to read.

This is easy to read.

This is not easy to read.

This is not easy to read.

8. Use Apps to Block Distracting Sites

The SelfControl app helps you to avoid distractions by blocking websites for a certain amount of time. Discover more student apps to make student life easier in our blog post "12 Student Apps You Don't Want to Miss!".

9. Watch a Documentary on the Topic

Documentaries are an entertaining way of compacting an entire story into a short timeframe. This will help you remember key details from a story plus you may even get extra credit for mentioning that you took the initiative and watched a film about the topic!

Check out the infographic in this blog post which helps you decide which documentary to watch.

10. Search Google Like a Pro

Save time when researching sources online by mastering the biggest search engine in the world; Google. Follow the tips in this image to find what you need at your fingertips:

Search Google Like a Pro

You know how to Google, but do you do it like a pro?

Here are a few simple yet very helpful search operators to help you Search Google... like a Pro

| "Quotation Marks" | "I love you Mom" |

Using quotation marks in your search terms lets you search exactly for that word. It means, all your results will have your search terms in them.

| - Dashes | dolphins -football |

If you want to exclude a term from your search include a hyphen before that word.

| ~ Tilde | music ~classes |

Use tilde when you want also its synonyms to appear in the result. The above query will search for music classes, lessons, coaching etc.

| site: | site:ndtv.com |

Use this operator to search within a specific website only.

| | verticle bar | blouse | shirt | chemise |

This query will search websites that have any one/two/all of the terms

| .. Two Periods | movies 1950..1970 |

Include two periods when you want to search within two number ranges

Sources:
www.google.com

Infographic by : Splashsys Webtech
www.splashsys.com

Splashsys

11. Create Flashcards for Quick Memory Buzz

Quickly test your knowledge of key concepts, definitions, quotes and formulas with flashcards. Sign up to GoConqr now to create your first Flashcard deck like the one below now!

12. Take Regular Study Breaks

When your brain is working, you need to take regular study breaks to help your brain absorb more information but also to keep you motivated and focused when you are working. Take a short break after 45-50 minutes study as your focus and concentration will become impaired after this period, anything new after 1 hour 30 minutes does not get assimilated.

13. Listen to the Correct Type of Music

In our blog post "Music for Studying: 10 Tips to Pick the Best Study Music" we looked into the area of how the correct types of music can lead to more productive studying by elevating your mood. Have you made your Mozart Spotify playlist yet?

14. Make Your Study Space Portable

We may be creatures of habit with favourite seats in the library but information retention actually improves when you vary the places where you study. Check out this Buzzfeed video for more study hacks:

15. Practice, Practice, Practice…

Practicing sample answers to past exam questions can help train your brain to retrieve information. Create realistic, exam-like condition and test your understanding by using our new Quiz tool. Try our general Knowledge Quiz below:

16. Don't Stay Up All Night Before an Exam

Make sure to get adequate rest the nights leading up to your exams. When you sleep, your brain assimilates the information you have learned when studying so getting a good night's sleep will help you remember those pesky maths formulas you need for your exam!

Don't make this your sleep schedule:

17. Discover News Ways to Learn

Trying new methods of studying can help you find what really works for you. Use technology to your advantage by watching educational TED Talks or downloading useful dictionary apps for example. Read more about the benefits of using technology to study.

18. Use Scents or Gum to Jog Your Memory

This may seem a bit random but spraying an unfamiliar scent while you're studying can help jog your memory when you spray it again just before an exam. Chewing a strange kind of gum will work the same way.

19. Study in a Group

Studying in a group can help you collect new insights to enhance your learning experience. The ExamTime Groups tool is an innovative spin on the traditional study group formula. Our Groups tool helps you share resources, discuss ideas and interact with members of your team or group project. Sign up here to get started!

20. Meditate (Note by Tayba: Muslims can use dhikr and fikr practices to substitute for meditation)

Studies say that meditation can help students stay focused when studying. Not only will meditation help you concentrate when studying but it will help reduce pre-exam stress as it improves both mental and physical health.

Check out this Meditation Education infographic on Edutopia which details the educational benefits of meditating:

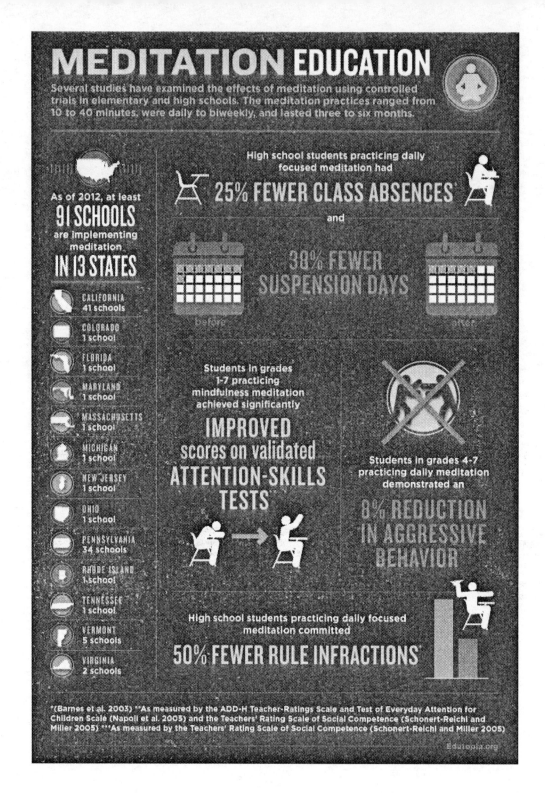

Our final piece of advice for those of you sitting exams is to stay positive. It's amazing how a positive attitude can impact on your exam results or motivate you to complete *that* assignment when all you want to do is go to bed!